CUTTING EDGE RADIO

HOW TO CREATE THE WORLD'S BEST RADIO ADS FOR BRANDS IN THE 21ST CENTURY

Jim Aitchison

Prentice
Hall

Singapore London New York Toronto Sydney Tokyo Madrid
Mexico City Munich Paris Capetown Hong Kong Montreal

Published in 2003 by
Prentice Hall
Pearson Education Asia Pte Ltd
23/25 First Lok Yang Road
Singapore 629733

Pearson Education offices in Asia: *Bangkok, Beijing, Hong Kong, Jakarta, Kuala Lumpur, Manila, New Delhi, Seoul, Singapore, Taipei, Tokyo*

Printed in Singapore

5   4   3   2   1
07   06   05   04   03

ISBN 0-13-009315-7

CONTENTS

THE STUDIO CAST
(In order of appearance)

Lionel Hunt

Tim Crook

Austin Howe

Hugh Mackay

David Holmes

Bill Tragos

David Ogilvy

Marshall McLuhan

Al Ries

Jack Trout

Mel Blanc

John Immesoete

Yukio Nakayama

Lim Sau Hoong

Rob Martin Murphy

Antony Redman

Bill Bernbach

Keith Reinhard

Warren Berger

Steve Henry

Christine Coyle

Danielle Sterrie

Steve Elrick

Jeremy Bullmore

Neil French

Paul Fishlock

Jack Vaughan

Michael Conrad

Michael Newman

Brent Hahn

David Alberts

Clive Desmond

Bob Dennis

Garry Abbott

Kash Sree

Calvin Soh

Lane Atkins

Les Francis

Mike Fromowitz

Steve Owen

David Droga

Chris Kyme

Brad Power

Elspeth Lynn

Lorraine Tao

John Culverwell

Ian Reichenthal

Linda Locke

Ralph Van Dijk

Adrian Holmes

THE STUDIO CAST

Street Remley	Kenn Delbridge
David Flint	Rennie Gomes
Philip Webster	Scott Whybin
Cary Rueda	Tham Khai Meng
Tony Hertz	Joan Warner
Paul Ruta	KC Tsang
Peter Souter	Ravi Deshpande
Simon Collins	Borhanuddin Osman
Andy Lerner	Yasmin Ahmad
Mark Rivett	Ted Lim
Peter Clark	Tony Lee
Carl Jones	Horacio Mancilla
Ken Bennett	Jorge Soldevilla
Nigel Dawson	Efren Murillo
Paul Burke	Miguel Ullivari
Alexsandra Lyall	Miguel Morena
John Kyriakou	David Guerrero
Emma Hill	David Ferrer
Mike Edmonds	Bhanu Inkawat
Rob Townsend	Khanitta Khanittanan
Barbara Levy	Andrew Bell
Thomas Hripko	Saul Gitlin
Adam Furman	Dennis Chang
Orson Welles	Andrew Craissati
Jim Berinson	Rowan Dean
Mandy Wheeler	Frank Todaro
Adrian Reith	Arthur Bijur
Paul Tan	Mike Cozens

FOREWORD

This is the first time I have been asked to write a foreword for a book.

(I even thought it was spelt forward until I looked it up.)

In that respect you could say I have been somewhat backward in coming foreword.

Not that you could say that about the author, Jim Aitchison.

Hot on the heels of his highly acclaimed, and already definitive, works on television and print advertising Mr. Aitchison has picked the brains of 104 of the world's top creative talents and got them to tell everything they know, and more, about how to do great radio advertising.

Actually that's 105 of the world's creative talents when you include the author himself.

Which is precisely the unique value of this and his other two books.

Instead of being the views of just one person, this is the collective wisdom of just about everybody who is anybody in the world of creative radio advertising, expertly edited and introduced by an author who has won many advertising awards himself and is also an accomplished radio broadcaster.

Nevertheless, I am not the least bit surprised that Jim has left radio advertising until last.

Everyone in advertising always does.

You could call it the poor relation of advertising media.

Which is a bit strange when you think how rich it makes all those rock singers and their managers.

It's also a bit strange when you think about how deeply involving radio can be.

FOREWORD

As a child in England I can distinctly remember sitting around the radio with my family completely engrossed in *Lost in Space*, absolutely mortified by *Little Red Monkey* and totally creased-up by *The Goon Show*.

And my parents wouldn't have missed their 6.45pm daily dose of *The Archers* for all the programmes on television. And never did for over 30 years.

These are radio programmes, of course, not ads, but it just goes to show how riveting radio can be when it's done properly.

Still, I'm as guilty as anyone else to putting radio at the bottom of the pile and I've been trying to work out why.

Is it that there are no exotic overseas locations as you might get in a TV ad? Maybe. But why not go to Buenos Aires to capture the unique sound and get the right voices?

Is it that the production budgets are too small? Possibly.

But why not use the old production rule of thumb and spend 15% of the total media on production?

With a million dollar radio campaign you'd have a very handsome $150,000 to spend on production.

Or is it, as a writer, when it comes to radio there's really nowhere to hide?

That, I suspect might be it.

But, have no fear.

Read this book today and I defy you not to want to come up with a great radio campaign tomorrow. And have a better than even chance of pulling it off.

After all, radio is the only advertising medium I know of where you can rely on the audience's imagination as much as you can your own.

You see, the job's already half done for you.

An irresistible proposition for any writer, surely?

Lionel Hunt
Chairman and Creative Director
Lowe Hunt

WITH SPECIAL THANKS

To everyone who so generously contributed his or her time and talent to my search for wisdom, my sincerest thanks. To Britain's Radio Advertising Bureau, Commercial Radio Australia, and the US Radio Advertising Bureau, my gratitude for supplying such invaluable material. And to all those busy people who worked miracles for me, kindly supplying scripts and arranging permission to reproduce them, my very sincere thanks.

Cover design: Andrew Clarke
Cover artwork: Paul Clarke

ACKNOWLEDGEMENTS

The Itzhak Perlman story was reported by Jack Riemer in the *Houston Chronicle*, September 2001.

Every attempt has been made to obtain permission to reproduce material included in this book.

1

THE GREAT STEAM WIRELESS SHOW

"Radio separates the men from the boys," says Lionel Hunt, chairman and creative director of Lowe Hunt & Partners Australia, chairman of the Lowe Group in Australasia and co-founder of The Campaign Palace. "You've got to be able to write, and to have a good idea, and there's nowhere to hide. You can't normally go to an exotic overseas location for a radio commercial, and you can't normally hide behind a brilliant TV director who can make your dull idea look beautiful, and there are no pictures for the art director to fiddle with."

According to legend, radio was invented on Madison Avenue. Late one night in a big American advertising agency, a bumbling Italian cleaner was working in the conference room. His broom handle accidentally smashed the screen of the TV monitor. Next morning all the agency folk could receive was the sound, which they called radio. The old cleaner's name was Mr. Marconi.

The truth was somewhat different.

In 1897, the great Italian inventor Marconi developed the first commercially successful spark-coil transmitter. His radio signal "flew" across his father's garden. Within two years, he had the distance up to two miles. Come 1901, Marconi's wireless spanned the Atlantic.

The AWA Radiola Super Six was state of the art in 1926.

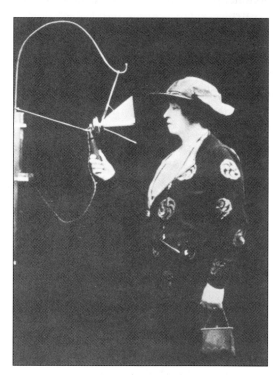

Dame Nellie Melba broadcasting "live" from London, 1920.

(From the Marconi Collection.)

The first radio station in the world was KDKA Pittsburgh, which broadcast the 1920 presidential election. By 1922, 560 stations were on the air in America and radio advertising had started. At first, restrictions forbade any commercials. Sponsors were only permitted to add their names to a programme's title. One such sponsor, the Colgate-Palmolive-Peet Company, found an ingenious solution: its musical variety show, *The Palmolive Radio Hour*, featured two singers conveniently named Paul Oliver and Olive Palmer.

A world away in Australia, Sydney stations 2BL and 2FC started operations in 1923. At first crystal wireless sets, in which a "cat's whisker" tickled a lump of crystal, were all the rage. Soon more sophisticated wireless sets were on the market, including a Japanese receiver shaped like a swan: tuning was accomplished by twisting its neck to the desired position.

In those early days, recorded music was broadcast using a spring-loaded gramophone. A microphone was placed near the mouth of the horn-type amplifier and the music went to air, complete with background noises.

In Australia, "live" studio performances were always conducted in evening dress. After all, you never knew who was listening.

Not everyone welcomed the new medium. "One has only to think of the sinister possibilities of the radio," warned George Orwell, "to realise that *'the truth is great and will prevail'* is a prayer rather than an axiom."

THE big networks dominated America's golden age of radio: the National Broadcasting Company (NBC) headed by David Sarnoff, the American Broadcasting Company (ABC), the Columbia Broadcasting System (CBS) operated by the advertising manager of a cigar company, William S. Paley, and the Mutual network.

NBC's Sarnoff was already a legend. On 14 April 1912 Sarnoff was a young telegraph operator at the Marconi station in New York when he picked up a message relayed from ships at sea: "RMS *Titanic* ran into iceberg, sinking fast." Sarnoff stayed at his post for the next 72 hours, broadcasting in Morse the world's first news of the disaster. He climbed the ranks at the Marconi company and in 1915 wrote a memo to the great man himself about a vision he had of a "radio music box" which could broadcast music into every American home. In those days radio was mainly used in shipping and by amateur wireless enthusiasts, and Marconi thought his idea crazy. But after the First World War, General Electric formed RCA to absorb Marconi's US assets — including Sarnoff — who then put his plans into action. So while Marconi may have invented radio, he actually did not invent Radio.

Kolin Hager, programme director of WGY in Schenectady, New York, a General Electric Company station, invented American radio drama in 1922. His concept was *One Man's Family*, which later became a major daytime serial on NBC until the 1950s. Meanwhile in Hollywood, great screen stars stepped up to microphones to perform "live" plays twice on the same night: once, for East Coast standard time transmission and again, at a later hour, for the West Coast.

It was during one network drama in the 1940s, NBC's *Mystery in the Air*, that listeners heard what is perhaps the most bizarre and appalling commercial announcement ever broadcast: "According to a nationwide survey, more doctors smoke Camels than any other cigarette."

In Britain, radio drama was broadcast "live" starting in 1923 with a play broadcast from the BBC's Savoy Hill studios, behind the Savoy Hotel. Longer plays began with four or five minutes of overture music. Music was played between the acts. The actors crowded around a single microphone. The advent of the revolutionary drama control panel in 1928 meant that producers could mix "live" from one studio to another. When Broadcasting House opened in 1932, "noise rooms" were fitted with large hydraulic tables with six separate surfaces on which different effects were created. Teams of sound effects men laboured over tubs of water, smashing plates of glass with hammers, crinkling cellophane to replicate a fire, and rolling pumpkins off ladders to simulate falling bodies. Val Gielgud, older brother of famous actor Sir John Gielgud, founded "The National Theatre of the Air". BBC radio drama defined the genre. Arguably, its finest moment was 25 January 1954: the first broadcast of Dylan Thomas' poetic play for voices *Under Milk Wood* starring Richard Burton.

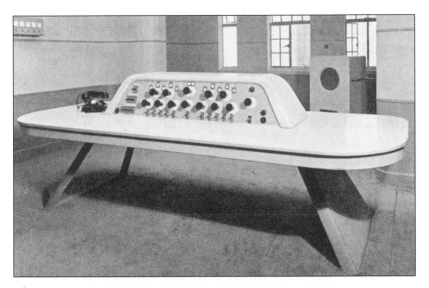

Not Star Trek, *but the BBC London in 1932. This control panel could mix the output of as many as 11 different studios at the same time for the broadcast of a complex radio drama.*

This studio housed the Wireless Military Band and orchestras. It boasted the new type of adjustable microphone stand.

The gramophone effects studio.

The main sound effects studio occupied a depth of two floors. The table in the foreground was divided into six different surfaces allowing a variety of sounds to be created by friction. Water effects were created in the tub at right.

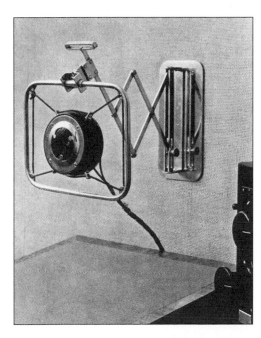

"This is the BBC…" A 1930s microphone with lazy-tongs suspension.

The Religious Services studio replicated the atmosphere of a church.

This Talks Studio calmed "on air" nerves by making speakers feel as though they were in a comfortable study. George Washington's picture over the "fireplace" indicates the studio was used for broadcasting talks to America.

Photography by M. O. Dell, H. L. Wainwright and Shaw Wildman.

FROM the late 1920s, radio could be recorded on machines like the massive Blattnerphone or the Marconi-Stille. Sound was recorded magnetically on rapidly spinning reels of fine steel wire. Edits were made by cutting the wire, removing the unwanted section, then tying the wire together again. By the mid-1930s, shellac or lacquer discs were cut. Studio suites developed gramophone effects areas, playing sound from banks of 17-inch-wide turntables. Echo was created by playing sound into an empty tiled room with a microphone placed at the opposite end.

Meanwhile in Australia, "live" sports broadcasts were achieved in the studio. When Australia played England at cricket, for example, messages came over the phone from London and were hastily scribbled down onto pieces of paper. They were passed to the announcer who read them aloud and tapped a pencil against a matchbox to simulate the sound of the batsman hitting the ball.

AS time went by, "live" drama gave way to transcribed drama. Plays and serials were cut onto a wax disc from which a matrix would be made for pressing copies that were distributed to hundreds of different stations. There was no time for rehearsals. Actors learned to "sight read" their scripts. If someone made a mistake on the last page, the wax disc was destroyed and everyone started again.

America invented the radio "soap opera" in February 1932, so-named because Colgate-Palmolive's Super Suds sponsored the first daytime serial on the NBC network. Not to be outdone, Procter & Gamble's Oxydol leapt into the fray and a new genre was born.

Australia rivalled America in transcribed drama. Some Australian radio serials ran for over 4,000 quarter-hour episodes. One epic lasted 21 years. By 1958, the Australian radio transcription business was worth US$1.25 million with programme sales to New Zealand, South Africa, Canada, Singapore and the West Indies — even Sierra Leone.

Peter Finch and Rod Taylor cut their teeth in Sydney radio drama. Finch called them the happiest days of his life.

Australian radio drama continued long after American stations had switched to Top 40 formats. In May 1964 one Sydney station took all its drama off air on the same day. Others followed. Soon, countless thousands of episodes of old radio shows were sold off and melted down to surface new expressways.

AT the BBC in the 1950s, a new kind of radio comedy evolved which impacted on two generations of radio copywriters. Previously, broadcast comedy was mostly stage comedy spoken into a microphone. Suddenly, a new programme went on air that presented a combined lunacy of voices, sound effects and music that could only be pictured in the mind of the listener. *The Goon Show* was the brainchild of Spike Milligan and featured the talents of Milligan, Peter Sellers and Harry Secombe. For the first time, the theatre of the mind became a comic asylum of odd characters that owed their existence purely to sound. The likes of Neddy Seagoon, Moriarty, Eccles, Bluebottle, et al, could never be duplicated in any other medium.

AMERICAN writer Brock Bower bade farewell to the radio shows of the past: "Nothing like them will ever be done on television because they demand the very thing TV has scotched: imagination."

Or, as Stan Freberg put it, television stretched the imagination — up to 21 inches!

THE demise of radio was forecast as early as the late 1940s. America boasted 2,600 commercial radio stations in 1948. By 1995, that number had soared to 11,700 — not bad for a "dying" medium. Five thousand were AM, 6,000 were FM, with over US$10.5 billion in advertising revenues.

By the end of the century, radio advertising topped US$12.4 billion a year, with virtually 80% of revenue derived from local advertisers.

THE advent of FM eliminated the crackle and static in radio signals. Under the old system of amplitude modulation, AM radio signals travel through air waves and ground waves. The signal bounces off the ionospheric layer and follows the curvature of the earth. AM stations also have a ground mat under the transmitter that sends part of the signal out through the ground, which is why AM transmission masts are often located on wet, marshy ground for better conductivity. At night, when the ionospheric layer is lower, AM waves can travel hundreds, even thousands, of miles beyond their approved coverage areas.

On the other hand, FM uses frequency modulation; it does not rely on varying the strength of radio waves, but varying their frequency. Rather than follow the curvature of the earth, FM signals travel through the air on the same line-of-sight principle as television signals. FM's greater fidelity means that music can be heard without interference from a passing electrical storm.

TODAY'S radio is format driven. Syndicators have taken over from networks. Targeting is ultra-specific. For example, America's most popular format, Country, is subdivided into real country, pop country, progressive country, modern country, easy country, bluegrass, Nashville, country blues and country gospel. AOR (Album-Oriented Rock) also has endless permutations: classic rock, new rock, hard rock, adult album alternative and heavy metal Z-rock. Other tightly defined formats are AC (Adult Contemporary), ARROW (All Rock and Roll Oldies), CHR (Contemporary Hit Radio), News/Talk, Spanish and Urban Contemporary/Black.

Radio has reinvented itself. And curiously, in certain quarters, the wheel has turned full circle. Since 1974, Los Angeles station Newsradio KNX1070 has rebroadcast old radio dramas from the 1940s and 1950s. Shows like *Dragnet, Gunsmoke* and *The Adventures of Sam Spade* have made its *Drama Hour* one of the most-listened-to nighttime hours in southern California. Globally, author Tim Crook reports that radio drama is in "a continual state of creative flux with the invention of new form and content". He calls the mind's eye "a continually playing movie for the imagination". Radio drama flourishes in Japan, he says, while the Korean Broadcasting System produces over 200 plays a year, supporting a 500-member dramatists' association and 400 actors. In 1996, France broadcast 358 hours of radio drama. Active radio drama centres can be found in places as diverse as Australia, Austria, Canada, Egypt, Hong Kong, India, Malawi, Mongolia, Shanghai, South Africa, Sweden, Switzerland and Uganda.

As radio continues to evolve, one passionate practitioner of radio creativity calls for more radical experimentation. At Radioland in Portland, Oregon, Austin Howe believes: "Radio has been stuck in the same cookie-cutter formats for years. I think the time is ripe for a return to the old school. Recording radio "live" with bands, sketch comedy, interviews ... especially with the advent of satellite and digital radio, there is going to be an explosion of need for content."

UNLIKE television viewers, radio listeners are station loyal not programme loyal. According to the marketing department of Commercial Radio Australia, the industry federation, they spend 83% of their listening time on average with their station of choice, usually selecting their secondary station for specific programming such as "live" sport coverage. As social researcher Hugh Mackay reports, "Radio stimulates the sense of a particular station being 'my station', a particular presenter being 'my friend' or 'my kind of person', and a particular programme being tailored to the listeners' needs or tastes."

Radio, he says, offers "the intimacy of the telephone."

The same factor applies in Britain. Millward Brown research for the Radio Advertising Bureau UK confirmed: "When they say it on television, they're saying it to everybody, whereas when I hear it on the radio they're saying it more to me personally."

If television is broadcast, radio is narrowcast. And significantly, radio commercials cannot be "zapped".

Listener loyalty aside, radio's economy is enviable. While a TV spot on a show like *Seinfeld* costs US$600,000, a national radio ad on shows by Don Imus or Howard Stern costs in the vicinity of US$10,000. Imus was ranked one of America's 25 most influential people in 1997 by *Time* magazine. Stern commands a daily syndicated audience of 5.4 million. And radio audiences are powerful: Larry King got his start as an all-night talk show host in Miami, before being networked to 300 stations by Mutual and eventually becoming one of the world's most visible faces on CNN.

GIVEN all its advantages, why is radio the most misunderstood medium? And why is radio creativity the poor cousin of print and television?

It shouldn't be, according to the great British art director and illustrator David Holmes. Holmes, a founding partner in Holmes Knight Ritchie-TBWA London, argues that sound is as important to us as vision. "It seems to me that we develop the given preferred faculty from an early age. Life's more comfortable that way and we take the easy road on the whole. To play the game of 'If I were blind', would any of us not be completely focused on the importance, the delights, pleasures, surprises, discoveries, the uplifting nature of what sound can give us? Sound helps me in the form of music. It's stimulating. I'm motivated by the messages the music is portraying." A wonderful sound, he says, can be just as exciting as a great visual idea. "Radio is all-powerful. Art directors should treat it with respect. If it were the only alternative on earth, we'd hear great radio commercials."

2

RETHINKING RADIO

B ill Tragos of TBWA once called radio "a new medium to some companies because it's been ignored for so long". David Ogilvy described it as the "Cinderella medium". Garrison Keillor said: "There's no romance in television: it's just the Wal-Mart of the mind. Radio is infinitely sexier."

Legendary media guru Marshall McLuhan explained radio in these terms: "The ear is hyperaesthetic. The eye is neutral. Given only the sound of a play, we have to fill in all of the senses, not just the sight of the action. So much do-it-yourself completion or 'closure' of action develops a kind of independent isolation."

While sight is arbitrary, sound is discriminatory.

"Listening to a message is much more effective than reading it," argued Al Ries and Jack Trout in a Battleground Reports newsletter published in *Marketing* magazine, June 1995. "The mind holds the spoken words in storage much longer, enabling you to follow the train of thought with greater clarity. And the tone of the human voice gives the words emotional impact that the printed words can never achieve."

Mel Blanc, the voice behind Warner Brothers cartoons, called radio a medium of illusion, capable of blurring the line between reality and fantasy.

On 30 October 1938, famous actor Orson Welles demonstrated radio's awesome illusory power. His adaptation of H. G. Wells' *War of the Worlds*, broadcast on *The Mercury Theatre on the Air*, created panic across America. Thousands believed that Martians in flying cylinders were vaporising New York and New Jersey. So convincing was the acting, and so inventive were the sound effects, that one woman was ready to swallow poison rather than die at the hands of the Martians. Undoubtedly, countless Americans sought the comfort of chicken soup after the show. Campbell's sponsored it.

"Radio can paint a picture that only the listener can imagine." Double Mercury Award winner John Immesoete is senior vice president and group creative director at DDB Chicago, where he created the Bud Light *Real American Heroes* campaign. "The human imagination is boundless and personal — therefore if the writer chooses his words carefully, the potential of the radio ad is boundless. The radio writer can hypothetically be more powerful than his television or print counterpart by virtue of what he can imply rather than has to show. Radio is also in many ways the most personal medium for the storyteller. A radio ad seems less of a 'mass' communication than a TV ad or print ad, or even an Internet ad." Immesoete believes a radio ad can become communication in a purer form. "If you're successful, you hold a captive listener with few distractions. Great standup comics are never funnier than when they're on and it's just them, a stage and a microphone. Their other diluted movie and TV performances often pale in comparison. This analogy applies to the radio writer who is in peak form."

Yukio Nakayama has written and produced over 3,000 radio commercials. He started as a radio writer. He voices tracks himself and even creates his own sound effects. He has won the ACC (All Japan Radio and TV Commercial Council) Radio Grand Prix, the Fuji-Sankei Advertising Awards Radio Grand Prix and the Dentsu Advertising Awards Radio Grand Prix three times each. Today he is creative director of Creative Division 1, Dentsu Tokyo — and still a passionate advocate of radio. "I believe the essence of radio commercials lies in words. There is a huge amount of information around us these days. However, man is dying to listen to words that inspire him, encourage him, give him empathy. I am eager to listen to human words. They never become old. They never become new. Human words are old and new any time."

"For TV you have eye contact, but for radio you have to touch the heart of the person with only the voice." Chinese-language advertising guru Lim Sau Hoong, CEO and executive creative director of 10AM Communications Singapore, imagines the audience is there, facing her. Some are paying attention; others aren't, so she has to find ways to attract them.

"Radio is the most under-utilised medium by far," says Rob Martin Murphy, executive creative director of Euro RSCG Partnership Singapore. "It is an inexpensive and very effective way for client's brands to start conversations with consumers. More clients should take advantage of radio. There's a lot of bad stuff out there and it's not too difficult to make a brand stand out."

"When you're writing TV or print, you're basically showing off your imagination. When you're writing radio, you're showing off *the listener's* imagination." Antony Redman, writer, former creative director and now indie movie director, believes radio is probably the most vivid form of advertising. "No director or photographer or actor can ever match up to the pictures we create in our own minds."

YET radio advertising is riddled with conventions. Characters in commercials are heavily stereotyped. Seventy percent of radio ads contain information about availability. Ninety percent of radio ads use a narrator or voice-over. Many employ the donut principle: music top and bottom with a voice-over hole punched in the middle. Worse, the same commercials are run too long and at too high a frequency.

Many of Bill Bernbach's observations hold specific meaning for radio, explains Keith Reinhard, chairman of DDB Worldwide. "Bill said, *You cannot sell a man who isn't listening* and *If your advertising goes unnoticed, everything else is academic.* In creating for radio, the first job is to get the 'listener' to listen. And there is no end to the number of ways we can arrest attention — a musical gliss, a surprising word, a hushed tone, a mysterious sound effect, or by eavesdropping on a private conversation." Reinhard quotes another Bernbach principle: *Word of mouth is the best medium of all.* "Radio lets us put a catchphrase on millions of tongues or plant a jingle squarely in the humbox of every shower singer in the country. Bill also said, *There is practically nothing that is incapable of boring us.* And Lord knows, there are enough boring radio commercials to prove that point."

Radio is a creative wasteland, says American advertising commentator and author Warren Berger, editor of The One Club's *One* magazine. "Radio is the least respected form of advertising in the United States. It relies almost entirely on humour, but because subtlety is hard to use on radio, it is usually very obvious hit-'em-over-the-head type humour, very loud and juvenile. There has been occasional good work — Motel 6 by the Richards Group is considered a shining example."

Steve Henry calls radio a difficult medium. "Probably more rubbish is produced for this medium than any other." Henry is creative partner at London's Howell Henry Chaldecott Lury & Partners. "The wear-out factor is very high for all broadcast media, but radio suffers from it very badly. The usual argument put forward is that radio briefs are given to junior teams, and senior teams don't give it the attention it deserves. There's some truth in that, but it's a chicken and egg situation. Maybe senior teams fight shy of it because the medium is so intrinsically unrewarding? We can all quote examples where radio was the lead medium, or a significant part of the marketing mix, and where great work resulted, but crucially those examples are few and far between."

The legendary Dick Orkin started The Famous Radio Ranch in Los Angeles in 1979. Orkin's work is the reference standard in American radio creativity. Creative partner Christine Coyle describes the majority of radio commercials as: "Either wild, over-the-top, jokey, implausible situations, or copy that is dull, derivative and boring, delivered with a cloned announcer sound." Much of it is written by agency juniors who know little about creating emotionally-based commercials for today's consumer, or written and produced by local radio stations with the same knowledge issue. Creative copy gets short shrift, she says. "We take the time to make sure our advertising is relevant, researched, and reaches out to the listener with a compelling story that is strategically sound, stories that break away from the tired, announcement-driven standard ad form."

TITLE: MOTEL 6 "DEER"

One of many brand-building monologues delivered by Tom Bodett. Duration: 30 seconds.

SFX: *COUNTRY-STYLE FIDDLE PLAYING THROUGHOUT...*

TOM: Hi, Tom Bodett for Motel 6. When a deer sees headlights, he just stands there in the middle of the road.

You know why? Because he's stupid.

When people see the light, they stop throwing away money and go to Motel 6.

You know why? Because they're smart.

Be smart. Save some ... doe. I'm sorry. Save a buck. Ooops.

Anyway, call Motel 6 and we'll leave the light on for you.

Arguably America's most celebrated radio campaign in recent years: Motel 6 from The Richards Group Dallas. Each commercial was in the form of a folksy monologue promoting the budget motel chain with unashamed honesty. The campaign is explored in detail in Chapter 5 of this book.

TITLE: MOTEL 6 "PRESIDENT"

SFX: *COUNTRY-STYLE FIDDLE PLAYING THROUGHOUT...*

TOM: Hi, Tom Bodett for Motel 6 with an open letter to the President. Well sir, you asked us all to contribute to helping shrink up the deficit. And since what's good for the goose is good for the gander, I've got a painless way for you to contribute along with the rest of us — Motel 6. Instead of staying at those big fancy places when you go out on business, you could stay at The Six. You'd get a clean, comfortable room for the lowest prices of any national chain and a good night's sleep to go along with it. Those guys in the suits and the dark glasses that follow you around could stay in the room with you for just a few extra dollars. Heck, maybe you could all watch a free in-room movie or make a few free local phone calls or something. It'd be a blast. Oh sure, you'd have to do without a shower cap and that fancy guava-gel conditioning shampoo, but all in all, Mr. President, I'd say you've probably already spent enough money on your hair, anyway. I'm Tom Bodett for Motel 6, and we'll leave the light on for you, sir.

Danielle Sterrie, vice president of London International Advertising Awards, started her career at London's Hobo Radio and Music Productions. She identifies a common fault in weak radio commercials: "Trying to pack too much information into the time they have. There's so little consideration for how they're going to sound, and how people are going to absorb the information." Silly voices are another hallmark of poor radio. "They can't think of an idea. They don't put any effort into being creative."

BBH Asia Pacific Singapore executive creative director Steve Elrick blames lack of creative motivation. "How many people do you know who actually read the radio scripts in the award books? Most creative directors won't even ask to hear radio spots or look at scripts in portfolios. Too much effort — radio translated to the page is such a poor communication of the medium."

As Britain's Jeremy Bullmore once asked, "I have sometimes wondered what radio advertising would be like if radio commercials cost as much to produce as television commercials do."

RADIO'S STRENGTHS AND WEAKNESSES

Neil French, worldwide creative director of Ogilvy & Mather, sums them up: "Its strengths are the possibility of using sound to create pictures in the mind, and its cheapness. Its weakness is that radio is usually a background to another activity — unless it's the BBC World Service!"

"Radio is no place for subtlety," comments Paul Fishlock, creative director of Brown Melhuish Fishlock Sydney. His work was selected for the *D&AD Copy Book*. "Assume your audience is less than half listening and that there is enough background noise to at least half bury your message. If there isn't, you're way in front already." However, he argues, you can be very personal in terms of the stations that you buy and the times that you put your spots out. "If we've got a tightly defined market we shouldn't be shy about identifying them. 'If you've got a child under two...' may not be the most creative opening to a radio spot, but it will sure get everybody with a child under two paying attention."

Jack Vaughan believes relevancy is critical on radio. Vaughan, of

Sydney's Principals, has held the posts of executive creative director and chairman in London and Australia at agencies like Young & Rubicam, George Patterson Bates and The Campaign Palace. "I know radio is often cast as a background medium, but I've never been quite convinced about that. I'm not sure our archetypal housewife using radio as 'company' is able to tune out the way it is said she does. And if she is that insensitive, no amount of loud noises, brash jingles or other attention-seeking banality is going to cut through." Vaughan considers that most people have a subconscious that is continually monitoring the world around them for interesting, but not necessarily loud, things. "If your message is relevant, even if it's *sotto voce*, it will cause them to listen. We know that's what happens in real life. You can be in a crowded room, full of people, filled with conversation, and yet we can still pick up on key words in a group three metres away if they interest us." Vaughan points to more conscious listening habits, especially in drivetime. "A lot more radio these days is drivetime. Women driving to schools or shops or the job. Men commuting. More traffic means more time with the radio and more conscious active interaction. So again, even more relevance is needed. Their attention shouldn't be taken for granted."

On radio, relevance converts hearing to listening.

"CREATE room temperature," advises Michael Conrad, chief creative officer, Leo Burnett Worldwide. "It is important to determine where the listener will be located — driving in a car versus ironing shirts at home. At what time will the commercial run? How often will it run? What stations will it be on? A more energetic execution might work better in the morning, and a calmer execution might work better at night — but this does not mean putting people to sleep. A good going-in position might be like talking to or with a friend."

"Radio can do anything," avows Michael Newman, former executive creative director at Saatchi & Saatchi Sydney and now principal director of brandnewman, an ideas company devoted to brand property development. "It's immediate. Radio is a tactical response unit. Fast turnaround in production means that radio can be as powerful as press when it comes to topical or guerilla ideas." But it's also for the long run, says Newman. "It's an habitual medium, so you can build storylines and characters over multiple executions over many years. It can reach people where nothing else can. It can be more target specific than any other medium, which means you can talk directly to people…" As Newman points out, the US dropped radios on Afghanistan.

Too often, radio is the poor man's television. Brent Hahn's take on that: "If the TV concept, the Big Idea, is a good one, why not embrace it? It's fundamentally smart branding and genuine, selfless team play. And it's an opportunity to show the TV guys that you can execute their concepts better than they can." Hollywood-based Hahn is founder and creative director of RadioActive! Commercials and winner of many major radio awards. His creative palette ranges from unadorned monologues to music-and-sound-design epics. For Hahn's money, radio's strength is the fact that it has no pictures. "We can create any scene, any universe, quite simply." Compared to television, clients often view radio as insignificant. "If you're lucky, they'll trust you to do a good job and leave you alone."

"To do great radio, you have to think of that 30-second window into people's ears and how you can take them somewhere else." Sydney-based David Alberts is regional creative director of Mojo Partners. Radio takes a lot more imagination than TV, he contends, because you don't have the safety net of pictures. "People forget the environment that their ad is played in. By nature radio is either predominantly music or words, so you have to play off what's expected." He references a radio campaign he did in London at Chiat/Day for Hutchison Telecom, a mobile phone company. "The brief was that they were opening a new chain of retail stores. So we used talkback radio, and we went around London and got the numbers of public phones. We'd ring the public phone and just let it ring and see who answered, because people can't ignore a ringing phone. *Someone* would answer. And it would be a *real* person. They'd say, 'Hello, hello?' And the deejay would ask their name and say, 'Where have you been? I've been looking everywhere for you. Don't you have a mobile phone?' And they'd say, 'No', and the deejay would tell them where to get one at Hutchison's…"

The results were entirely unpredictable — and made compelling radio:

SFX:	*PHONE RINGS.*
COURIER:	Hello.
DEEJAY:	You're a difficult man to pin down, I've been trying for days.
COURIER:	No, mate, you've got the wrong bloke.
DEEJAY:	I don't think I have. Do you have a mobile phone?
COURIER:	Yeah, mate. I'm a cycle courier. I just picked up the phone.
DEEJAY:	Do you have a telephone on your bike?
COURIER:	No, I don't…
SFX:	*PHONE RINGS.*
INDIAN MAN:	Hello, you are in a phone box.
DEEJAY:	That's right.
INDIAN MAN:	There is nobody here.
DEEJAY:	There is, you're there.
INDIAN MAN:	Hello?
SFX:	*PHONE RINGS.*
LIVERPOOL MAN:	Hello.
DEEJAY:	Hello, can you help me, please?
LIVERPOOL MAN:	Err … this is a public phone box you're ringing.
DEEJAY:	Slow down, slow down, you have a funny voice.
LIVERPOOL MAN:	It's my Liverpool accent.
DEEJAY:	Listen. I need your help. Can I contact you on a pager?
LIVERPOOL MAN:	On a what?

DEEJAY:	You can pick up a phone at Hutchison Telecom's new store in the Arndale Centre.
SFX:	*PHONE RINGS.*
CHINESE MAN:	You've got a long number.
DEEJAY:	I've got a very long number.

Alberts believes a lot of radio dialogue sounds very set-up. "So we got people involved in *spontaneous* conversations…"

Radio: A Primary Or Secondary Medium?

"Every medium can realistically be a primary brand builder." Vaughan believes it doesn't happen as much for radio as it does for TV or print due to a number of causes. "Because it is cheap, quick and flexible, because you can write it in one day, record it the next and run it the day after, radio is so useful tactically that that's become a self-perpetuating thing."

For Vaughan, the whole question of "radio sovereignty" may well be linked to the issue of creative administration in agencies. "Say you're in creative charge of an agency that believes every ad it sends out should be of an equally excellent standard. You have a client with a three million-dollar budget. The choice is TV or radio. Here's the dilemma: a radio spot requires just as strong an idea as a TV spot — in other words, the same amount of time and creative talent. Yet radio burns up material faster. With its cheaper airtime, you need six spots or more to match one TV spot. But because the airtime is cheaper, you don't get the same return on the revenue, even on a fee basis. In this scenario, it's hard to justify six times the creative hours and effort. If it happens often enough, your business model isn't viable. You need more people in the department to keep the standard up for radio, but your return on investment is less." He also points to a lack of understanding within agency account service departments that there aren't "grades" of ideas or craft. "They feel that because radio is less revenue-generating, you don't need 'as much of an idea' and as much time and effort to complete the task."

Conrad thinks it is an excellent, smart option to consider radio as a primary brand-building medium. "If it makes sense with the target, a brand could *own* the medium." However, he adds, "Brand teams do not think media neutral when they approach ideas. They think 30-seconds TV first." Conrad is excited about a new radio medium in development: "Intercontinental radio on the Web might provide new targets and promote fresh radio advertising in the future."

Fishlock lends his support for radio as a primary medium. "Not knowing if any other media was used, I'm confident that the Motel 6 radio campaign would have built a fantastic, unapologetic 'budget-motel-with-attitude' brand."

Newman references the launch of a new sports category, Indoor Cricket, using only radio. "Radio can launch new products without the help of any other media. You can even drive multimedia campaigns from your radio idea."

"Radio is the prime brand-building medium for many of our clients," reports Coyle. "For 18 years we've been doing highly successful campaigns for two car dealers — Toyota Carlsbad in Carlsbad, California and Keystone Motors outside of Philadelphia. Toyota does some minor TV, and both dealers do print, but radio has been the medium that has set them apart from their competitors. In fact, the Toyota Carlsbad dealership competes with several multi-location dealers, one that has 16 branches, one with 12 and another with 10. Yet when any kind of local polling is done, Toyota with one dealership consistently holds top-of-mind awareness. Usually there is a question centring on name, and Toyota Carlsbad is one of the top three answers given." Coyle says The Famous Radio Ranch also works for a local bank in St. Louis, and again radio is the prime brand-building medium. "On a national level, we have created spots for the Maui Visitors Bureau, which have been very successful at branding Maui as *The Magic Isle*."

RADIO alone can build awareness and increase reach, and Britain's Radio Advertising Bureau offers the proof. From October 1999 to April 2000, Millward Brown International continuously tracked consumer awareness and attitudes for brands advertised in two comparable British regions — Derby and Coventry, both in the

Central ITV region. Seventeen brands were involved. Nearly 5,500 telephone interviews were conducted among people aged 16 to 44. For each brand, one of the towns received radio advertising while the other did not. Television advertising was common across both. The study showed that adding radio to TV has a 15% multiplier effect; that is, if 10% of a given TV budget is redeployed onto radio, the campaign's efficiency in building awareness increases on average by 15%. Radio in isolation was only three-fifths as effective as television at raising advertising awareness — but its effectiveness was achieved at only one-seventh the cost. The most effective radio campaigns outperformed even the average for TV.

Curiously, there was clear evidence of misattribution: consumers often thought they had seen a campaign on television when in fact only radio had been used.

The study also probed radio's ability to go it alone. Seven of the brands in the study were tracked when they were only advertising on radio. One brand had had no media activity in the Midlands area for eight months. In February 2000, the brand continued to stay off TV but ran a four-week burst of medium weight radio in Coventry. In contrast, there was no radio advertising for the brand in Derby. When the responses from radio listeners in both areas were compared, a clear uplift in advertising awareness was obvious in Coventry. Again, television was cited as the source.

Interestingly enough, television stations, movie companies and newspapers are among radio's biggest users. In fact, in 2001 entertainment and the media represented Britain's top radio advertising product sector.

SELL THE FLAVOUR, NOT THE FEATURES

Radio can sell one thought — and a thousand feelings. Radio can't communicate a shopping list of features. It sells the flavour of the product. One well-executed theme can leave a strong picture in a listener's mind and, as the psychologists have told us, hearing memory in humans is stronger than sight, touch or smell memory.

"Radio operates in a circuitous manner," observes Clive Desmond, co-owner of Toronto music and sound design specialist Louder. "When skilfully constructed, it hits responsive chords in the listener.

You don't have to say everything. You just have to say the right stuff to lead the listener to jump to his or her own conclusions, to let the listener's imagination take over and fill in the blanks."

Unfortunately, too many radio commercials do try to say everything — and end up communicating nothing. Each commercial should set out to achieve one main goal, not many.

"A radio commercial is not a press ad, and unfortunately a lot of advertisers treat radio as though it were." Australian Bob Dennis is vice president creative services at Singapore's MediaCorp Radio, heading a unit that creates and records commercials in four languages for 13 radio stations. He writes, directs and voices radio commercials, and has notched up over 350 Australian and international radio awards. "A bad radio commercial is one that you don't actually hear while it's playing. It doesn't grab your attention and make you want to listen to it. One main problem is an excess of information. While this problem isn't unique to radio, I believe its negative impact is far greater in radio than other media." Dennis questions whether prices should be used in retail radio commercials: "I don't think people remember the prices. If you said '20% off everything', people will remember it, it sounds like something. But if you said 'now $30', or 'now $40', it's a waste of time." Dennis thinks radio works well for branding and image building. "It works for features, to a certain degree, but you've got to be very careful as to how much information you put in." According to Dennis, tonality is a critical element. "People will listen to something because they're interested in it or entertained by it. I don't think people like being shouted at. There's enough noise in their life without giving them more. Hard sell is like loud sell, whereas you can make something not quite hard sell but still urgent."

Singapore creative director Garry Abbott believes radio gives the audience a sweetener, and lets them fill in all the rest. "Radio is the medium of the imagination. It fills spaces in people's minds." Abbott says radio is under-used and abused. It is a one-to-one medium that gets straight into people's heads. "Radio is the perfect medium to entertain people and take them along with the message. Radio can be a very sensual experience if it's done well, and a very painful experience if it's done badly." Abbott employed morning drivetime radio to sell business lunches for a five-star hotel. The commercials used humour to sell the flavour of the proposition, not the details. "Thirty seconds is the bare minimum to establish an idea. Anything longer simply lets the copywriter indulge in overwriting." If radio is doing its job, he adds, you don't need to support it with television and press.

Says Kash Sree, Cannes Advertising Festival Grand Prix winner in 2002, and now senior vice president and creative director at Leo Burnett Chicago: "A lot of people just treat radio as a cheap medium to say a hundred and one different things, which is a shame. I feel radio should be treated like TV. It should make one point, and it should reward the consumer for listening."

"The old adage, less is more, is sadly never applied to radio," observes Calvin Soh, president and creative director at Fallon Singapore. "Everyone tries to cram a half hour news read into 30 seconds." It is a pity, he argues, because sound is critically important in life. "Your sense of hearing is more acute than sight when you are newly born. And it's the last sense to leave when you die."

Personalised Pictures: Everyone's Dog Is Different

"We can paint more accurate and personalised pictures on radio than with any other medium." Reinhard talks about the way audiences identify with advertising. "Think about it. Instead of asking viewers to identify with a 'typical' family sitting down to a 'typical' dinner table in a 'typical' kitchen constructed on the set of a 'typical' television commercial, we can evoke the picture of the listener's very own kitchen simply by uttering a reminder, 'Tonight as your family sits down to dinner…' Eight words summon up a million separate kitchens in the minds of a million separate listeners — each picture entirely accurate and customised to the individual consumer. A million pictures for a lot less money than the 'typical' picture you tried to paint on TV." Radio, says Reinhard, has always been an interactive medium. "If I'm a listener, you supply the words, I supply the pictures."

Lane Atkins, vice president and creative director of BBDO Miami, also perceives radio as interactive. "The consumer becomes intimately involved in the creative process. What he perceives in his mind is, in large part, his own creation."

"As an engineer, a great love of mine is creating the pictures." Les Francis grew up listening to radio plays. From 1983 he was an engineer at the legendary Street Remley Studios where his passion for radio commercials developed. Today, as a producer-director-engineer Francis concentrates on the total perspective of the track. "When I see a script, I have a picture in my mind of how I think I'd like it to sound. The first thing I say is, does this have to be done in the studio? If there's any outside movement involved, I go outside. You can make it sound like you're outdoors with equalisation and bird noises, but if there's any 'movement' you'll hear the room working." Francis uses footsteps, even clothing movements, "whatever's necessary so that the commercial comes to life."

"A radio commercial cannot be illustrated, except in the mind of the listener," argues Mike Fromowitz, senior vice president and senior creative director, BBDO New York. "If a picture is worth a thousand words, then the right sound effect in a radio spot is worth 10,000 words. The sound of a train whistle immediately transports the listener to exotic countries along the Silk Road. The ominous sound of footsteps and a broken pane of glass immediately set the mood for a few words on home security."

Steve Owen, senior creative at Manchester's Key 103, elaborates: "Radio is a close personal medium. Radio has the ability to beam personalised images into people's heads using just sound." Owen emphasises this point by playing his clients the sound effect of a dog barking, then asks them to write down a brief description of the dog. "Everyone's dog is different. No two descriptions are ever the same. What a fantastic medium…"

TITLE: MITSUBISHI MOTORS AUSTRALIA "YETI"

SFX: *HIGH MOUNTAIN AMBIENCE, HOWLING WIND, AND THE YETI'S FOOTSTEPS. WE HEAR THE YETI ROARING THROUGHOUT.*

VO: Up here, in the thin air of the mountains, the Yeti has survived all these years, safe from its biggest threat — Man.

SFX: *SLOWLY FADE UP THE SOUND OF AN APPROACHING VEHICLE…*

VO: Where conditions are simply too harsh for Man to roam, the Yeti — with its white fur — remains hidden against the snow…

SFX: *THERE IS AN OMINOUS METALLIC CLUNK AS THE VEHICLE DRIVES PAST, FOLLOWED BY A DULL THUD AS THE YETI HITS THE GROUND.*

VO: There's no place a Mitsubishi Pajero four-wheel drive can't go, because it's perfectly adapted to abominable conditions.

Selling the flavour not the features: an award-winning spot for Mitsubishi Motors Australia from Young & Rubicam Adelaide, written by Jeremy Southern and Kevin McNamara, engineered by Pete Best at Best FX. The spot runs 30 seconds and minimal copy allows time for voice spacing and sound effects.

TITLE: KRAFT VEGEMITE "WAKE UP CALL"

An efficient operator and a lethargic-sounding young man.

SFX: *PHONE CONVERSATION.*

OPERATOR: Hello, wake up calls, what time please?

MAN: Oh, yes, um, can I book a wake up call for 6.30?

OPERATOR: 6.30am. Thank you, we'll call you then.

MAN: Hang on.

OPERATOR: Yes?

MAN: And one for 6.45.

OPERATOR: 6.30 and 6.45?

MAN: Yes. And 7. And one at 7.30 and maybe 7.45 please.

OPERATOR: I see.

MAN: Oh, and you'd better put me down for a 7.50 too.

MALE VO: Need some energy in the morning?

           Vegemite* — one of the world's richest known sources of Vitamin B.

MNEMONIC: *VEGEMITE MUSIC FANFARE UNDER.*

Selling the flavour with one singular message in 30 seconds. And if it has to be a telephone conversation, make sure it's relevant to the idea and product. Written by Andy Lish, engineered by Jason Murphy at Song Zu. Agency: Mojo Partners Melbourne.

*Australians spread Kraft Vegemite, a yeast extract, on their morning toast.

3

WHAT WORKS BEST ON RADIO

Radio is an art form. And, according to Bertolt Brecht, "art is not a mirror held up to reality, but a hammer with which to shape it."

The question is: what kind of hammer works best?

Lionel Hunt sees great radio in the same terms as great print and television. "Good, fresh, entertaining ideas, brilliantly conceived and executed."

Michael Newman says: "A great radio idea is the same as a great advertising idea."

While print and television advertising are embroiled in debates about form over substance, there is no question that having an idea is essential on radio. Simple ideas, with singular propositions, relevant to the listener, will stand out from the pack.

David Droga, executive creative director, Saatchi & Saatchi London, always looks for ideas in scripts. "Ideas that allow for as much theatre as possible. If the product or benefit is at the centre of the drama, then you will have *genuine branding*."

"Radio should be approached the same way as everything else — with an idea," says Chris Kyme, creative director and partner of new Hong Kong agency Bang! "So many run-of-the-mill radio ads tend to be conversations between people talking about the product. And that's not an idea." As an example of great idea-driven, product-centred dialogue and acting, Kyme references the brilliant British radio campaign for Philips in the early 1980s, starring comedians Mel Smith and Griff Rhys Jones. In the definitive sketch of the campaign Mel, the customer, goes into a shop to buy a video. He insists it has to be Japanese because they have all the good bits. The salesman, Griff, shows him a Philips. When Mel says that it "doesn't sound Japanese", Griff quickly corrects himself: "*Firips*, it's a *Firips*." More executions, with Mel and Griff portraying different characters, followed.

"The better radio commercials have ideas in the scripts and whether you put sound effects with them or not, they'd work because there's an idea." Brad Power directs radio commercials at STELLARadio Sydney, the specialist radio commercial division of Stellar Sound. Radio campaigns are rarely if ever researched through focus groups and Power sees that as a creative advantage. "Ideas remain intact. Once you go into research, ideas start to get whittled down, almost to a nonsensical point."

"When you have an idea, the spots write themselves," says the award-winning Canadian creative team Elspeth Lynn and Lorraine Tao at Toronto's Zig agency.

At Sonovision, South African radio guru John Culverwell pinpoints the hallmarks of great commercials:

1. They should be simple and contain a great idea.
2. They should be entertaining, whether you use humour or drama. "Entertainment" is what draws the listener in, engages them, and leaves them with a positive feeling about the product.
3. They should be well cast and produced. No shortcuts — great voices, actors and production are essential to make the scenario depicted credible.
4. They should understand the listener's environment or culture, and should speak the listener's language.
5. They should meet the brief and the advertising objective.

Cliff Freeman & Partners New York creative director Ian Reichenthal was responsible for the award-winning Hollywood Video

Library radio commercials. Reichenthal asserts: "It's not a general rule or anything, but a lot of the radio ads that I like best create a picture in your mind's eye. You can almost see what's going on."

Reichenthal believes the hallmarks of great radio ads are the same as the hallmarks of any other kind of ads:

1. They should be simple.
2. They should get, and hold, your attention.
3. They should make you feel something.
4. Directly or indirectly, they should make you want to go buy the thing.

SURPRISE

Great radio often contains a surprise in terms of idea or execution. Sometimes the very fact that a particular product is advertising on radio is in itself a surprise — for example, a paint company selling colour without pictures.

Linda Locke, regional creative director and chairman of Leo Burnett Singapore, cites surprise as a hallmark of great radio commercials. "Setting me up in a certain way, taking me down a certain route, then ambushing me with a twist. It might entertain me and make me laugh, or it might even shock me, make me stop and think." Listening, she says, is a solitary experience. The level of intimacy with which you can talk to someone, and surprise them, is more intense on radio. Another form of surprise: Locke advocates going against the station format and being intrusive. "You can leverage the listening environment and do the opposite to whatever mood that environment is creating."

Ralph Van Dijk, a director and co-founder of London's renowned Eardrum, identifies surprise, simplicity and relevance as key requisites. "If the first five seconds don't intrigue me, I'm not bothered by the next 25. The idea should remain pure *from start to finish*. If you have to deviate to accommodate other information, write an additional script."

Title: 2DAYFM PUBLIC SERVICE "CHILD ABUSE"

A little girl is playing and talking to her doll.
Duration: 45 seconds.

SFX: *MUSIC BOX PLAYS THROUGHOUT...*

LITTLE GIRL: Dolly, let's go upstairs and play dress up.
There's some very nice clothes, dolly. I
think you will look pretty in your pink
dress.

Come here, dolly, don't be scared. I won't
hurt you. Just pull down your panties. It's
okay, Mummy knows.

Come on, I'm just showing you some
affection. Don't cry, all Daddies do this
to their little girls.

SFX: *A SINISTER MUSICAL DRONE HELD UNDER...*

FEMALE VO: Children who have been sexually abused
often learn to accept it as normal
behaviour, and go on to harm others. If you
suspect any form of child abuse, please
contact your local Family Centre
immediately.

*The element of surprise works with harrowing effect in this public service
commercial sponsored by Sydney radio station 2DAYFM. Agency Doorley Abram
Davis & Chapman established innocence before twisting the situation.*

TITLE: NO FRILLS FUNERALS

A straight, unemotional voice-over used throughout.
Duration: 30 seconds.

VO: This is what it sounds like when you're buried in a
     $25,000 funeral.

SFX: *SIX SECONDS OF SILENCE.*

VO: This is what it sounds like when you're buried in a
     $2,000 funeral.

SFX: *SIX SECONDS OF SILENCE.*

VO: No Frills Funerals.
     Call 9247 6895.
     When you're gone, you're gone.

Strategic simplicity — plus the emotional power of silence to make the point.
Written and voiced by Jay Furby, engineered by Simon Hicks at Song Zu.
Agency: Saatchi & Saatchi Sydney.

SIMPLICITY

"We must be simple, brutally simple," asserts Michael Conrad. "In film it's good when you have a 5-second idea within a 30-second commercial, like *Runner escapes from beer belly* for Reebok. The 25 seconds or so can be used to give a brutally simple idea breadth and room."

Adrian Holmes is chief creative officer at Lowe & Partners Worldwide. His advice on writing television commercials applies as much to radio: "First be clear, then be clever. Clarity of message has become unfashionable. I always get the impression that some people think that to be understood is somehow reprehensible…"

"You don't have to go to the dark side of Pluto to get an idea," says Street Remley, recommending absolute simplicity. An American, Remley has called Australia home for over 30 years, firstly as creative director of Young & Rubicam Adelaide, and then as founder of his own legendary radio creative house Street Remley Studios. "If a commercial is for a leakproof pen, then the fact that the pen doesn't leak should be the central core of the idea. You don't have to borrow interest, or go to Hollywood, and then sticky tape the product to that borrowed interest. You make sure that the idea evolves directly out of the leakproof pen." Remley condemns derivative work. "Most often ads are not original ads at all. They're derived from an old Schwarzenegger movie, or a *Seinfeld* episode, or a current hit song or an old rock song they've bought rights to. In an idea sense it's a cop out, it's bad if you can't generate your own ideas." Remley's ideas and productions have won over 600 awards, including metal at the International Broadcasting Awards in Hollywood. He influenced a generation of Australian radio copywriters, voice talent and studio engineers. And, in the same way that Fallon made Minneapolis famous for advertising, Remley made Adelaide the epicentre of Australian radio creativity.

"People get lost in too much production, they get too clever with words." David Flint of Melbourne's award-winning production house Flint Webster argues for clear communication and a simple strong message. "Bad radio commercials generally have no idea, far too much happening, the wrong voice, and try to fit in too many words."

"It all starts with the writing, with the idea," says his engineer

TITLE: BROOKE BOND "CHOICEST" TEA

Throughout this 60-seconder, the voice progressively changes from a rather "twee" chap to unaccented British and concludes as a rather threatening Cockney.

VO: I say, could we have a bit of quiet, please. I'm going to do the Brooke Bond Choicest commercial now. Thank you. (Ahem…)

It wasn't too, too long ago that Brooke Bond Choicest was rather exclusive tea. You know, drunk by the right sort of chaps out of the right sort of cups, with jolly little cucumber sandwiches and that sort of thing. Of course…

times have changed quite a bit and nowadays Brooke Bond Choicest is enjoyed by many different kinds of people who want a really fine tea, particularly on special occasions. And since Christmas is a very special occasion, Brooke Bond are making a special offer…

which consists of two quarter-pound packets of Choicest Tea, banded together and on sale at special prices…

So what you want to do is this. Nick round the shops, look for the special packs of Choicest where words "Special Tea at a Special Price" are printed in big letters… And buy a packet 'cause at times like these it's nice to have a tea like Brooke Bond Choicest, that's a bit special, 'cause you never know who's goin' to drop in, do yer?

Tony Hertz kept it simple for Brooke Bond Tea: the power of the single voice was magnified as the voice progressively changed throughout the commercial.

partner Philip Webster. Webster was Street Remley's first sound engineer. Flint Webster tracks have won major awards at Clio, the London International Advertising Awards, the New York Festivals and the International Broadcasting Awards in Hollywood.

Cary Rueda, creative director at Dentsu Young & Rubicam Malaysia, calls radio "billboards for the ears". "Radio works best when the task is immediate, when the message has to be digested in the shortest possible time."

"SIMPLE is usually better," attests Tony Hertz, of London's HERTZ: RADIO and Other Clever Advertising. Hertz, an Anglo-American whose passion for radio has spanned 30 years, is the only writer-director to win a Gold Pencil for radio at Britain's D&AD Awards. His other radio awards include a D&AD Silver Pencil, 22 Clios, 2 Gold and 16 Silver ILR awards and numerous gongs at the London International Advertising Awards. "If you've got a good message, try not getting in its way. There's something really exciting about a beautifully crafted and presented straight commercial."

His commercial for Brooke Bond Tea was classically simple. Consumers perceived the brand as really exclusive, "only for snobs", and the commercial had to make it more accessible. Hertz began by asking: "What symbolised snobbery — and 'unsnobbery' — in England, and it's the way people speak. George Bernard Shaw said, 'As soon as an Englishman opens his mouth, another Englishman hates him.' I had this idea of somebody very, very posh becoming very, very common." Hertz was determined to record the ad in one take. "I knew I could edit it together, but I really wanted to find a guy who could do it in one take." He chose actor Peter Hawkins, a talented dialectician. "Apart from the voice, the writing was key. There are certain words in 'English' English that become giveaways of class. The way you pronounce the long 'a'. The way you do a glottal stop with a 't', when somebody of a certain class says 'butter' and when somebody else says 'bu' er'. The writing of the script was structured so that I gave the actor key words to change on. Hawkins loved it. He stopped being a 'voice'… what he did was play a number of different characters, rather than simply switching voices." Hertz believes a lot of people who write advertising are more involved in

TITLE: IMPERIAL WAR MUSEUM "LETTER"

A young, British male voice reads this poignant letter.

SON: To the best Mum in the world.

Dear Mum,

This letter I hoped you'd never receive, because it's just a verification of that terse, black-edged card which you received some time ago.

Tomorrow, we go into action. No doubt lives may be lost, but if this leaves the world a slightly better place, then I'm perfectly willing to make that sacrifice.

Don't get me wrong though, Mum, I'm no flag-waving patriot. No, my little world is centred around you and Dad. You are worth fighting for, and if it strengthens your security in any way, then it's worth dying for, too.

I want no flowers, no tears, no epitaph. Just be proud, and I can rest in peace knowing I've done a good job. Surely there's no better way of dying.

I loved you, Mum. You're the best Mum in the world. Goodbye,

Your son.

MVO: This letter was written by a young private the night before he died in battle. At the Imperial War Museum, we don't try to glorify the War. We try to give you an idea of what it was like to be part of it. We're open 10 until 6 every day. Nearest Tube is Lambeth North.

The Imperial War Museum. Part of your family's history.

Neil French's favourite radio commercial: "It could hardly be simpler."
A letter from a young soldier to his mother made an emotional 90-second
communication for the Imperial War Museum from Ogilvy & Mather London.

what they write, rather than what needs to be said. "The stuff that works is the stuff that you don't expect. Well-observed real moments are the source of great writing and great advertising. So watch people yourself and write what you see. Then you'll never have to write another quiz-programme, courtroom-scene, phone-in, psychiatrist-and-patient or film-trailer pastiche as long as you live, and the world will sound a lot better…"

PAUL RUTA believes Asian print work offers a universal learning for radio writers. Now based at D'Arcy Toronto, Ruta had served as a creative director in Asia. "The best print work from Singapore, Hong Kong and Thailand is uncluttered, uncomplicated, pure, and true to the idea. I'm sure this arose as a cultural and linguistic necessity, but along the way it has also become the envy of the global advertising community. Why is radio seldom so pure and simple…? Maybe because radio is words, and words are free, so we keep cramming them in till the time runs out." Ruta believes you should write what you believe is a good script for the length of your spot, then prune the words by half. "It's incredible how little it takes to fill 30 seconds." More so than other media, he stresses, radio ads have to be easily absorbed. "People typically listen with a fraction of their attention. Simplicity and directness are the main disciplines I've learned."

Neil French pioneered the minimalist approach in Asia. He strives for simplicity in print and television work, stripping ads down to the idea. The same, he says, applies to radio. He references the Imperial War Museum radio spot. "It could hardly be simpler, and it's by far my favourite spot. *Firips* is my second favourite — they're not just 'funny' voices, but character voices, known to the audience, and marvellously underplayed."

Mike Fromowitz is another veteran of Asian advertising. His award-winning creative output was centred in Hong Kong. "Radio is poorly suited for a multitude of messages within one commercial. The idea is to keep it simple. So you search for that one idea and stick with it. The addition of a second or third idea almost always results in lower recall, interest and comprehension of the first." Fromowitz also believes in repetition. "The major selling promise should be stated at least twice." Like French, he prefers minimalism.

TITLE: VIRGIN ATLANTIC "UPPER CLASS"

A 45-second "demonstration" by a measured, upper-class British voice.

MVO: Chances are, you're listening to this in your car, a perfect opportunity to take part in a simple demonstration.

Put your hand on that little lever under your car seat, the one that moves the seat forward and backwards.

Okay. Now, move it to the very forward position.

A little cramped?

Next, move your seat as far back as it will possibly go.

Now ask yourself which position you'd rather be in for ten hours…

(SLIGHT PAUSE…)

Because when you fly Virgin Atlantic Upper Class, you can expect up to 75% more leg room than other Business Classes.

Thank you for taking part in this demonstration. You may now return your seat to the upright position.

A simple, economically-written demonstration of leg room,
targeting the drivetime business audience, by Net#work Johannesburg.

"Most radio these days tends to be noisy, loaded with music, voices, sound effects — a wall of sound from start to finish. I find myself liking a more minimalist sound for cut-through reasons. To stand out, why not try something other than humour? Drama works wonderfully well. So do informative ads." *Fromowitz has faith in the power of the single human voice.* "Some of the best radio uses just one voice — but it is a voice with attitude. And when the voice delivers the material, it makes it compelling — be it thoughtful, witty, sarcastic or cynical…"

SUBVERSION

At Portland's Radioland, president and creative director Austin Howe looks for subversion in radio concepts. "Most scripts we get from agencies aren't at all subversive or mischievous. They're polite, and obedient, and boring."

"Quite honestly, I look for an element of 'We can't do that on the radio, can we?' Even if the commercial is just a single voice and serious, I look for some element of honesty or truth or execution that is mischievous. To me, big, subversive ideas are the key to great radio. The best commercials leave me with a sense of 'I can't believe they got away with that'."

He cites the famous Mel and Griff spot for Philips. "It's very funny, but the fact that the straight announcer signs off with '*from Firips*' is, to me, that element of subversion that makes it so great. Or the British RSPCA campaign where we hear a sick guy dying and find out later that it's actually a dog talking, whose owner is having him put down. Or a beer company making fun of their old advertising in *Real American Heroes*."

Even the mandatory legal copy at the end of a commercial can be subverted. "We did about a dozen spots for LA Cellular. They all had some different cookies for the listener at the end of the legal copy: 'Curb your dog', 'I think I love you', 'Lay off the eggnog' and 'I just need you to hold me'."

DAVID ALBERTS subverts radio by quickly changing the paradigm and creating culture. "You can start playing games at a low cost and have a high frequency." He demonstrates his agency's philosophy of

TITLE: HEALTH EDUCATION "THE DEPARTMENT OF SUICIDE"

OFFICIAL: Can I help you?

APPLICANT: Oh yes, I'd like to commit suicide, please.

OFFICIAL: I see. Something dramatic? We have an opening on the Forth roadbridge.

APPLICANT: No, I can't stand heights.

OFFICIAL: Oh. Gas ovens are still very popular.

APPLICANT: No, we're all-electric.

OFFICIAL: Pity. How about a nice overdose? That's very quick and neat.

APPLICANT: I'm not *really* in that much of a hurry.

OFFICIAL: Oh, why didn't you say so? I've got the very thing. Smoke.

APPLICANT: You mean, cigarettes?

OFFICIAL: Yes, a natural. Slow, expensive, unpleasant for those around you, and you can go in so many different ways.

APPLICANT: Really?

OFFICIAL: Oh yes. Lung cancer, throat cancer, emphysema, heart disease.

APPLICANT: That's marvellous. Thank you very much.

OFFICIAL: All part of the service. I should warn you though, it may take a while and there is a possibility that you might live.

APPLICANT: No, I'll chance it. Got a light?

OFFICIAL: Yes.

SFX: *MATCH STRIKES.*

APPLICANT: Thank you. *(INHALES)* Oh, I feel worse already. *(COUGHS...)*

Tony Hertz subverted conventional anti-smoking advertising: he delivered the salient facts in this hilarious, tersely written comedy sketch.

Uncommon Commonsense: "A client came to us and said Cointreau Lime & Soda had been delisted from clubs, and we need a one-off radio ad that says it is available in 'off-licence' (hotel bottle shops and liquor marts). When someone says 'I need a one-off ad', it's not going to be a great use of their money, so instead of making an excuse for it, we set up Cointreau Lime & Soda against the clubs. We ran a competition where we asked people to send in, either over the Internet or on a recorded message, their worst story of what had happened to them in a night club. And then we turned those entries into ongoing ads. Someone would ring in and say, 'I went to a night club and this guy came up to me and kissed me and then threw up on me, and it was the worst thing ever.' Then we'd add the tag, 'Cointreau Lime & Soda, fortunately available in off-licence.' We got 1,200 entries. Now we have a deejay who's going to record a club version of it, sampling the entries, and we're going to release it on the charts with a video called *Night Club Nightmares*. And that," swears Alberts, "will allow us to get back into clubs."

For another liquor brand, Alberts developed five radio ads that sounded like a series of legal disclaimers. The ads, in fact, whimsically disclaimed all responsibility for people's behaviour after they'd been drinking the product — for instance, "We take no responsibility for people who think they look like Tom Cruise..."

Not surprisingly, Alberts has no time for the conventional straight voice-over announcement. Radio, he says, is wonderful for creating a whole world around something.

SONIC BRAND TRIGGERS

Without visuals, pack shots and logos, how can radio commercials be branded? Radio mnemonic devices, also known as sonic brand triggers (SBTs), come in different forms and create virtual TV in the listener's mind. The SBT could be a distinctive sound effect that triggers the brand — for example, "Army soldier, (*SFX: Boots stamping to attention*) be the best". It could be the consistent use of a distinctive voice. The SBT could even be musical, like a match striking followed by the Hamlet cigar theme. SBTs work effectively for brands with nothing new to say, low interest brands, or brands with a long purchase cycle.

John Immesoete reviews the audio mnemonic: "Anything you can use in the medium to make the consumer remember your ad or your product is important. A phrase, a sound, a lyric, or a sound effect that does is invaluable. Anything that helps the consumer retain knowledge so he can pass it along to others is valuable."

Humour

"Comedy," says Conrad, "should be deadly serious. Humour is always good in advertising, but it's hard to do. The laugh or smile has to be created in the listener's mind, and not in the commercial."

Peter Souter, creative director of Abbott Mead Vickers BBDO London, once warned: "People try to be funny too often, when maybe they can't be that funny or maybe the particular topic of the ad doesn't warrant it." Souter believes that being funny is a common knee-jerk reaction to the need for radio commercials to engage and entertain. Creatives feel they *have* to be funny, he says.

For his part, French condemns the so-called "funny voice". "A 'funny voice' is no substitute for wit and humour."

"Humour is an innate quality, and writers either have it or they don't." Les Francis winces at the thought of yet another *Lone Ranger* or *Robin Hood* commercial. "Humour in radio writing suffers more casualties, more often. It is so subjective and it can get blown out of the water by any one person." How does Francis recognise and nurture a genuinely funny script when it comes in from an agency? "Firstly, there's more chance it's going to be funny if it's not borrowed interest, if it hasn't been done before. Another problem is that the script will be too long, so some of the humour in it will have to go. The best scripts I've worked on were workshopped in the studio, so just the bare bones, the plot and some funny lines, were written. *Most of the writing was rewriting.* A lot of the humour came out of the day in the studio, not out of the month before." How did it get recorded and produced? "Because the client understood radio and absolutely embraced radio."

Remley has an inclination towards humour. "Humour is not always possible or suitable. I love it when a client lets himself be the brunt of the humour because I think it makes for great advertising. Most of the people we really love in life are people who aren't afraid

TITLE: MAGNA MOVERS "BRAS AND PANTYHOSE"

This 40-seconder starts with an innocent enough conversation between a mother and daughter… before reaching a totally unexpected proposition.

GIRL: Hello, Mummy.

MOTHER: Hello, darling.

GIRL: What are you doing, Mum?

MOTHER: I'm getting dressed.

GIRL: What's *that*, Mummy?

MOTHER: That's my bra, sweetie.

GIRL: And *that*?

MOTHER: Those are my pantyhose.

GIRL: I want to wear bras and pantyhose!

MOTHER: My darling, you can't.

GIRL: *Why*?

MOTHER: Because bras and pantyhose are for grown-up ladies, for Mummies.

GIRL: And for Daddies.

MOTHER: *(LAUGHS)* No, darling, Daddy doesn't wear bras and pantyhose.

GIRL: He does!

MOTHER: Don't be silly.

GIRL: He *does*! When you go out to visit Granny, he does. I've *seen* him!

MVO: When you need to move in a hurry, call Magna International Movers. We'll get you moved quickly.

Lateral humour from South African hotshop TBWA Hunt Lascaris Johannesburg. The very natural-sounding performances heighten our sense of eavesdropping.

to laugh at themselves, who are a little bit self-effacing, and who don't take themselves too seriously. Clients who apply that to advertising, and in a tasteful way let themselves be the brunt of the humour, do themselves such a favour. And I've spent half of my life trying to convince clients of this."

Like Remley, Jack Vaughan will almost invariably write humorous radio, "unless it's for some life-and-death public service issue, and even then I'm not sure that the Voice of Doom isn't too predictable." In the case of radio, he says, never was it more relevant that listeners are attracted to people with a sense of humour, people who are fun and entertaining to be with. "When you're eavesdropping in a crowded party or bar, you'll tend to tune in on the joke-teller, rather than the guy with the sad story 'earbashing' the barman. Mind you, I'm not talking about belly laugh stuff. I'm talking about gentler versions of humour, whimsy perhaps."

Keith Reinhard likes radio that makes you laugh and love the brand. "DDB Chicago got laughs and won the US radio industry's top prize two years in a row." The award comes with US$100,000. "With tongue very much in cheek, the Bud Light campaign salutes *Real American Heroes* like Mr. Foot Long Hot Dog Inventor, Mr. Garden Gnome Maker and Mr. Really Bad Toupee Wearer. John Immesoete, the creative director who thought up the campaign, points out that you have to understand the irony — how to poke fun without being too mean-spirited. To make it all work, John found a bombastic-voiced announcer, backed by booming rock ballad singers, who is basically clueless as to what he's saying."

"Radio is ephemeral," contends Simon Collins, executive creative director of J. Walter Thompson Australia. Advertisers, he argues, should face the fact that people don't make time to listen to radio in the same way that they sit down to watch TV or read a newspaper; people listen when they are doing something else like driving. "Listening to the radio is the opposite of a group activity. Like the Internet, it is largely a solo activity. Generally people turn the radio on to lighten the atmosphere. Even in semi-serious radio, like talkback, the commercial breaks are light relief. Today, unless you live somewhere like Bosnia or Afghanistan, radio is a medium which accommodates humour better than anything else."

TITLE: BUD LIGHT "MR. SUPERMARKET FREE SAMPLE GUY"

SFX: *MUSIC UP…*

ANNCR: Bud Light presents … Real American Heroes.

SING: *Real American Heroes…*

ANNCR: Today we salute you, Mr. Supermarket Free Sample Guy.

SING: *Mr. Supermarket Free Sample Guy…*

ANNCR: Though man dreads few things more than a trip to the supermarket, you offer us shelter in a storm.

And maybe… a free mini-weenie.

SING: *Weenie freebie…*

ANNCR: Like a savvy trapper, you snag us at our lair — between the chip aisle and the beer aisle.

SING: *Stockin' up, yeah!…*

ANNCR: What exactly do you have? Who cares. If it's on a toothpick and it's free, it could be plutonium and we'd eat it.

SING: *You're feedin' me…*

ANNCR: So crack open an ice-cold Bud Light, Mr. Supermarket Free Sample Guy. *(SFX: BOTTLE TWIST OFF)* Without you, a trip to the supermarket wouldn't be nearly as super.

SING: *Mr. Supermarket Free Sample Guy…*

ANNCR: Bud Light Beer. Anheuser-Busch, St. Louis, Missouri.

At DDB Chicago, John Immesoete used humour and music to celebrate American icons for Bud Light.

TITLE: BUD LIGHT "MR. FOOT-LONG HOT DOG INVENTOR"

SFX: *MUSIC UP...*

ANNCR: Bud Light presents ... Real American Heroes.

SING: *Real American Heroes...*

ANNCR: Today we salute you, Mr. Foot-Long Hot Dog Inventor.

SING: *Mr. Foot-Long Hot Dog Inventor...*

ANNCR: When conventional wisdom said no one could make a hot dog longer than six inches, you dared to dream.

SING: *Dared to dream...*

ANNCR: You knew the limitations of a regular size hot dog bun, and you ignored them.

SING: *Can't stop me now...*

ANNCR: You made a ten-inch wiener and people cheered...

SING: *Oh...!*

ANNCR: But you weren't satisfied. You said, "Wait, I think I can still give you two more inches..."

And so the foot-long was born. So crack open an ice-cold Bud Light, Mr. Hot Dog Hero.
(SFX: BOTTLE TWIST OFF) Because you gave every single one of us our fondest wish — a bigger wiener!

SING: *Thank you, thank you, thank you...*

ANNCR: Bud Light Beer. Anheuser-Busch, St. Louis, Missouri.

TITLE: BUD LIGHT "MR. PICKLED PIGS' FEET EATER"

SFX: *MUSIC UP...*

ANNCR: Bud Light presents ... Real American Heroes.

SING: *Real American Heroes...*

ANNCR: Today we salute you, Mr. Pickled Pigs' Feet Eater.

SING: *Mr. Pickled Pigs' Feet Eater...*

ANNCR: Ignoring all you know about pigs, and where they live, and what they step in, you look at their pickled paws and say, "Yummy..."

SING: *Lookin' tasty...*

ANNCR: Craving only the most daring meal, you pass up the cow tongue, skate by the head cheese, dismiss the Rocky Mountain oysters...

SING: *Rocky Mountain oysters...*

ANNCR: But a pig's foot soaked in pickle juice — now *that's* good eatin'.

SING: *Save me a big one...*

ANNCR: So crack open an ice-cold Bud Light, Mr. Pickled Pigs' Feet Eater. *(SFX: BOTTLE TWIST OFF)* Because it takes guts to eat those feet.

SING: *Thank you, Mr. Pickled Pigs' Feet Eater...*

ANNCR: Bud Light Beer. Anheuser-Busch, St. Louis, Missouri.

TITLE: CONDOMS

A young man speaking conversationally.

VO: You know, it's a funny thing but a lot of people are embarrassed about using condoms.

   If you are, then I suggest you look away because I'm holding one.

SFX: *SLIPPERY SOUND OF A CONDOM PACK BEING SQUEEZED.*

VO: This is a condom, and besides being a contraceptive, it's the only protection you have against AIDS, apart from no sex at all.

   And yet, some people are still embarrassed about using condoms. There's nothing to be embarrassed about. Look...

SFX: *CONDOM PACK IS OPENED.*

VO: There it is.

   And they're easy to use. To show you how easy, I'm going to put it on.

   This microphone'll do. Just take the condom and place it over the tip.

SFX: *A DULL, SLIDING SOUND.*

VO: And gently roll it down from the top...

SFX: *A HEAVY, VIBRATING SOUND AS THE CONDOM SLOWLY ROLLS DOWN OVER THE MICROPHONE.*

   THE VOICE BECOMES MUFFLED:

VO: There. See? Simple. So there's no need to die of embarrassment.

   Use a condom.

In this classic Australian commercial, a young man demonstrates how to use a condom — on radio. All the pictures are created in the listener's mind as he talks.

At Santa Monica's Radio In The Nude, Andy Lerner believes humour lets you give a glimpse of the brand's personality. His company has majored in humorous commercials for clients like Coca-Cola, Kodak, Miller Beer and Cadillac, winning awards at Clio, the One Show and London International. "The reason that I think so many commercials use humour is simply that it works. I don't think anyone really wants to sit in their car listening to an announcer calmly listing the attributes of a product. If the message can be put across in a fun way, not only have you delivered the message, you may have also made a friend — or at least cast the product in a positive light. If you've done it right, you've captured the listeners' attention, related to them in some way, and made that moment they listened a little more enjoyable and possibly, hopefully, memorable."

Aural branding, he says, can be achieved through the personality of the commercial. "If you understand the brand, you should be able to communicate that through all aspects of production — the kind of humour, the actors, the music, the style of production."

HERTZ sounds a note of caution: "In the UK, creatives have become besotted with humour. They think radio has to be funny, or deeply tragic, or utterly shocking, to win an award. I think it's a shame because an awful lot of brand values are being chucked out of the window, and clients are allowing it to happen, simply because everyone thinks radio has to be two people talking funny to each other." As a result, he says, beautifully crafted brand-building radio commercials have become exceptionally rare because they don't win awards.

"Humour is the genre of first resort for too many radio writers," agrees Newman, "and not every good writer is a funny writer. There aren't enough really funny ads; too many are just ad-funny. Why are there so many clichéd caricatures masquerading as wit in radio commercials? Goofy voices and cringing puns aren't really funny, just forced." Newman considers there is a world of emotions we can touch in people beyond their funny bones. "If you're going to go funny, make sure it's a real giggle on the cold, pale page, even when the account executive reads it. Maybe then the talent can make it a belly laugh in the studio. Certainly, the opportunity of using a longer length commercial — even a 60- or a 90-second ad — makes genuine humour more possible. But it also leaves more room for error." Newman used humour for the Australian Labor Party campaign in a Federal Election and won awards for political ads. "Humour helped sweeten aggressive messages in a way that wasn't possible on TV."

Steve Henry discusses how to avoid the pitfalls of the not-very-funny radio ad. "Even more than in other media, know what elements of the script you want to protect from external influence, know what battles you need to win — and win them." Henry suggests collaborating with professionals. "The trouble is, everybody thinks they're funny and most people think they can write a funny radio ad. But the truth is never that simple. There are lots of professional comedy writers out there who'd love to help you put together your radio spot."

Lane Atkins recommends listening to comedians who get laughs *without* the use of expletives. "Their humour is much more thoughtful and imaginative."

THE JINGLE JANGLE

"Music is incredibly important," argues Henry. "It's been said that music is at least 50% of the power of a TV ad. More tellingly, it's fair to say that music is the most emotive thing in the world. All art aspires to the condition of music. Music can take you to places that no other appeal to your senses can do. It strikes deep at the heart of people's emotional lives."

Music is one thing, the typical radio jingle is another. Is the singing commercial the lowest form of advertising life? Here are some classics:

```
"Brylcreem, a little dab'll do ya,
"Brylcreem, you'll look so debonair,
"Brylcreem, the girls will all pursue ya,
"Simply rub a little in your hair…"

"How can you be sure
"There are no white ants in the floor,
"Borers in the door,
"Silverfish galore,
```

"Call the Flick man, that's your answer,
"Remember one Flick (*FLICK SOUND*) and they're gone!"

"Murray Mints, Murray Mints,
"Are too-good-to-hurry mints."

Over the years, music has effectively registered many campaign themes in our minds. Marlboro and Coca-Cola are prime examples. In fact, Alberts cites the case of an air crash in Spain: "The black box recorded the pilot's voice as the plane went down. Without thinking, he started singing a jingle from when he was seven years old." For PowerAde sports drink, his agency created a jingle that was aired heavily for a month before becoming a background 'irritant' in the minds of sportsmen in the next flight of commercials, thus subverting the process of having a jingle.

Music has performed many miracles on radio. Indeed, the first singing commercial on American network radio saved the famous brand Wheaties from extinction. Faced with flagging sales, General Mills was about to kill the cereal. Then, on Christmas Eve 1926, the Wheaties Quartet sang a little ditty called *Have you tried Wheaties?* and the rest is history.

"I denounce the cheesy jingle style as much as the next adman, but I do think the pendulum may have swung too far the other way." Music is one of radio advertising's greatest assets, asserts Paul Fishlock, and why a good deal of a radio audience is listening anyway. "Music can be radio's pictures. People who've never consciously heard your ad can find themselves singing along to it. Sometimes we're far too cool about the way we use music for our own and our clients' good."

Conrad believes it all depends on how fresh the jingle is. "*Real American Heroes* from Budweiser is very funny and I guess very successful with the people. We awarded that campaign with Gold at the Clios."

For French, music isn't a priority on radio. He's got a CD player for that. "I expect there have been great jingles, I just can't recall any. And if radio is music, how does a jingle break the clutter...?" French takes the view that radio is more complicated than other broadcast media because of its precise audience differentiation. "Too many

TITLE: DEFENDER SNAIL PELLETS "YOU MADE ME LOVE YOU"

VO: A snail serenades Defender Snail Pellets…

ENGINEER: Cue the snail!

SINGER: ("AL JOLSON" VOCALS)
You made me love you,
I didn't want to do it,
I didn't want to do it…

VO: Snails are only human, they don't want to die. But with Defender, they don't have a choice in the matter. Rain or shine, the smell of Defender makes them fall in love with the pellets — and love can hurt…

SINGER: *You make me feel so bad…*
Gimme, gimme, gimme, gimme what I cry for,
You know you got the kind of kisses
That I die for…

VO: Defender, the pellets snails are dying for, for about half the price of the number two brand…

SINGER: *You know you made me love you…*

VO: In the garden-green pack at your supermarket, hardware or nursery.

One of the rare occasions when Street Remley used music: old-fashioned love ballads made the point that Defender Pellets attracted snails, then killed them. Mandatory copy points are seamlessly incorporated into the script.

TITLE: DEFENDER PELLETS "I ONLY HAVE EYES FOR YOU"

VO: A snail serenades Defender Snail Pellets…

ENGINEER: Cue the snail!

SINGER: ("AL JOLSON" VOCALS)
           Are the stars out tonight?
           I can't tell if it's cloudy or bright,
           'Cause I only have eyes for you, dear…

VO: When snails slither out at night to munch on
           your garden, you can be glad they only have
           eyes for Defender Pellets.

           Or actually, noses.

           Snails are attracted by the smell of Defender,
           which is the last thing they know before the
           lights go out…

SINGER: *I don't know if I'm in a garden,*
           Or on a crowded avenue…

VO: And yet Defender Pellets only cost about half
           the price of the number two brand…

SINGER: *I only have eyes for you…*

VO: Defender, in the garden-green pack at your
           supermarket, hardware or nursery.

people think 'radio' and forget the ambience of the station. The ad should depend entirely on the type of radio station it's going on. A country and western station is not the place for a rap ad, and vice versa. Classical FM is not the place for Spice Girls rip-offs or 'funny' voices. Actually, *nowhere* is the place for 'funny' voices…"

Hunt also takes issue with jingles. "I think jingles got a bad name because most of them were so bad. Also, I think many of them were very poor communications as you couldn't hear most of the words. There's nothing wrong with music though, it can obviously have a very powerful emotional pull and underscore what's being said. Having said that, given that most radio stations play nothing but music and most radio ads are using music, I like to hear just the spoken word. Churchill didn't need background music for his radio broadcasts."

"The mistake is to use music as a replacement for an idea." Mark Rivett is a partner, creative director and composer at Australasia's biggest music and sound design company, Song Zu. Rivett has won many accolades for his film and television music. "Jingles almost don't exist these days. They've given way to music tracks. Music is not a cop out, it never was, but you still need an idea if you're using music and it had better be a good one." Rivett recommends finding the right person to collaborate on a music track. "Radio was made for music, and music was made for radio. It is true, however, that music on radio is tricky and very easy to get wrong."

While Hertz does not like the majority of jingles, he believes certain phrases "sing well". "They feel good when you sing them. And that is my criterion. If it happens, then I'd write a jingle." But it should not be a case of if you can't think of an idea, sing something.

Newman recalls he once used an angelic choir in baroque style, on a rock station, for a car dealer. "The canniness of the engineer and the authenticity of the production helped keep the rewards-for-listening coming."

Reinhard has no qualms about music. "Radio is a good way to get people singing your song. I'm a big fan of music in advertising and even worked with a talented friend once to write a song about why:

```
"Usin' music in your spot,
"Cuts the copy down a lot,
"Gives your proposition power,
"When they sing it in the shower.
"Usin' music in your ads,
"Has 'em dancin' 'cross the land,
"And you'll be steppin' out
"From all them other brands."
```

BUT what kind of music separates brands best? An original music track or buying the rights to an established song?

"Rule One for me is that the creative device doesn't overtake the branding." Peter Clark of Sydney creative house CLAX is an agency-trained copywriter, a classically trained composer and musician, and a voice-over. His radio jobs included music producer, newsreader and deejay. His father headed Australia's biggest radio network, Macquarie, and his mother was an opera singer. "There's always the danger that you'll pay a music publisher $60,000 for the rights to a song, revitalise everyone's memory of the song, but not do a single thing for the product. Sometimes a great song is so all-consuming, you lose sight of what the brand is. If you can't remember the brand, it's not going to do anything." Would changing the lyrics improve the branding? "It's very dangerous. If it's a silly song, a funny song, you can do what you like. But if it's a serious song, it's sacrilege to start carving it up and risk offending people."

Clark believes there are two kinds of jingles. "There's the classic jingle, some persuasive copy put to music which the Americans pioneered, like:

```
"You'll wonder where the yellow went
"When you brush your teeth with Pepsodent…"
```

"They're punchy little trademarks. They're just like learning your multiplication tables, you can still remember them 30 years later, and you don't have to like them for them to work."

The other kind of jingle is what Clark calls the concept jingle. "We pioneered those in Australia. They had more substance and more the qualities of pop songs." The genre was defined by the work of Alan

TITLE: CHANNEL SEVEN SPORT "UP THERE CAZALY"

This jingle celebrated the spirit of the Victorian Football League's Aussie Rules game and promoted the television coverage by Channel Seven. (Although the song was first heard in a TV ad, it demonstrated the awesome power of the right music in advertising.)

SUNG: Well you work to earn a living,
But on weekends comes the time.
You can do whatever turns you on,
Get out and clear your mind.
Me, I like football,
And there's a lot of things around.
When you line them up together,
Footy wins hands down.

Up there Cazaly, in there and fight.
Out there and at 'em, show 'em your might.
Up there Cazaly, don't let 'em in.
Fly like an angel, you're out there to win.

Up there Cazaly, you're out there to win.
Up there and at 'em, don't let 'em in.
Up there Cazaly, show 'em your height.
Fight like the devil,
The crowd's on your side.

The crowd's on your side.

Ron Mather, national creative director of The Campaign Palace Australia, describes advertising success as when an ad becomes "currency". In 1979 the agency's ad for Channel Seven Sport featured the jingle Up There Cazaly *written by Mike Brady, which became the first commercial song to reach the Australian pop charts and receive countless thousands of free exposures on radio.*

Morris and Alan Johnston, founders of the Mojo agency, and included *I feel like a Tooheys or two*, which became the anthem of Australian beer drinkers. A lot of detractors say that a jingle is taking the easy way out, but Clark disagrees. "A lot of famous campaigns are founded on music."

Jingles were at their peak in the days of cigarette advertising. Every brand had a full orchestra playing its song, with musicians called back constantly to record alternative versions — country and western, Dixieland jazz, rock, folk. The tobacco companies kept the musicians and studios busy, as Clark recalls: "They were dealing death, but they were the 'angels'…"

STORYTELLING

Stories define the human condition, especially when they hold a cracked mirror to life. Radio is the medium made for stories.

"Some of the greatest stories throughout history were handed down through the oral tradition," attests Steve Owen. "These stories were created to be told, not read."

In Hertz's book, "The purest, and in many ways the most satisfying radio ad, is one person talking. No effects, no music, just someone — woman or man or child — talking. It is the direct line from the oral storytelling tradition, and it can be an immensely powerful advertising technique."

Batey Ads Singapore used children's stories to create awareness of animal cruelty. Each story started innocently enough with lines like "This little piggy went to market" and "The owl and the pussycat went to sea", before they described in graphic detail how animals are slaughtered for food. Bob Dennis and Antony Redman worked on the production at MediaCorp Radio. Their key decision was to leave the storyteller's voice "cold", with no added music or sound effects, allowing the contents of each story to create disturbing pictures in the minds of the listeners. As Dennis recalls, "It's often better to let the words tell the story, rather than add another element which can confuse the listener and take a lot of drama away from the idea." The campaign won Best of Show for Radio at the 1996 London International Advertising Awards.

"Many ads are part story, part sell," advises Newman. "Radio

TITLE: VOLVO "PAUL DOBEY"

We hear the unemotional voice of Paul Dobey throughout.

DOBEY: My name is Paul Dobey and this is what happened to me last February.

I was feeling sick while I was driving along the M6, and I decided to pull onto the hard shoulder in my Volvo Estate.

After a short while, I felt better and I put my safety belt on to continue my journey. But it wasn't just nausea that hit me that day.

I looked in the mirror and to my horror, I saw a lorry speeding towards me on the hard shoulder. I thought, that's the last thing I'm ever going to see in my life.

I was hit from behind with incredible force. My Volvo was spun around, tipped onto its side, and pushed 200 yards up the motorway into a ditch.

I climbed out of the car and I discovered that I had been struck by a 40-ton articulated lorry with a JCB earthmover on the back.

Now I reckon if it hadn't have been for the Volvo's passenger safety cell, I'd never have known what hit me.

MVO: Volvo. A car you can believe in.

Storytelling: this convincing 60-second first person narrative conveys horrific visuals through the human voice. Agency: Abbott Mead Vickers London.

should be more seamless, so I prefer to make the sell part of the story."

Yukio Nakayama recalls a 2-minute radio story scripted by his wife that he directed for Suntory Whiskey. "A thirty-something man talks about his memory of his father, as though he was speaking at his father's funeral. When the man was just a child, he asked his father to buy him a new bicycle. At that time, however, his father did not have much money so he had to abandon something in order to buy the bicycle for his son. He gave up drinking whiskey at night, which was his only reward for the tough job he did every day. He kept it a secret from his son. One day he had saved enough money to buy his son the bicycle. The son, now a middle-aged man, remembered not the whiskey his father drank but the whiskey his father did not drink." As Nakayama explains, the son understood his father's sacrifice when he had his own child. "We tried to express the reality of the product that did not exist. The father gave up his most favourite thing, his whiskey, and in turn realised his little son's dream." The commercial won Japan's ACC Radio Grand Prix in 1985 and was selected for the ACC Hall of Fame.

"Radio is very good at creating suspense, drama and humour," says Carl Jones, vice president and creative director, BBDO Mexico. "Like the *Friday Fright* dramas on the Canadian Broadcasting Corporation. Good radio is radio that involves you and has a twist."

"There's always some kind of conflict in any great story, drama or comedy, and it's true for radio spots as well." Ken Bennett is the Mercury Gold award-winning creative director at Outer Planet, located on Bainbridge Island, Washington State, a 35-minute ferry ride from downtown Seattle. Bennett believes scripts should contain tension or conflict of some kind. Characters should be strongly drawn, and remain consistent throughout. "Also, I love situations that have been pushed into the realm of lunacy, as long as there's a basis in reality. Radio is a great place to go for the absurd."

"WE believe wholeheartedly that in an age where consumers have seen it all and heard it all, stories are a fresh alternative." Christine Coyle refers to stories as any kind of dramatic narrative. "We prefer comedy because we find most things funny and there is a reward to the listener for the time spent. But a good story can be funny or not, a monologue or a dialogue."

But, stresses Coyle, the stories must come from real life, and radio copywriters must be willing to self-disclose. "Every moment of every day presents us with fodder for good advertising. Just yesterday, Dick Orkin and I were at lunch. He wanted to order the onion soup, but the waitress heard him say 'pea soup'. When he corrected her, she said 'What?' and he corrected her again. She said, 'Right, the onion soup'. So what did she bring? The pea soup, of course. Now I don't know how we'll use that, but we'll file it away and it will find its way into a commercial some day." When you pull from your own life, says Coyle, even the most seemingly outrageous incident is grounded in a very real emotion. "And it resonates for listeners or viewers in a way that 'made-up' stuff doesn't. That said, as storytellers we recognise that moments pulled from our own lives will only remain moments if we are willing to dramatise them, and that is where imagination and play come in."

Coyle confirms that self-disclosing takes courage. "It means you're dealing with messy things like feelings, fears and fantasies that interfere with the projection of our perfect self to the world. Like, 'What would the boss think if he knew that at 38 I'm still afraid of the dark and need to sleep with a night light…?' Our own lives are a well that never goes dry. Yet some writers feel they're not being 'creative' unless they're creating out of 'thin air', which can result in commercials that are more like *Saturday Night Live* sketches. Or they believe it's easier to simply regurgitate the kind of commercial we have all heard countless times on radio — the dull, boring announcement spots delivered in a cloned, droning voice."

THE THREE WORST WORDS ON RADIO: "THAT NUMBER AGAIN…"

"It's a waste of time," swears Bob Dennis. "If the phone number is going to be there once, it might as well be there twice, because nobody's going to remember it once. And the question is, are they going to remember it after hearing it twice?" Dennis recalls a taxi company's radio campaign in Adelaide: "The only time I've heard it work well is when the whole commercial is built around the number, so the phone number becomes the feature. But tagged on to the end of a commercial you'd have missed it." Dennis believes telephone numbers take up too much valuable time. "I have never written a phone number down from a commercial. I have never taken my hands off the wheel and grabbed a pen."

A far better option: put the client's name in one more time rather than put in the phone number. At least that way, says one radio marketer, the client's name gets into the brain one more time and people will look up the phone number.

Sometimes radio writers get lucky, as Newman recalls. "When forced to add the phone number to my Indoor Cricket scripts, I realised that the digits had no 'fours' or 'sixes'." Because fours and sixes are key scores in the game, he was able to incorporate the number into the commentary, "without it feeling like an add on".

"The only time a phone number works in radio is when the spot is about the phone number," Ruta suggests. Any Canadian, he says, can sing this jingle:

```
"Nine six seven, eleven eleven,
"Phone Pizza Pizza, hey hey hey..."
```

Adds Ruta, "It's also the only excuse for a jingle I can even fathom."

"There's a great body of research out there, from the radio advertising bureaus of both America and Australia, that establishes that phone numbers on radio are a waste of time," says Remley. The only two clear exceptions, he believes, are cab companies and air conditioning companies. "Even the idea of doing a whole campaign around a phone number is pretty old hat. Obviously someone out there will do it very originally and cleverly in the future, but clients should be discouraged from putting in phone numbers. As soon as they put in their phone number and address, 30 seconds is suddenly 23 seconds."

4

WRITING BETTER RADIO

"Radio writing is the purest form of writing left for the advertising professional." John Immesoete explains his passion for radio. "Television, because of its cost and scope, invariably involves many layers of people and many 'hands'. Producing television is also a very collaborative art involving many people. Print can similarly have a lot of people touching it because everyone, wrongly, thinks they can do print." Immesoete calls radio the last bastion of individuality left for the writer. "Many times, the writer is the sole person creating and producing the product. Clients rarely attend radio productions, much less other agency staff. The satisfaction of writing and producing a great radio commercial is probably akin to that felt by a man who designs and builds his own house as opposed to the man who just buys one." Radio, says Immesoete, became his salvation. "I started at a very large agency. The politics and hyperbole of TV could get pretty thick. It was nice to take on the radio assignments and be left alone to create. I think I learned things early on in those studios that made me a better creative overall…"

Award-winning Grey Worldwide Melbourne creative director Nigel Dawson views radio from a similar perspective. "It's as pure as a poster that contains only words. It is curiously liberating to have only a single tool at one's disposal — sound. There's no need to think about clever pictures, or visual techniques, or supers or headlines or logos. You can shut your eyes and flood your mind with every conceivable sound, one of which will give you the kernel of an idea. So many commercials just use the dreaded MVO, but there are hundreds of other possibilities out there from which you can create entertainment and involvement." On radio, Dawson stresses, you cannot hide. "There is no clever photographer or director to replace your lack of an idea with beautiful images. When you sit down to write a radio commercial, it is more important than with any other medium that you don't get up until you have that Holy Grail — an idea."

How should you write better radio? "Do not try to make a radio commercial," advises Yukio Nakayama. "Express human life and emotion through sounds. Narration or dialogue. Music. And sound effects. Just three elements can make the idea reality. Needless to say, the relevance between human emotion and the brand is very important, but it does not have to be rational. We like to read between the lines. We do not want to express everything in words. That is our culture. We know that words often betray people."

"The majority of people don't think in sound, they think in words." Steve Owen says the written word is the dominant form of communication because that is how we are taught at school and college. "If I took your PC, and all your pens and paper, and left you with just a DAT recorder and some music and sound effects CDs and a phone, you could still produce a radio commercial. We don't work in the written word, we work in sound." Key 103 employs three full-time writers and one full-time producer. The specialist radio company creates and produces about four to five campaigns a week for national, regional and local clients, the kind of workload that Owen says, "would put the average agency creative in a mental home".

PETER SOUTER once said radio ads are very much like conversations: being boring, or patronising, or overly complicating things, is taboo. "What would you do if you were talking to a friend or someone in your family? You wouldn't shout unnecessarily, you wouldn't drone on and on and on and on…"

BMP DDB copywriter Paul Burke reminds us that writing skills have diminished as advertising became more visual. "You must have natural dialogue. No one talks about 'class-beating luggage space'." Burke also warns against cramming too much in. "You need to let a commercial 'breathe'..."

As Australian radio marketer Alexsandra Lyall observes, "The emotion you can get into a silence is incredible."

AUSTIN HOWE spells out his standards for great radio: it has to be unforgettable, it has to be singular, and it has to be entertaining or engaging. Howe has conducted an exercise with his clients, primarily direct advertisers, in which he asks them which recent ads they remember. "If they can remember a spot, I ask them what points, if any, they remember from it. Usually they remember a spot but they don't remember whom it was for, and they rarely remember a single point that was being made. Interestingly, the Richards Group's Motel 6 campaign comes up a lot, and it hasn't been on air for years."

Howe tells his clients what they should reasonably expect from their radio commercials:

1. That people will remember the advertiser's name.
2. That people will get a sense of the brand personality.
3. That people will decide whether they like the brand or not, and whether the brand understands them or not.
4. That people get a sense of what drives the advertiser, what the advertiser cares about.
5. That people might take away one key thought, IF (and probably *ONLY IF*) that point is the hero of the spot.

"The commercials that work best on radio are those that do all these things exceptionally well. And that can be with humour, or seriousness, or charm, or intrigue, or interest. Or white space, just like a good print ad."

"WRITING and producing great radio ads is almost an intuitive process," says Mark Rivett. "The good writer seems to effortlessly draw upon life's experiences and distil them down into 30- or 60-second micro-audio plays. Many good writers seem to have come into the industry after having other jobs and experiences. They have a great insight into what makes people tick. Their scripts are fresh, their ideas and dialogue are simple and never pretentious. Radio is the medium that allows the imagination to run wild and is far less bound by budget and other restrictions. Radio certainly sorts out the good, the bad and the ugly..."

Rivett offers his list of what makes a bad radio commercial:

1. Phone numbers
2. Historical settings (Napoleon and Josephine, etc)
3. Overacting
4. Playing the TVC audio track on radio
5. A bad jingle
6. Overwriting
7. Underwriting
8. Bad writing

"If it ain't on the page, it ain't on the stage." A lame script is a lame script, says Clive Desmond, and offers his own list of taboos. "I discourage the use of children under 16 — it's usually painfully cute. I discourage the use of sirens and cell phones ringing — it's dangerous. I have shot cows in a radio commercial, and people partying in a pool. What things would I never do? I wouldn't make light of genocide, the civil rights movement, unusual sexual persuasions or physical disabilities, but I would poke fun at religion, politics, radio, school, family, ad agencies, car companies, certain occupations, the police, the court system, the press, television, death and sexual excess — if someone would let me..."

CREATIVE METHODOLOGY

Jack Vaughan considers writing for radio as not that different from creating other media executions of a campaign concept. "You're looking for an executional idea that works best for that medium. It's a matter of finding a way that expresses the core thought that *isn't* the TV soundtrack or an audio version of your print." Vaughan believes the radio idea should be organically radio. "For me, the exercise is to not think visually, which is tricky, because I'm a writer who's visually led. You have to think with your ears rather than your eyes." Vaughan goes back to the core idea or strategy of the campaign. "Let's say it's 'reliability'. You try to think of ways to depict reliability, or lack of it, in an aural way. It may be totally different than the way you express that core thought in TV or posters, but that doesn't matter, as long as it sheets back to the central strategic idea."

Vaughan demonstrates how he would develop a campaign thought for radio. "Take the example of the 'reliability' core thought. I'd go through the usual repertoire of approaches — maximisation, minimisation, reversal, et cetera — and perhaps think about demonstrating unreliability. What comes to mind? Tradesmen; it's universal. How does their unreliability manifest itself? Phone messages. Excuses. Fantastic lamebrained excuses for not turning up. 'I had a brain tumour…' I kid you not, I've had that one twice! So I'd have a series of excuses on a telephone answering machine. Then turn it round to talk about the reliability of the product or service I'm selling." The opening line will write itself, Vaughan attests, "in a way that's true to your inner ear. You just listen to it in your head, and copy it all down. In this case, the opening device is probably the 'beep' of the answering machine."

"Shut your eyes," suggests Owen, "and think of a sound that creates an emotional response. If the response is big enough, you don't really have to say that much after it to get the message across. Think in sound, not in words." The big award winners, he reminds us, tend to be the simplest of ideas.

"Think like a blind person," agrees Steve Henry. "It's a cliché, but blind people are supposed to have more acute sensitivity in their other senses. Because radio misses out on that one crucial sense — the visual — you have to compensate for it by concentrating even more on the sound side of things."

STREET REMLEY tells copywriters to take briefs to heart. "When you get a brief, don't just flip through it once. Rewrite it the way human beings talk. Write it in your own fashion, even if it starts with, 'Now what this client is on about, he makes tomato sauce, but he's got a new bottle for it because with the old bottle, the stuff would never come out. So what he wants to talk about is, the new bottle's got a big, wide mouth, so the tomato sauce comes out, and tastes better as well…' A lot of writers don't even go to that stage, writing in terms that are meaningful to themselves." Out of that process, Remley says, could come the lines.

Remley also references Dick Orkin and "experiential" thinking: "Understand the brief, then get the product category into your mind. Say it's a washing machine. Then take that broad area of dirty clothes, and washing machines, and laundry rooms, and detergent, and just go up the street with your mates and tell real-life stories, funny or serious or bittersweet or poignant or tragic, things that have happened to you relevant to washing machines. Not jokes, but *real things* that happened to you, or things that you've heard about second-hand. Start to draw on your experience as a copywriter. Make little shorthand notes of all the stories you hear doing this, and take them back and apply them against the brief, and suddenly you're writing like a real human being, rather than contriving as a copywriter does."

Remley's writing process invariably starts with the ending. "I'm of the school that before I go very far with it, I'd better find how I'm going to get out of it, I'd better find an ending. It makes a lot more sense, if it's humorous or dramatic or a fairly narrative approach, to find out how you're going to get out of it that's going to be pleasing. One of my *penchants* is to avoid voice-overs or tags completely. I like to do really 'humourfied' commercials where whoever's doing the talking delivers the whole thing, rather than having to slap a voice over on the end to explain everything that happened earlier." He references his award-winning Wrangler *Hare Krishna* commercial for The Campaign Palace. "It was based on Lionel Hunt's thinking, all I was doing was making radio out of his outdoor boards. One of them was a *Hare Krishna* band, the bright orange beautiful people, and in the middle of the *Hare Krishnas* was a guy with a Wrangler shirt on. His back was turned, he was walking out of the frame, and it said *If I can't wear my old Wrangler shirt I'm not going.*" In Remley's commercial, all the conversation took place between the *Hare Krishna* members, and it ended with the sounds of the band fading away up the street.

TITLE: WRANGLER JEANS "HARE KRISHNA"

At its heart, this 60-second commercial contains merely a 20-second nugget of dialogue.

SFX: *FOR THE FIRST EIGHT SECONDS, WE HEAR ONLY HEAVY TRAFFIC...*

THEN, OVER THE NEXT 17 SECONDS, WE CAN HEAR A HARE KRISHNA BAND SLOWLY APPROACHING. THE DISTINCTIVE CHANTING AND TAMBOURINES GROW LOUDER AND LOUDER...

SUDDENLY, 25 SECONDS IN, THE CHANTING STOPS AND WE HEAR A MALE HARE KRISHNA ACOLYTE ADDRESSING THE OTHERS.

MALE: Hold on … where's Goose?

GIRL: He's not coming.

MALE: Oh. *(COUNTING THEM IN TO SING AGAIN)* One, two, three... *(HE STOPS)* Why not?

GIRL: Why not what?

MAN: Why isn't Goose coming?

GIRL: He said, "If I can't wear my old Wrangler shirt, I'm not going".

MAN: *(SHRUGS)* Oh well, he couldn't carry a tune anyway. *(COUNTING THEM IN)* One, two, three...

SFX: *THE CHANTING STARTS AGAIN AND FOR THE NEXT 15 SECONDS WE HEAR THE HARE KRISHNAS MOVING OFF INTO THE DISTANCE.*

When Street Remley turned Lionel Hunt's Wrangler Shirts poster into a radio commercial, there was no VO tag. Remley calls it a "humourfied" commercial "where whoever's doing the talking delivers the whole thing, rather than having to slap a voice-over on the end to explain everything that happened earlier." Agency: The Campaign Palace, Australia.

THE first thing Paul Fishlock usually does is write a dead straight announcer-style ad. "It teaches me how much has to be said and in what order. It helps me relax knowing I've got a 'banker' should a worse case scenario loom. Sometimes, a twist on the announcer format can become the idea. Some of my favourite radio commercials are exactly that." As he writes, Fishlock has no illusions. "I assume that people aren't listening and that you have to earn their attention. I think far too many people who write radio assume that consumers still use radio the way they did before TV — whole families hushed and huddled around it for their evening's entertainment." What does he *never* do? "I never set out to write a funny 30-second radio play. Shop bell SFX followed by toe-curling Pythonesque-except-not-funny dialogue, 'I'd like to buy a banana,' 'I'm sorry, sir, this is a bank...' And then it's downhill from there..."

Michael Newman starts with a sentence. "Lots of other people seem to start with a situation or a joke. But if I can describe a script in a line — without honed dialogue, production wizardry, acting skills, music or theatre of the mind — then I know I have something production-proof to work with. An idea, rather than just a construct." Being able to sum up the idea in just a sentence helps Newman underwrite his script. "It means every phrase has to add something to the initial thought or it's not worth its place. The art is to omit. I leave plenty of space. If it's a 30-second spot in my mind, I make it a 45-seconder in reality. I question the right of every word to be there before I get to the studio." Newman actually hears the script in his head as he conceptualises. "I can have the idea in amongst the general hubbub of a frantic agency, but then I need to go away and 'listen' to it in quiet solitude. If the idea is clear enough in my mind, and if it communicates something interesting in a single sentence, then it will almost always write itself if I can listen well enough."

Desmond thinks about location first. "Where is all of this going to happen? So I think visually off the bat. I have to see what or whom I'm writing about before I can begin to construct something." Desmond's search for ideas begins by elimination. "There are only a handful of successful radio commercial formats, and the fun comes in working the same old format in a new way, using the same ingredients as were available 50 years ago. That's where the creativity comes in. Is the spot a narrative? Or dialogue? Would a sound design demonstration be effective? Is this a place for comedy or drama? Man on the street or music? Sometimes I combine more than one format into a spot." Then he considers the basic structure, the plot, the characters, the things they have to say. "Before I ever write a script, I figure out the ending because it's more effective to know the outcome of the script before you actually sit down and write it. Writing the script takes me no time at all. Plotting the script eats up a lot of time…"

Toronto-based John Kyriakou starts with a story. Kyriakou, formerly chairman and executive creative director of J. Walter Thompson Singapore says: "Radio is about stories. It's the deejay who tells stories about performers and their music. It's the talk show host who relates stories about people, places and events. It's the listeners who call in with their own personal stories. This is what makes radio such an engaging medium." With that in mind, Kyriakou begins writing by imagining "a great voice, a pure voice, a storyteller. I then write a monologue for that voice, without any concern for time or length. I don't get stressed searching for an idea. I find that the story usually leads to one. The story also helps establish a tone for the brand or product. The story becomes the framework or guide. The spot may remain a monologue or become a dialogue. Music and sound effects are used to enhance the story, to set a mood, to place it in a situation. But the starting point is always a reminder that you don't watch radio, you don't read radio, you listen to it. *And there's nothing more captivating than the human voice with a story to tell.*"

BOB DENNIS is convinced that the idea for the script should always come from the product. "The old school of thinking was that you had to mention the product name at least three times in a 30-second commercial. I don't support that theory because every project should be addressed individually. You can have a dull script that mentions the product name four times and no one will remember it. You can have a good script that mentions the product once and everyone remembers it. The bottom line is, it's important that the listener is left with no doubt as to who or what the commercial is for, and that's why the idea for the script should always come from the product."

Dennis writes down the unique selling proposition on a piece of paper and sticks it on the computer. "I'll think of a direction, and scenarios around that direction, and I'll be looking for bizarre or interesting lines of thought. The opening is vital." It doesn't have to be a "big" opening, Dennis stresses, but it should make the audience wonder "where is this going?" And it should be engaging enough to make them listen right to the end. Like many writers, Dennis has an ending in mind before he starts writing, yet he remains alert to new possibilities, even if it means starting all over again. "I've often written scripts and spent hours working on the first bit, then I'll be typing in the final voice-over copy when suddenly it suggests something else. And I'll keep going to see where it takes me, and at the end of it I might think, yes, this is the direction."

"Writing for radio teaches you how to economise on words, and how to let a sound effect set up a situation so that you don't have to spend five seconds trying to explain where you are and what you're doing." He identifies the three most common failings of radio scriptwriters: trying to fit a 60-second idea into 30 seconds, trying to fit a product into an idea, instead of letting the product or u.s.p. suggest the direction; and being unwilling to cut words so that the pace of the read ultimately suffers. While there are many visual conventions in television commercials — leaves swirling around a new car as it zooms up a tree-lined street, the runny cheese in a pizza commercial, the smiling faces in bank ads — Dennis believes there are generally fewer aural clichés. "Because you can't see the product on radio, you've got to describe the *feeling* or the *look* or the *taste*, so you tend not to be able to get too clichéd with it."

TONY HERTZ starts work from a consumer's point of view. "One of the things I respect the big agencies like McCann-Erickson for is that they are very, very good on consumer insight. They start off from a very good basis of knowing what people want. They investigate the relationship that consumers have with the product. What is it I am trying to sell that is interesting? What is it that I have to say that is going to be interesting to someone? What is it about this car, or this tea, that I need to convey? More often than not, and it frightens me sometimes, the first idea I come up with is the right idea. But I think it's important to go through the process of trying to destroy that first idea and seeing if you can find something better." As a breed of people, Hertz says, we are paid to be intuitive, and intuition doesn't come to order.

"I don't know whether this is cynical or not, but one of the things I try to do, particularly with radio, is to say how can I do something which the other guys wouldn't do? I know that nine times out of ten, faced with a communication problem, most copywriters will try and write a comedy dialogue."

Hertz experiments with what he calls "mixed media" and creates free form commercials: "You have three lines of dialogue in the middle of something else, so you don't necessarily have to have a dialogue commercial, or a jingle commercial, or a sound effects commercial. Why can't you do them all? One of the reasons I like Robert Altman as a film director is that he really understands sound. This is a guy who will have nine recorders going at the same time, and he really captures life, and you can hear it." (Altman started exploring sound with cheap tape recorders in his high school days. He directed TV series like *Bonanza, Maverick* and *Combat!* before his first movie success, *M*A*S*H*.)

Hertz "free associates" with words, music and sound textures. "Chuck Blore, one of my idols in the 1950s and 1960s, did a commercial for the Bell system. He took microphones out onto the street, captured little snatches of dialogue, and integrated them into free form radio structures."

Hertz disputes the conventional wisdom that says we should use sound to create pictures in the mind. Instead, we should use pictures to create the sound. "You may think there are brand or product elements that radio can't communicate: colours, textures, shapes, flavours, landscapes, patterns, relationships..." The truth is otherwise, he says.

"WHERE you set a radio ad is half the job done," believes Emma Hill, an award-winning senior writer at Clemenger BBDO Melbourne. "With our briefing system, you're given the one single thing the client wants to say. I sit down with that and I wait for some kind of picture to come into my mind about where it's going to be. I like to think of a real-life situation where you can keep the dialogue really minimal, use a lot of space, a lot of effects, but as less voice as possible. When I first started I was told when you're writing 30-second radio, always time it out to 22 seconds."

She talks about her radio for Yellow Pages, an account for which Clemenger Melbourne has long done brilliant work. "The Yellow Pages 'Closing Soon' brief comes up time and time again — if you're not in the Yellow Pages you'll be sorry. I thought, how could you do that on radio? And I had the idea that you would be just sitting there, doing nothing…" She made the connection that sitting there, doing nothing, was just like being in a Yoga class. In Hill's commercial, we hear a typical female Yoga instructor speaking calmly and meditatively — with appropriate pauses between each instruction — until the whole situation is eventually turned around:

> "For the next few moments, empty your mind… (PAUSE) Put your pen down… (PAUSE) Your hands by your side… (PAUSE) Find an object in front of you and stare at it… in silence… Sitting there, staring… (PAUSE) Now, that's what you'll be doing all next year if you forget your ad in the 2001 Yellow Pages Directory. It's your last chance… Call 13 23 78…"

Hill always considers what has been done before. "There'd been a very successful campaign about two years before by Tony Greenwood. His idea was if you weren't in the Yellow Pages, you'd have to go out and sell yourself. He did mock street moments where people were approached and told, 'You look as if you need a haircut, I could do it for $15 dollars.' Another line the agency developed was, *If you're not in the Yellow Pages you'll go missing* and that lent itself to a 'missing persons' campaign."

With all her work, Hill takes the single claim, or the one thing the client wants to say, and asks herself: "How would Emma say it? How would I *speak* that to someone? Like, 'if you're not in the Yellow Pages you'll be doing nothing', or 'you'll have a lot of spare time on your hands' or 'you'll have to find something else to do'." By exploring all the different ways of saying it, she finds one expression that sparks a fresh direction. She also makes it a habit to write down an idea on the bottom of the brief before she leaves the briefing. "A lot of people say they'll think about it in a couple of days because they've got something else to work on. But if you sit down and listen to what they want to say and even if you write down a better way to say it, then you've walked out with a little spark already." Very often her best ideas come quickly. "A lot of the time you come up with something, and you think it's so obvious that someone's bound to have done it before. Then you realise that no one's done the most obvious ones, and that's why you feel unsure whether you should present them or not." Hill's writing style is well-defined. "I've never written a straight voice-over ad. And I don't write conversations between people in a straight situation either. I'm not a big believer in end lines so I tend to start writing from the beginning of the script. I love American ads, and I love American end lines, but a lot of our clients don't have them."

Hill says her agency is structured to inspire better creativity. "You're given a budget on the brief, just like you are with television, and it's always enough. The good thing about Clemenger's is you're surrounded by such good people that you don't want to do same-same, you want to strive to do better."

PETER CLARK explores the brief and relies on intuition to direct his thinking. "I'd usually just get a feeling that this should be a situation commercial, or it should have some musical content." His thinking is also influenced by what competitive brands in the same category were doing. "If they were using strong music tracks, I'd go to the other end of the scale." Once he develops an idea, Clark always judges it in terms of branding. "Have I done such a great job for the idea that the branding will be lost…? That's always my worry."

Mike Fromowitz turns off his computer. "I use large layout pads, with a pen or pencil. I work on radio the same way I work on print, and cover the walls with ideas first. For the first day or two, either alone or with a partner, we'll throw rough ideas on paper — never a full script. We may talk about 20 to 25 'ways in', but only five to ten concepts — short version scripts — actually get put on paper. Then we decide to write up the ones we feel best about, maybe five to six spots."

Fromowitz likes to write quickly. "I don't care if the English is right or wrong, or if the grammar is off. That can be fixed later. I often write the words big, for extra emphasis, or small, depending on how they sound to my ear, or how I see them visually in my mind's eye. So the words begin with no precise structure. They're all over the page. I do this because it is important to first find and establish a distinctive voice for the spot so it will stand out from the clutter. I stay aware at all times of trying to say too much. The client will ask for more. It's important the listener feels the pace of the commercial and is comfortable with what is being said and what is being heard. The ear has a way of mishearing what is not said clearly, or if the pace is too fast." Fromowitz discusses music's place in the scheme of things. "Music can be an advantage in a radio commercial. However, I have outlawed beginning a script or idea with a jingle. It's a cop out. You need to begin with the bud of an idea. Music comes later." He also sounds a warning about humour. "In many US agencies, creative people oftentimes start out trying to make the radio humorous. Many spots often fail because humour takes a special writing talent. Not everybody is funny. And what's funny to you may not be to others."

Calvin Soh sticks to the strategy and generates ideas. "They shouldn't be medium-specific at this stage. Once you start culling, see how the good ones that remain could work on radio." Soh calls radio probably the most imaginative yet affordable medium at your disposal. "You could conjure rich, colourful characters merely through sound — or any place on earth, without having to build a set. But start with a good idea, and embellish as you go." He recommends listening to comedians on tape. "Analyse how they can make you laugh without visual aids. You'll find it's really down to *what* they say first, then *how* it is said, the delivery. *Those are the two cardinal rules of radio, whether you're making funny or sad spots.*"

HOW does Immesoete write radio? "All advertising has to start with an objective; what do you want this commercial to do? Do you want to create store traffic, enhance a brand image, change a brand image, announce something new? It sounds simple, but we all know it can be the most complicated thing in our business. *Simplifying the objective as much as possible is the most important thing facing the radio writer, so you can communicate simply and clearly."* Once the objective is clear, Immesoete starts to consider tone. "Should the communication be humorous, serious, informative, straightforward, or something else? This depends of course on the target market and the product. Put yourself in the consumers' place — what's the best tone to communicate with them? Many writers fail at this point by writing in a tone they're comfortable with, rather than the tone appropriate for their consumer."

Depending on the time he has, Immesoete might do nothing other than jot down ideas for a couple of days. When he is comfortable that he has enough ideas, he starts writing scripts. "I believe more is more in this case. I write as many scripts as I possibly can in as many different campaign areas as I can think of." Scripts, says Immesoete, are like lottery tickets. "The more you have, the better chance of winning the jackpot. I crank them out till I'm exhausted." The next stage is bouncing them by other people, weeding out some, refining others. "If you're fortunate enough to work with other good writers, use them. Share your ideas with them and listen. Worry about the credits in the award shows later. *It's better to share credit for a winner than own sole possession of a loser."* Don't be afraid to toss out scripts at this point, he says. "If something struck you as brilliant early one morning but the rest of the world doesn't get it, then the rest of the world doesn't get it. The client is paying for mass communication, not for your personal amusement. Toss out the idea and move on."

WRITER-DIRECTOR David Mamet is famous for his superb dialogue and rapid-fire wit. His screenplays include *Glengarry Glen Ross* and *State and Main*. His output is prodigious. Mamet observed in the *Hollywood Scriptwriter,* "I tend to write a lot, which I think is the secret to being prolific. That's the only secret I know, and I've been doing it ever since I started."

Nakayama recounts a similar sentiment. "I wrote scripts every day for the first three to five years, even on weekends. I wrote 50 to 100 scripts for each assignment. At last the most senior creative people started coming to me and gave me lots of opportunities to write. I also produced and directed myself. I phoned the agents of young promising actors and actresses to get new voices for my work. Sometimes we recorded their voices for free, making demonstration audiotapes that helped them find new opportunities." Nakayama's wife Sachiko shares his passion. She is a writer-producer-director at Random House, a specialist radio production company. They have worked together for almost a quarter of a century. "I read a lot of books, met a lot of people, went to factories and laboratories and thought, then wrote again and again until I was tired. When I'd finished writing, I'd ask some reliable persons to read my scripts. They often gave me great inspiration to improve my work. It is very important to think, then try again in the studios. We experimented through sound itself. We understood how to use sound including spoken words, which are so different from written words." Nakayama attributes his dialogue skills to the theatre. "From the time I was three years old, my mother took me to see popular plays. That is why I like stage performances to this day. I once saw more than 100 plays a year. Those experiences helped to develop my 'ear'."

If agency creatives want to develop their ear for dialogue, Desmond tells them to study acting and improvisational performance. "Improv is dialogue driven. Acting requires you to develop keen listening and observational skills. It's not a casual study. You have to understand a lot about acting, how acting works, how actors approach dialogue. Writing and acting go hand in hand. It's a worthwhile effort on the part of the writer to study acting, even if the goal is not to become an actor."

Henry also emphasises dialogue. "A lot of great writers from the real world learned their trade in radio. It's a great place to hone your dialogue skills." His point is valid. Great playwrights like Samuel Beckett, Bertolt Brecht, Tom Stoppard, Harold Pinter, Alan Ayckbourn, Robert Bolt and John Mortimer can trace their roots to radio drama. In America, Arthur Miller and David Mamet have acknowledged their debt to the medium.

MONOLOGUE is usually better than dialogue, argues Dawson. "Dialogue is so often as predictable as a game of tennis, with lines being lobbed from one end to the other, and usually the last line ends up in the net. This is inevitably true if the dialogue is about the product." Citing Mel Smith and Griff Rhys Jones for *Firips* as a "magnificent exception", Dawson says "real people don't actually talk about products very often."

With monologue — "one voice literally speaking his or her mind" — the writer can deliver information with charm, whimsy, force, whatever you like. The talking head on radio, says Dawson, will be visualised by the listener as a charmer or a nutter accordingly.

Monologues can also be sung. Dawson used a typical Gilbert & Sullivan tune to sell a new real estate section in *The Herald-Sun* newspaper; the characteristically jaunty nature of the song and clipped, precisely sung lyrics were ideal for demonstrating a vast list of house numbers and street names. "Music is a much underrated tool, probably because we think it will be too expensive and not worth the bother. But a good use of music, not just a jingle, can have a huge cut-through when surrounded by the spoken word."

If you are going to attempt dialogue, Dawson believes you need to be a great listener. "Listen to how people really speak. Listen to the way you speak on the telephone, which is basically a two-way radio. Listen to how reporters speak on the radio. Listen to how your Mum tells you to take care. Listen to stand-up comics and particularly their timing. Analyse all this and dialogue ideas will start to come alive. So often you get radio writers who come up with a dialogue script and say 'it fits 30 seconds, I timed it out'. The trouble is that they timed it out without pausing to take breath. People don't talk with a machine gun clatter, nor can listeners take it. If a script 'fits into' 30 seconds, it is probably 20% overwritten. Give it air, let the words sink in, read it like people speak, with time to think what they are going to say next."

DAVID DROGA treats radio a lot like television. "Instead of spending time crafting a few scripts, I prefer to put an idea down in a few lines and then move on to a new one. Once I have dozens of ideas, I can decide which are worth fleshing out to a finished script."

It's worth investing the time, he argues, especially for young creatives. "The best thing about radio briefs is that most senior creatives don't want to do them. Which is kind of ridiculous, considering there is a lot of fun and glory in brilliant radio ads. I can't remember who said it, but it's true: 'Your only major overhead is your imagination'."

"THINK of ideas first, style second." Mike Edmonds, one of Australia's most awarded radio writers and creative director of Marketforce Perth, avoids setting out to write any particular kind of commercial. "I usually start thinking of ideas and see where it takes me. Naturally, like most radio writers, I love humour, but some of the spots I'm most proud of have been serious." Radio, he stresses, doesn't have to be funny. "Don't try to be funny if you're not a funny person. Award CDs are full of funny radio ads, but radio stations are full of bad ones. There are lots of great ways to make a point with sound."

Edmonds believes the purest radio commercials have no end tag lines. "I try to have the idea do the sell without an end line at all. I only write a voice-over tag if I absolutely have to, to finish the point I'm making."

Edmonds stresses that he is "always, always, *always*" inspired by the product he has to advertise. "I delve into that first and seek inspiration from that before anything else." Nine times out of ten, he says, an idea will occur while he is tasting, testing or investigating the product.

You don't have to start with a script, he believes. "Radio is an unusual medium. Don't get sucked into thinking you start writing great radio by writing great radio. You don't. You start with an idea. An observation about life, a twist of logic, a surprising point you want to make. *Then* you write the script. Draw boxes if it helps. One of the best radio writers I know writes his initial ideas in boxes, some with little drawings, before he starts conceptualising rough scripts."

Edmonds offers ten ways to kick-start a creative idea:

1. **Exaggerate the benefit:** If the proposition is something like "Firehouse Chilli Sauce is hot", you simply write on your pad "Firehouse Chilli Sauce is so hot that..." you need asbestos oven mitts, or it sets fire to the food, etc.

2. **What it's like:** This is pure analogy and you hear it all the time in some very good spots. For example, the ball bearing commercial of a few years back where the guy says something like, "If nuclear weapons were ball bearings, this is how many you'd need to wipe out all life in America..." and you hear two or three ball bearings dropping on a polished floor. Then he says, "And this is how many nuclear weapons there are currently in the world," and you hear about 20 seconds of thousands of ball bearings dropping. Great stuff and a terrific analogy.

3. **What's funny about that?** Sometimes, something in the brief will strike you as funny, bizarre, sad, shocking, etc. The best example I can think of is actually one of the first radio ads I worked on. A butcher came to my country radio station and asked me to do a radio ad telling people he'd kill their pigs for Christmas hams, which is common in the bush. He said he couldn't afford TV and the local newspaper wouldn't let him run an ad with a headline "I will kill your pigs". I thought it was an hilarious proposition and so wrote a very funny spot about a farmer trying to get the family pig into the back of a pickup truck before the kids saw him. But this technique can work with sad things, too. On a Quit Smoking brief, it said smoking can strangle a foetus. It made me think of a dozen compelling radio ideas straightaway.

4. **Play what if:** A traditional creative game. Take the brief and twist it all ways to unlock a fresh idea. For example, mufflers: what if cars drove around upside down? Or life insurance: what if you could see into your future?

5. **What's the key feeling?** Sometimes, isolating the tone of voice can lead to some interesting radio ideas. A commercial was done here years ago for littering that featured a guy trying to wake up his dog. It turns out it had choked on litter and died. I'm sure that concept started with someone saying, "I think littering is kind of..." and the feeling could be joy, hope, fun, etc.

6. **What's the key word?** I did a commercial once that won a few big awards and achieved record sales for the client, and it

was simply a play on words. It was for a Thai Food Festival, and I just had two guys sitting at a restaurant. One said, "Hey, nice tie," and the other replied, "Thanks. Want a bite?" The listener heard "tie" and we revealed "Thai" at the end. Virgin has done a lot of these, too. So look at the names on the brief and see what pops up.

7. **Who's the target audience?** Examine whom you are talking to. What do they talk like? What do they listen to, watch or read? What films appeal to them? Sometimes this unlocks an idea.

8. **All you need is hate:** This comes from Steve Dodds, a great Sydney radio writer. He hates bad advertising. He once wrote a spot where a voice-over guy was told to get out his pencil because the lawyers had made a few changes to the script for a Toyota Corolla. The engineer then instructed him to take out "faster than an F18 jet" and "guaranteed to get you a date with Kylie Minogue", etc. So look at other ads in the same category as the product you're advertising and subvert them. It's fun and consumers usually love it.

9. **Hey, why don't we just...** Sometimes you look at a brief and a thought pops into your head that goes something like, "Well, if that's the case, why don't we just..." Example: we did a commercial for The Gallery, a wooden blind company. The brief said their cedar slats are sanded finer than others so they're not rough to the finger. Our commercial featured a guy rubbing a competitor's slat on the microphone cover. It made a horrible, scratchy, splintery sound. Then we rubbed one from The Gallery and you heard only a soft "whooshing" sound.

10. **Do the opposite:** A time-honoured creative technique similar to "What if..." Take the proposition and do the exact opposite to make your point. Example: Slimmo Pills make you slim, so what makes you fat? Another example: Porsches are quick, so what's slow? It's simple, but you can unlock new ideas in a tired, unconfident brain.

Edmonds warns against overwriting. "It's more professional, and a lot cheaper, to edit the script in your office than in a \$300-an-hour studio with $500-an-hour talent waiting. Read your 30-second script out loud, real loud, and if it comes in at exactly 30 seconds, cut some more out. A 30-second script should time to 23 or 24 seconds in the office." Time expands in sound studios, says Edmonds. "Don't kid yourself in the office by racing through 90 words in 40 seconds and think it's on time!"

Dialogue only works when it sounds real. "Don't have people say things in your script that they wouldn't say in real life, like, 'Wow, Sue, I love your new couch. It's so soft and plush', 'Thanks, Barb, I got it from Whizzo Furniture on Steven Street opposite McDonald's and only five minutes from the train station'. If your dialogue isn't reading real, do another idea. Nobody can shoe-horn irrelevant product information into normal-sounding conversation."

IDEAS come first, agrees Rob Martin Murphy. "The idea behind the radio spot really dictates the genre. I have used humour a lot, even for serious subject matter. But there is no rule to say one genre is more effective than another. If you look through any award book, you'll find all the genres there."

His writing methodology: "I just start writing. All different thoughts, scenarios and ideas. I never try and write the script straight off. I find that tends to box you in, and you end up writing radio spots where the characters start regurgitating the brief back to each other. You hear that stuff all the time. 'Hey, John, you look great, what have you been doing?' And John says, 'Oh, you know, just using Brand X.' And the woman continues, 'Brand X?' and John answers, 'Yeah, Brand X with twice the amount of Z...' That makes for really boring and telegraphed radio."

RALPH VAN DIJK warns against trying to think of a so-called "radio" idea. "You'll probably end up in Clichéville." He believes the idea could come from anything — a strap line, the way the product looks, or a scene you can visualise. "Once you have the idea, then see how best to communicate it on radio."

Van Dijk begins by distilling the brief and identifying the core message that has to be communicated. "Once I've done that, a number of broad approaches come to mind. I then try and twist these initial ideas to make them more interesting. After writing a line or two for each, I flesh out the ones with most potential."

It helps to think visually. "If I can 'see' the idea, or have a picture of the person who will be voicing it, the rest falls into place a lot easier. If I'm having trouble moving on from a particular train of thought, I'll sometimes pick up a sound effects catalogue and start thumbing through. Each description of a sound forces my mind to picture a completely different scene as a setting for the product."

WHEN he's writing for radio, Antony Redman uses the same technique as he does for print and television. "I'll still fill 50 boxes on the page with ideas. I only keep the boxes out of old habit and instead of filling them with pictures and headlines, they'll be filled with stories, or the seeds of stories, kind of set-ups like the first lines in jokes. The only way I'll know if they are going to work is if I go through the fun process of actually writing the ads." Redman's scripts are influenced by the way people listen to radio. "I think people have a peculiar relationship with radio that probably can't be said of other media. It's almost more affable than the newspapers or TV. TV ads just get in the way of the movie. Press ads get passed over for the articles. But it's a bit hard when you're driving to change radio stations to avoid the ads. Or when you're working, it's the same. I don't know anyone who constantly switches radio stations. They find what they like and stick to it. So I reckon this plays a big part in how you come up with a radio idea. People don't change stations, so they know when the ads are on and will persist with the station. So you are duty bound to give them some kind of surprise, something unexpected." Redman advocates what he dubs the Old Trick of Contrast: "If it's a talk station, use anything other than words. If it's heavy metal, do something different like a *Hare Krishna* chant. Remember, they aren't going to change the station so you've got them. The same old adage for all advertising is a good thing to hang onto: give me a benefit, intelligently dressed, and I'll buy it."

Is There An Ideal Length?

"It would have to be 45 seconds," considers Remley. "I've only written a handful of 30s that I'm really proud of, and because I overwrite I find it very hard to do 30s that have a really nice listenable pace, have the humour that I hope to achieve, and yet achieve everything the client wants to achieve. In fact," he confesses, "I spent my whole career cheating a lot and letting commercials go out the door that ran 33, and then playing dumb when I got those terrible phone calls from the radio stations."

The dimension of the idea, says Remley, should drive the length of the commercial, not the other way around. In some markets, he notes, radio time can be bought in 5-second increments. "I wish I could buy 35, 45, 55. It shouldn't be the media guy block-buying 30s cheaply then imposing 30 seconds on you before you even get an idea. In America they offer a big discount and a 60 is nowhere near twice the cost of a 30, so you're encouraged to do 60 seconds even though you know it is a bit too long." Many commercials are padded out unnecessarily. "Even if they're really well done, they might involve the listener for 35 seconds, and the last 25 you lose him."

Clark shares Remley's preference for 45-seconders. "Often you don't need a 60. Sixty seconds has been a fantastic luxury length for doing a great theatre of the mind commercial, whereas 30 can sometimes make it just a little tight, especially if you're stuck with obligatory dealer tags and locations and phone numbers that have to go in at the end. Thirty is usually not enough while 45 is more than enough."

Too many commercials are too long, asserts Michael Conrad. "It's important to finish the commercial once the message is nailed and the height of the drama created. Very often radio commercials go on and on, probably because radio is not so expensive, or the time was booked before the idea was created."

Ian Reichenthal equally abhors the kind of radio commercial that turns you off early — "and there's still 45 full seconds left to go!" When Reichenthal finds himself struggling to expand a radio script into 60 seconds, he kills the script. "I figure, *if it's a struggle to write, chances are it'll be a struggle to listen to.* If we could, as an industry, stop those kinds of radio ads, we will have not only improved advertising, we will have improved life as a whole."

"Much like writing any good ad, have a very simple idea, take away everything that is extraneous, and just allow that idea to sing out." Linda Locke believes people overwrite radio. "Radio is best when it's short, sharp and sweet."

"If it's a fairly simple message, 30 seconds is probably quite enough," observes David Flint. "It's an art for a lot of writers to write the right amount of words for 30 seconds. If it's a complex idea and you have to set up a situation, you might need 60 seconds." It might help to break the well-established format of situation, voice-over wrap-up, and final situation reprise. "We might break up the voice-over section. We might go a few seconds with dialogue, then have one line of voice-over, then some more dialogue, then another line of voice-over, but not doing 'your-turn-my-turn'. We might even overlap them and have them together."

Philip Webster believes: "Any length will work extremely well if it's written well." He instances 60-second dialogue commercials with what he calls too much "advertising" conversation; they would work better tightened up as 45s. However on another occasion, a series of 60-seconders flowed perfectly at 70 seconds. Rather than cut them back, the agency renegotiated with the stations to air them.

"I love 30s, and I'd love to do 10s and 15s," says Hill. "I've only ever written one 45, for a health insurance client. And I've listened to it over and over again and I actually think it's too long. It's about two guys doing knee surgery in their home garage to save money. It required a fair bit of set-up, and a chunk of copy had to go in with rates and a phone number. But if I shortened the tag I could make it work in 30." Hill has disciplined herself to write economically. "I used to write wall-to-wall scripts, but it was drummed into me, time and time again, to keep everything simple, and the whole philosophy that if everyone is yelling and doing wall-to-wall stuff, whisper and your ad will stand out. In my first year as a copywriter, Street Remley did a Radio Marketing Bureau workshop and it was the most frightening thing I've ever been to. They'd say, write a quick radio ad without any dialogue, or just use sound effects, or just use one voice." As Hill says, writers have to be honest with themselves about script length and simplicity of ideas — it isn't a case of removing single words. "If you start editing words you've got too much in there anyway. Maybe the concept isn't simple enough..."

Dennis loves attention-grabbing 15-seconders. "Everyone knows you can't cram in a lot of information, so you get to have a bit of fun with them." He hates 30-seconders, and considers 45 seconds the ideal length. "Most people buy a 30-second commercial and have 45-second expectations. It's very hard to set up and end a satisfying situation in 30 seconds that contains all the required information. In a 45, there's enough time to establish and resolve a situation. Sixty-seconders are good, but sometimes too long. I'd like to see clients do 90s, like mini-dramas, if the material is right." More experimentation is needed; for example, a campaign of 15-seconders could deliver one product feature per spot, with all spots rotated frequently. "What we're doing in radio now — 15s, 30s, 45s and 60s — is what we were doing 30 years ago. For radio, going into the future, I think we have to relook at that whole subject and work out what we can offer that's different."

While Howe believes 30-seconders force you to be singular in your thinking, he also calls for more experimentation. "Unfortunately, there seems to be an artificial 'radio reality' in terms of time and the compression of it. I try to avoid that 'reality' as often as I can. The longer the format, the better. I co-produced a Tillamook Cheese campaign with Sam Pond where we have a 2-minute spot and two 60s. The 2-minute spot just gives you so much extra breathing room. Sam actually thought it would be hard to fill the two minutes, but I love white space in commercials. Because it's reality. Not 'radio reality', but real reality." Dialogue, especially, requires time. "Jim Riswold at Wieden & Kennedy gave me some great advice early on. He encouraged me to *listen* to movies that have great dialogue *without the pictures*. I started by listening to the Coen brothers' movies and the reality is, good dialogue is messy, sloppy, illogical. I started listening more closely to actual conversations, for pauses, for logic. Real dialogue is even messier!" He writes his 60s as though he were writing 30-seconders.

Howe condemns what he calls the manufactured, edited, spell-checked, grammatically correct, scripted "radio reality" that goes on air every day. "And we wonder why we hate to listen to it…"

"YOU don't ever have to know how long a commercial will be until you've actually done it," Hertz observes. "Thirty seconds is a kind of

TITLE: BOB JOHNSTON CAR SALES "BIG CLAIM"

SFX:	*FANFARE UNDER ANNOUNCER.*
ANNCR:	Attention! Buy your new car from Johnston Car Sales because Bob Johnston's after-sales service is lavish beyond your wildest dreams.
AGENCY MAN:	Tasty, eh, Mr. Johnston?
JOHNSTON:	Don't you think you've overstated it a bit?
AGENCY MAN:	Really? How about this then…
SFX:	*FANFARE UNDER ANNOUNCER.*
ANNCR:	Buy your new car from Johnston Car Sales because Bob Johnston's after-sales service is incomparable.
JOHNSTON:	Too strong, mate. Run that and they'll expect the earth.
AGENCY MAN:	Okay…
SFX:	*FANFARE UNDER ANNOUNCER.*
ANNCR:	Bob Johnston's after-sales service is very good.
AGENCY MAN:	How's that?
JOHNSTON:	I'm a bit worrried about that "good" part…
AGENCY MAN:	I see…
SFX:	*FANFARE UNDER ANNOUNCER.*
ANNCR:	Bob Johnston's after-sales service is better than average.
JOHNSTON:	Yeah, that's it. Spot on.

Tony Hertz subverted typical car dealer advertising by making one exaggerated claim after another in this 45-seconder for Bob Johnston Car Sales.

inheritance from TV. Everything is done in 30 seconds. Media is planned in 30 seconds. In the UK and in most of Europe, time is sold on the metric system, in 10-second increments — 10s, 20s, 30s, 40s, 50s, 60s — and you pay accordingly. In the US, the norm is 60 seconds. And you can also get 30s. The fact is, if as a general rule 30 is too short, then 60 is too long, unless you've got 60 seconds of stuff to put in it. Most American commercials are way too long, because they don't have that much stuff so they repeat the telephone number five times." His Brooke Bond Tea commercial was a 60-seconder, because it could not have been done in 30 seconds. For car dealer Bob Johnston, Hertz did a series of 15-seconders, one outrageous claim followed by a little dialogue at the end, with Patrick Allen doing the voice-overs. "Then the client rang me one day and said, 'Other people's commercials are longer than mine, how much for a long one?' So I wrote *Big Claim*, which was a 45-seconder." Hertz has an easy formula for determining spot length: "You write the commercial, you get it correct, you read it out loud, and the number of seconds it takes is how long the commercial ought to be."

Concurs Van Dijk: "The ad should be as long as the idea dictates. Of my two favourite ads, one is 90 seconds and one is 20 seconds. *In most cases, 40 seconds is the minimum length required for an ad to have a setup, reveal, and call to action.*"

The Critical Opening Line

Many commercials fail because the first line does not grab the listener's antennae, or is so rushed that nobody understands the context of the idea or what the commercial is supposed to be about. There are no second chances.

Immesoete elaborates: "Every line in a radio ad is crucial. In a 30-second ad, you get 75 words, tops. Choose them wisely. That makes the first line the most important as it sets the stage for what's to follow."

"The strength of the opening line dictates how much attention the listener will give the rest of the ad," affirms Van Dijk. "It's vital that the listener is engaged or at least intrigued *after the first sentence*."

Cracking that elusive first line is the hard part. While Ernest Hemingway, Lewis Carroll and Virginia Woolf usually wrote standing up, and Truman Capote, Mark Twain and Robert Louis Stevenson usually wrote lying down, Emma Hill offers a less extreme solution.

She says it helps to think of the first line as a headline, and to put yourself in the situation of the listener, knowing what time the commercial is going to air, who you're talking to, what they might be doing at the time, and thinking how you can grab their attention right away.

"Your first line, or the first thing that happens in a radio commercial, is what's going to snag people," says Hill. *"Even the first sound they hear.* So if you're writing a 30-seconder to 22 seconds, you've got time for the first few seconds to be quiet, or for something to start slowly, rather than just yelling." In Hill's opinion, *"The first line is as important as the last line."*

Hertz recommends starting a commercial with what he calls a "bumper": "Write in a 'bumper' line, a line or a bit of atmosphere, that helps the listener separate your ad from the rubbish that's likely to precede it. Do the same at the end," he adds.

Conrad believes you can tell a good radio script from a bad one by judging the first sentence. "A couple of weeks ago in a cab to the Zürich airport, a radio commercial came on with the following words, 'If you have to say something important in advertising…' Nicolic, the taxi driver, switched to another music station." Conrad references a commercial about Transport for London. "It starts with a woman asking a question, 'Excuse me, should we shoot drivers?' I think Mr. Nicolic would *not* have tuned that out…"

"When creating for radio, I always remind myself that I am talking to someone who isn't listening," reflects Cary Rueda. "So it has to cut through and get noticed, then it has to be engaging enough to lead them till the end. *The first few seconds should grab them and distance you from the rest of the herd.* Finding those first few seconds can be harrowing. Much like being in a crowded ballroom, and you wish to speak to someone across the hall but you can't personally tap his shoulder. So knowing the ins and outs of his psyche is very important. Once you have a good idea of how and what he thinks, then more or less you can find your voice. Once you attempt to know your consumer, you can intrude his peace." Tonality is crucial, Rueda believes. "The consumer always knows whether

TITLE: JEANS WEST "SEX CHANGE"

A superbly underplayed chat between two young Aussie blokes in a bar. Duration: an economical 30 seconds.

SFX: *BAR SOUNDS LIGHTLY UNDER THROUGHOUT.*

BLOKE 1: How's it going, mate?

BLOKE 2: Pretty good. I'm thinking of having a sex change.

BLOKE 1: Yeah?

BLOKE 2: Yeah. The only thing stopping me in the past has been the cost of all the new clothes, but now Jeans West are having a twenty-nine ninety-five sale. They've got jeans at 29.95, skirts at 29.95, or two tops for just 29.95.

BLOKE 1: That's fantastic.

BLOKE 2: Yeah. At Jeans West I can get a whole new wardrobe in one simple inexpensive operation.

BLOKE 1: Get you another beer?

BLOKE 2: You're … not trying to get me drunk, are you?

MVO: The Jeans West 29.95 Sale. This week only.

The critical opening: within the first few seconds, every listener would have been paying attention. A classic Australian radio track written by Simon Collins that demonstrates how retail ads can become intrusive for all the right reasons. Agency: The Campaign Palace.

you're being effortless with your communication, or whether you're trying *too* hard…"

Dawson is convinced that intrigue works on radio. He recalls how one of the most awarded commercials he has worked on, for home builder AV Jennings, started life with a very predictable opening. "We were selling home improvements and someone had the thought that if you didn't have room to swing a cat, you needed AV Jennings. The thought was turned into a script, but at that stage it was somewhat prosaic and started with something like, 'If you don't have room to swing a cat…' which left us nowhere to go. So we thought, let's start with a bit of intrigue. How about an argument with two people saying, 'It is', 'It isn't', 'It is', 'It isn't'. Without pictures, you have no idea what they are talking about. Then we resolved the argument with the wonderful sounds of a cat being swung around the room, knocking vases and furniture flying, to prove that indeed there wasn't room to swing a cat. Try doing that in any other medium!" As Dawson recalls, one radio station banned the commercial because they thought it would be too upsetting for their listeners.

SIMON COLLINS revisits his work for Australian retailer Jeans West at The Campaign Palace. Because the client was outspent by its major competitor, radio became a guerilla medium. "We were encouraged to do ads which might get talked or complained about, that might get a bit of free airtime simply by being controversial."

The opening dialogue in one such commercial was a young man telling a friend he is thinking of having a sex change operation — a definite attention grabber. "The only thing stopping me in the past has been the cost of all the new clothes," the young man confesses, "but now Jeans West are having a $29.95 sale. Jeans at $29.95, skirts at $29.95, or two tops for just $29.95…"

"I took the central proposition and steadily exaggerated it until it became funny." Collins demonstrates:

1. "Jeans West women's sale prices are so low that lots of young women will take advantage of them." *Not remotely funny.*
2. "Jeans West women's sale prices are so low that even old women will take advantage of them." *Still not funny.*

3. "Jeans West women's sale prices are so low that men will approve of their women buying things." *Hmmm.*

4. "Jeans West women's sale prices are so low that men may even take advantage of them for themselves." *Slightly funny.*

5. "Jeans West women's sale prices are so low that in order to take advantage of them some men are thinking of having a sex change operation." *Quite funny. Write it up.*

However, while Jeans West proved an exception, Collins warns: "Ads that deliberately try to creep up on their target audience via an irrelevant demographic run the risk of being completely overlooked by the target audience altogether."

GETTING AND HOLDING ATTENTION

Neil French says, "Write a 30-second script for a 60-second spot, and pro rata. There's too much gabbling and hysteria on radio. An ad is a chance to slow the pace and get attention that way. And the words can live better when they have air around them. Listen to 99% of radio ads and all you get is gabble, 'funny voices', and panic." French says what you write depends on the brief. "It could even be just sound effects."

David Holmes elaborates: "Radio ads can be produced without words. If that were a strict brief, we *can* do it. I once was asked by my client Avis Rent A Car to congratulate a commercial radio station on its first birthday. We contrived to have the eponymous *Happy Birthday to You* played on motor car horns for 30 seconds."

Chris Kyme also advocates the creative use of sound effects, "where you draw the listener in so that they actually picture the scene they are hearing. The worst kind of radio is the usual announcer yelling loads of information at you, none of which actually sticks in your ear, or badly acted conversation pieces which always sound so fake."

"Like in print, you've got to be prepared to use 'white space'," advises Clark. "A lot of radio is overwritten to blazes and people say, oh, you can fit that in, and you've got to read it at a hundred miles an hour to fit it in, and the person listening at the other end hasn't got a clue. It's just a load of gabble, particularly when you think about the

TITLE: AV JENNINGS HOME IMPROVEMENTS "THE CAT"

HUSBAND: It is.

WIFE: It isn't.

HUSBAND: It is.

WIFE: It isn't.

HUSBAND: It is, I'll show you…

SFX: *SOUND OF CAT SCREAMING, VASE BREAKING, AND CAT HITTING CUPBOARD WITH A THUMP.*

        PAUSE — SILENCE…

HUSBAND: You're right — it isn't.

VO: If your house isn't big enough to swing a cat, but you don't think you can afford an extension, talk to Jennings Home Improvements now. Our "Easy Extender" plan could give you that new room for as little as $25 a week.

        Talk to Jennings Home Improvements "Hot line" on 890 0721. Or see Saturday's *Sun*. But hurry! Offer closes June 30th.

HUSBAND: Now it is. Puss! Puss! Puss! Come on. Puss! Puss! Puss!

SFX: *SOUND OF CAT SCRAMBLING TO ESCAPE.*

Nigel Dawson believes intrigue works on radio, especially in the first few critical seconds. By starting the script with an argument, listeners were drawn into the 30-second commercial to find out what was happening. Client: AV Jennings Home Improvements. Agency: Foote Cone & Belding Australia.

residual noise factor, a lot of other potential distractions, and other things the listener may be doing at the time." Clark believes the spoken word is an enormously powerful tool. "If the idea is good, the simple, single voice will get through as well as anything."

How does Fishlock hold a radio listener's attention? "It's just a matter of having something of interest to say, and saying it in an interesting way. Think of some of the great announcements and speeches that have been delivered in audio. Good ideas endure whatever medium they are created in and whatever time length." If you are using a personality, he says, introduce them or have them say their name. "Even if people would 'get' who it is in the end, it's better they spend your commercial listening to the message than working out who the voice is." He condemns showy cleverness. "As an advertising medium, radio does have probably the least attentive audience and the smallest box of tricks with which to attract their attention. If showing how clever you are is top of your agenda when you sit down to write a radio ad, you're doomed to fail. Showing how clever you are and being creative are of course different concepts, far too often confused in the advertising arena."

"Most media, from print to TV to interactive, sits in front of us," Newman reminds us. "Radio spends its life in the background. We have to literally turn our attention to it. Humour can be a great start to engage the potential listener. It's also easy enough to get people to tune into your radio spot by writing against the grain of that particular station's sound. But the listener is reassessing his or her decision to keep listening every five seconds or so. You've got to be able to keep it up without dropping into a boring sales spiel that lets the listener off the hook at the most critical moment for the client."

"The listener will only stick around to the end if the message is entertaining or relevant," insists Van Dijk. "But they'll mentally switch off early if the script becomes formulaic, or the dialogue is compromised to make way for a heavy sell or call to action. If you can remain consistent and true to the idea throughout, you'll take the listener with you for the whole ride."

Brent Hahn defines a great commercial as: "*Anything that makes you want to hear it again, despite the fact that it's an ad.*" The hallmarks are a simple, clear message; great performances; artful editing and rhythm; and truth.

TITLE: YELLOW PAGES "MISSING"

What sounds like a police announcement, delivered by a typically expressionless yet official voice, interrupts the commercial break. Why are these two people missing...?

"POLICE" VOICE: Bill Burgess, plumber, dark brown hair, medium complexion, 180 centimetres, small birthmark on inside left ankle, married with three children.

Wife is Ruth, blonde, shoulder-length hair, 165 centimetres, brown eyes, slight build, no identifying marks.

They run a suburban plumbing business and were last seen in the 1999 Yellow Pages Directory.

MVO: This is your last chance for advertising in the 2000 Yellow Pages directory. Make sure you're not missing. Call 13 23 78.

Even a dull, monotonal voice can hold our attention — especially when it sounds like it is reading a police announcement. Created by Clemenger BBDO Melbourne for client Yellow Pages, and produced at Flint Webster.

TITLE: JOHN WEST "PERFECT"

The commercial parodies trailers for disaster movies.

SFX: *DRAMATIC   MUSIC   AND   STORM   EFFECTS
                  THROUGHOUT...*

AMERICAN VO: There had never been a storm like it...

HERO: *(IN AWE)* I've seen gales before, but this —
                   this is different...

AMERICAN VO: Waves the sizes of buildings...

WOMAN: *(SCREAMING)* You can't go out there, John!

HERO: You don't understand, Maggie! I have to!

AMERICAN VO: Winds with the force of nuclear warheads...

MAN: *(SHOUTING)*   We'll   be   crushed   like
                   matchsticks!

AMERICAN VO: Man against Nature...

HERO: *(GRIMLY)* We are going out there!

AMERICAN VO: Nature against Man...

MAN: You're insane!

HERO: Maybe I am, but there's something out there
                   I want.

AMERICAN VO: John West bring you the perfect tuna.

                   John West, enduring the worst...

SFX: *BURST OF RAGING GALE...*

AMERICAN VO: to bring you the best.

*A British Aerial award winner: John West Tuna from Leo Burnett London.
Exemplary scripting, acting and sound design created a credible movie trailer —
before the brand was revealed. Duration: 40 seconds.*

Radio: Theatre Of The Mind, Or Mindless Theatre?

"Radio's ability to activate the 'Theatre of the Mind' has been much discussed, but not as well employed." Keith Reinhard believes that Bill Bernbach's observations on the importance of emotion also apply to radio. "Bill said, *You can say the right thing about a product and nobody will listen. You've got to say it in such a way that people will feel it in their gut. Because if they don't feel it in their gut, nothing will happen.* I've always felt that we underutilise radio's power to be emotional and strike at gut level. For a reminder of radio's emotional power, replay some of the spine-tingling dramas or even the soap operas from radio's earlier days."

Reinhard cites a commercial that DDB Johannesburg created for a homeless shelter. "With a few well-chosen words and effects it brings home the wetness, the loneliness, the misery of life on the street..."

```
SFX:    INTERIOR HOME, RAIN FALLING SOFTLY OUTSIDE.

ANNCR:  This is how rain sounds inside your bedroom.

SFX:    INTERIOR CAR, HEAVY RAIN AGAINST WINDSCREEN,
        PUNCTUATED BY RHYTHM OF WIPERS.

ANNCR:  This is how rain sounds inside your car.

SFX:    EXTERIOR, DOWNPOUR.

ANNCR:  This is how rain sounds to street children.

SFX:    EXTERIOR, CONTINUE DOWNPOUR.

ANNCR:  If you don't enjoy getting wet, imagine what it
        feels like when you can't get dry.
```

Adds Reinhard: "What followed the narration, of course, was an appeal for listeners to support the shelter."

Newman says radio allows you to show things you can't in any other medium. "I once had a girl undo enough buttons on her split skirt to cause a road accident."

A word of caution from Hahn: "In TV it takes a split second to establish a scene. In radio, it can take much longer. And the point of view has to remain fixed. You can't cut back and forth between

TITLE: *MARIE CLAIRE* "PHOTOGRAPHER"

A bossy woman photographer is calling rather bizarre instructions to her model. We are compelled to listen and find out why...

WOMAN: Okay, Sue, just turn your head towards me so that I can see those bags under your eyes...

SFX: *CAMERA.*

WOMAN: Great, great ... err, now pull that sheet down a bit, yeah? Show me your cellulite...

SFX: *CAMERA.*

WOMAN: Super, super. Chins up — no, all of them...

SFX: *CAMERA.*

FVO: Would you let your boyfriend's ex-lover take revealing photos of you and publish them in *Marie Claire*? Four women did. See the results in this month's issue, out now. *Marie Claire*, writing that gets you talking.

WOMAN: I'm going to have to use a wider lens so that I can get the whole of your fat bum in shot, okay?

SFX: *CAMERA.*

A brilliant piece of theatre on radio — an intriguing 30-seconder, tightly written, well acted, economically edited. Written by Paul Silburn at Leith London.

cameras." Which is another reason why great radio scripts are timed to allow a scene to be fully established.

ANDY LERNER and writer Grant Sanders activated theatre of the mind for the Kodak Picture CD. The commercial had to help launch the new product and demonstrate its benefits — without visuals. Their brief from the agency: "Make it different from the TV spots. Really use radio, use sounds!"

Which is precisely what they did. They devised a 60-seconder in which a series of "what if" situations explored how far the use of the new product could theoretically, and humorously, take the consumer. The commercial began simply enough with the narrator saying that you have just taken a picture of a dog holding a flower in its mouth. You take it for processing and check the box for a Kodak Picture CD. Thanks to the CD's free built-in software, you are able to retouch your photo on your computer and email it to your friends. Your friends in turn email it to millions of other people, causing newspapers to write about it, and political leaders to talk about it, until it becomes a symbol for the unity of all mankind. The strapline: *Kodak. Take pictures … further.* The narrator's voice — underscored throughout by an original music track and seamlessly punctuated with spot sound effects and voices — anchored the storyline and kept the listener's attention focused on the new product. The commercial, appropriately called *Sounds*, won its category at the London International Advertising Awards.

"While TV budgets tend to be shrinking, you can write a radio script uninhibited by budget," says Redman. "Airdropping 50 bulls into a vegetarians' convention only takes a few sound effects. Imagine if you had to shoot that for TV?" More than any other medium, Redman insists, you can write those dream scripts. "You don't need to experience any of the things you write about first-hand, you just imagine it and it becomes reality. The best piece of radio ever done was Orson Welles' *War of the Worlds*. Look at the reaction it caused. Unbridled confusion and panic caused by words and sounds. And look where it got him. The next thing he did was *Citizen Kane*."

HERTZ is convinced that art directors, in many ways, do better radio than copywriters. "They don't get hung up on words. It's not just the 'pictures in the mind' — they think in blocks and shapes." Radio, he says, is like art directing a print ad; a search for a look and a style that focuses not only on getting the message across, but making it attractive, distinctive and satisfying. Hertz challenges sound design as a means of creating theatre of the mind. "Sound design uses sound to *accompany* pictures, not to create them." Instead of using sound to make the pictures, he recommends using pictures to make the sound.

His advice is to start with the image you want to create. "If you know what a scene looks like, the sounds will follow. Think about that picture you want to see. Do a storyboard or a key frame, or draw an image of any kind, and then find the sounds — words, sound effects, music — which make that picture. Imagine the microphone as a camera, and think about 'shots'." He references a still-life photograph of a plastic sandal sitting on the edge of a worn jetty just above clear green water — an image that evoked a sound: "An art director said he loved the shot because he could practically hear the sandal *squeak*."

The start and end point for creating, presenting and producing radio is always a picture, says Hertz. He realises pictures by visually plotting his commercials on paper, storyboarding wide shots and close-ups. And like print ads, voices, sound effects and silences are elements whose balance and proportion need painstaking adjustment. "Draw your scene and show it to everybody. The more the director, the engineer, actors and clients see it your way, the more likely you are to hear it your way."

HOWE also believes art directors — and ambition — are key to great radio. "Somehow, radio became the 'writer's medium'. The art director got to be part of the TV and print, but at nearly all agencies the writer goes it alone for radio without the benefit of Bill Bernbach's contribution to the evolution of the creative species. But in the UK, creatives grew up with the BBC and have a reverence for the spoken word, and creative teams are more likely to be more ambitious, conceptually, about a radio assignment."

Like Hertz, Howe storyboards radio ideas. "I think every spot has a 'storyboard'. The listener will see something, so we might as well guide what it is that they're seeing."

Howe likes commercials that mess with the art direction, and references a spot by GSD&M for Southwest Airlines that he judged at the Clios. "The premise was, 'there is good, and then there is better', a pretty straightforward retail proposition. In the commercial the announcer says, 'Take diving, for instance. There's good...' and we hear a guy jumping from a diving board, the crowd going 'Ahhhhh', and then the diver splashing into the pool, met with applause from the crowd. The announcer comes back: 'Then there's better...' There's the same bounce on the board, the same 'Ahhhhhhs', and a second or two passes and the crowd goes 'Oooohhhh', and then another second or two and they start laughing uproariously, and then one more 'Ahhhhhhhhhh', and then the diver splashes into the pool to wild applause. At which point the announcer proceeds to tell you how Southwest Airlines has these good deals, but if you go to their website you can get better deals." The art direction of the spot, Howe elaborates, is what makes it so memorable. *"It forces you to see it, and you like what you see."*

Another example: "A brilliant South African spot promoting radio. Two guys are playing Russian roulette with a gun and it eventually goes off. You figure one guy is dead. After a long pause, the other guy says, 'Hey, Cedric', 'Yeah?', 'Aren't you glad this wasn't a TV commercial?' And the end line was, 'Radio. It goes in one ear. And stays there.' "

Howe believes you have to know the rules to break the rules. Changes of pace, even quiet commercials, work well. Howe's all-time favourite radio campaign illustrates his point about art direction. "Dentsu Japan did 1-minute 20-second spots for the Imperial Osaka Hotel, each one dedicated to either the sound of shoes on the marble in the lobby, or the sound of the consommé in the restaurant, or the matchsticks they use in the bar..."

IN MEDIAS RES

It means "into the midst of things", starting a scene in the midst of the narrative or plot, with no introduction or preamble. Novelist

Stephen King believes every life is *in medias res*. It is the perfect way to start a radio script. Skip the phone ringing and the "Hello?" Forget the door bell, and "Oh, hi". Plunge right into the action and start the commercial *in medias res*.

"You can really cut to the chase by viciously editing your own dialogue and effects," suggests Clark, referencing story compression in American television shows. "The editing is so slick in the visual sense, they don't waste any time, they just jump, jump, jump. You can do the same in radio — you can jump to key dialogue lines and sound effects that will paint the pictures for you." He cites one example of a weak opening: If somebody's husband arrives home and he's had a bad day at the office, *don't* have the door open and the wife call out, "Had a nice day, dear?" to which the husband replies, "No, I've lost my job." Instead, says Clark, the commercial might start with a loud slamming door and a comment from his wife like, "Oh, *that* good, eh?" "It sets off an immediate picture in your mind that someone is in a foul mood and lets the husband go straight into saying 'I've lost my job,' or whatever. Instead of wasting five seconds, you've set up the situation in two."

"Stories don't need to have a beginning, middle and end," reflects Christine Coyle. "When we're doing 30s, they rarely have an actual beginning, or the beginning might be the middle of the story. And not all advertising stories have to have a traditional ending. Sometimes the commercial ends *without* the situation being resolved, much like life…"

BRAD POWER discusses the use of telephones to start commercials. "The phone rings, someone picks up the phone, and suddenly the other person starts the sell. I understand why the telephone has become a cliché. It's a mechanism to start a conversation, a mechanism to get attention, but the telephone conversation we end up hearing is generally the most unreal piece of dialogue. People do not talk the way that they tend to talk in commercials … like, 'Conditions apply though, Jack'. It's supposed to be a conversation between two friends, and you think what a strange relationship these two have got if this is how they talk to each other. You've got to make conversations natural. As soon as they start talking in a commercial way, there's no credibility. If the dialogue doesn't fit into a telephone conversation, then don't put it into a telephone conversation. If you've got to give information about '5.6% interest on the latest housing loan', then just get a voice-over in to say it. It's more honest, more open, and a much more effective piece of communication. Why try to pretend it's two housewives talking about it on the phone?"

Ironically, Power directed one of Australia's most compelling radio campaigns in recent years for the Australian Red Cross Blood Bank — and every commercial was a telephone conversation. The campaign, created by Publicis Wellcare/Mojo Partners Sydney, was awarded a Silver Pencil at D&AD.

Each commercial establishes a traumatic situation. In the phone call, a close relative is informed that a loved one has been in a life-threatening accident and they need to come down immediately and donate blood. Which is all very dramatic and emotional in its own right, but it's then that the loving mother or husband or daughter starts to come up with reasons why giving blood is inconvenient at that point — a hairdresser's appointment, a business commitment, a dinner date. The agency's executive creative director David Alberts says the campaign had to set up and create some sense of urgency, some sense of drama, that would make people give blood. "Radio is a great medium for this. You're listening and suddenly it turns on you very quickly."

Power discusses the conflict in the situations: "The beautiful thing about the Red Cross ads was that people didn't quite know what they were, so they started to listen and by the end they were horrified. They couldn't believe that someone would say those things because it sounded very real. If radio ads can get people to feel a range of emotions then you're really getting somewhere. Rather than just blasting information at people, you actually get people to listen..."

Power worked closely with agency writers Denis Koutoulogenis and Pat Richer. "We asked ourselves, what *would* a doctor say? We found out how people talk in those situations; it's very easy for us to *think* we know how they talk."

Executionally, Power broke conventional production techniques. "The thing about a conversation between two people is that it's inherently difficult to make it sound natural, because you know what the other person's going to say next. You're having a 'conversation' that's written down, whereas the way people really talk is that the other person doesn't know when I'm going to finish my sentence." Power arranged the recording so that the talent worked in separate areas: one was on the phone in one room, the other was in the recording studio sounding like they're on a phone. "Not only were the people separated, but when I gave them their scripts I gave them only their words. I didn't give them the other person's half of the script. So in take one and take two, they didn't know what the other person's last words would be, so we got interruptions, pauses, they even talked over each other. We ended up doing five or six takes in the end, and by take four they were starting to figure out what they were going to say. So we ended up going with the first takes because that's where the spontaneity was." By minimising the number of words in the script, Power knew that the first two spontaneous takes would fit comfortably within the overall timing, despite all the pauses and interruptions.

Technically, Power ensured that *both* voices sounded like they were speaking on a phone line — which was another break with convention. "Usually on a radio ad the phone rings and only one of the parties sounds like they're coming out of the phone. The other person sounds like the listener is standing next to them. By making them both sound like they were on the phone, we could really eavesdrop on their conversation." Power was prepared to sacrifice the clarity of the occasional word and used a real phone line. "It was a bit grubby, a bit hard to understand at times — but that's *real*. It sounded like we were bugging a telephone call, that we were privy to something that would otherwise be a personal discussion. The more you clean it up, the more you get that over-polished sound that isn't real."

Dozens of creatives have praised the campaign, Steve Elrick among them: "I was stunned when I heard it. So many human truths in one spot. How good did I think it was? It drew blood. I hadn't donated for over a year or two. I went down within the week…"

TITLE: AUSTRALIAN RED CROSS "BUSY SIS"

SFX: *TELEPHONE CONVERSATION.*

SISTER: Hello?

MOTHER: Kelly?

SISTER: Mum!

MOTHER: *(Sobbing)* Is that you?

SISTER: *(Shocked)* Yeah, what's wrong? Mum?

MOTHER: It's Emma. She's been in an accident.

SISTER: Oh God. What happened?

MOTHER: She was crossing the road after school.

SISTER: Oh God.

MOTHER: She needs blood…

SISTER: Right…

MOTHER: But they don't have any of her type left.

SISTER: So, you need me?

MOTHER: Yes. You're the only family member with the same blood type.

SISTER: OK, um, right now?

MOTHER: Mmmm. Where are you? Dad will come and pick you up.

SISTER: Mum, I'm just having dinner with Peter. He finally asked me out. He's inside waiting. And we've got tickets to a concert … I really should get back, mum.

MOTHER: Darling! Emma is dying.

SISTER: Mum, I'm so sorry. But I can't just get up and leave. I've got a life, too. Do you understand, mum?

"EMMA": Someone desperately needs your blood right now. Call the Red Cross Blood Bank on 13 14 95. Or are you too busy?

Telephone conversations with a horrifying twist addressed public apathy towards donating blood. Directed by Brad Power, the actors were in separate rooms with only their half of the script. Pauses and interruptions, combined with the use of real phone lines, made the commercials more real and compelling. Publicis Wellcare/ Mojo Partners Sydney. Agency producer: Amanda Peters.

TITLE: AUSTRALIAN RED CROSS "BUSY MUM"

SFX: *TELEPHONE CONVERSATION.*

MOTHER: Hello.

DOCTOR: Mrs. Wilson?

MOTHER: Yes?

DOCTOR: It's Doctor Fraser from St. George Hospital, Mrs. Wilson. I'm afraid your son Matthew's been in an accident, madam.

MOTHER: *(Shocked)* What? What? Matthew?

DOCTOR: *(Calmly)* Now he's going to be all right, but he needs an urgent blood transfusion.

MOTHER: *(Progressively more hysterical as the doctor explains the situation)* Oh my God! Oh my God! Is he all right?

DOCTOR: Yeah he's fine. He's OK.

MOTHER: Oh Matthew! What happened?

DOCTOR: Look, unfortunately, we have no supplies of AB negative blood.

MOTHER: Oh my God! Oh, my baby... *(Suddenly realising what the doctor has just said)* I'm AB negative!

DOCTOR: *(Relieved)* This is fantastic. When can you get down to the hospital?

MOTHER: Well it's just that um, I've got this hair appointment, and it's really hard to get into this salon.

DOCTOR: *(Surprised)* Er, Mrs. Wilson...

MOTHER: Oh, and then I've got lunch with Jane...

DOCTOR: Mrs. Wilson! Your son will die if you do not give blood!

MOTHER: Oh, um all right. Um... *(Pause)* What if I come down in the morning after tennis?

"HER SON": Someone desperately needs your blood right now. Call the Red Cross Blood Bank on 13 14 95. Or are you too busy?

TITLE: AUSTRALIAN RED CROSS "BUSY HUSBAND"

SFX: *TELEPHONE CONVERSATION*

BOB: Hello, Doctor Martin? It's Bob Davis.

DOCTOR: Oh, hi Bob.

BOB: How is she doc?

DOCTOR: Well, you know, she's resting now but she's lost a lot of blood.

BOB: Is she going to be OK?

DOCTOR: She needs a transfusion, Bob. Listen, you're A positive, aren't you?

BOB: Yeah…

DOCTOR: Well, that's great. That's great because we're going to need your blood.

BOB: Oh right. Um… look, can't someone else do it?

DOCTOR: *(Dumbfounded)* Bob, do you understand how serious this is? Your wife has lost a lot of blood. You're A positive. She needs your blood now.

BOB: Yeah, look it's just I'm flat chat today.

DOCTOR: It's your wife, Bob. Your wife. She needs your blood. There can't be any question of yes or no, it's got to be yes.

BOB: OK, OK, I hear you, I hear you. Listen, could she hold on till Wednesday? Because I've got a little break there in the middle of the day. I could probably fit you in —

"WIFE":   Someone desperately needs your blood right now. Call the Red Cross Blood Bank on 13 14 95. Or are you too busy?

IMMESOETE talks about structure. "A good starting point for any writer is collecting pieces you like and taking them apart. Write out all the words of ads you admire. *This teaches you architecture.* It also makes you a better listener. Learning structure from others isn't stealing — it's advancing your knowledge. Besides, doing things strictly 'your way' is seldom as fiercely original as you think. Just because you haven't done it before doesn't mean it's never been done."

Great radio tends to be cinematic, explains Redman. "Now that I've moved into writing and directing films, I find the old radio plays a great inspiration as the scripts were always so tight. I believe if you filmed some of those radio plays today they would make great films." By the same token, he suggests some films would make great radio. "I watched the Coen Brothers' *The Big Lebowski* for about the millionth time the other day and I reckon you can close your eyes and it makes a great radio play. The dialogue crackles along."

Words And Images

"Learn to paint pictures with words from the masters," advises Immesoete. "Before you can write, you need to read. Build up a solid literary base. Read and you'll pick up skills from other writers, usually without even knowing it. Hemingway spoke clearly in short, succinct sentences — good for the ad writer. Faulkner used flowery language and detail — good for the radio writer." Television, says Immesoete, is the medium of the noun and the verb; radio is the medium of the adjective and the adverb. "The adjectives and adverbs take the place of the pictures."

Reinhard elaborates. "The first radio award I won was for an insurance commercial. A poor guy's car was sinking in quicksand — you can hear the sucking sound as the car goes down. An agent shows up with the assuring words, 'Sir, that car is completely covered.' Corny, but very visual — a funnier picture in the mind than we could have painted on television." Reinhard references Stan Freberg's demonstration of radio's power to elicit fantastic images. "He dropped a maraschino cherry the size of Cleveland into the middle of Lake Erie. His point was that in radio, anything you can imagine is possible to portray." Reinhard quotes Eastern Airlines and

Fuller Paint as examples of great radio imagery. "The old Orson Welles series of radio spots for Eastern Airlines elicited irresistible images of Eastern's destination cities — New Orleans, New York, Miami and Atlanta. And years ago, an especially creative and dulcet-toned radio personality named Ken Nordine painted a series of sound pictures of colours — on radio — for Fuller Paint. Imagine quirky but well-placed sound effects and fragments of piano behind this riff on the colour green…"

```
NORDINE: As an intellectual vibration, smack dab in the
         middle of the spectrum, green can be a problem.

         That's because there's so many different greens
         inside of green and each one has a different
         IQ.

         There's the green that should never have happened
         … the stupid green. The green that is green
         with envy. Then there's the so-so green, the
         who-cares-anyway green.

         But somewhere in green is a green here and
         there that has something to say. A truly
         intelligent green.

         A green with some integrity. That's the kind
         of green for you and me. There's a green to be
         seen with. Vivid. Vibrant. Living alive! We
         should spend the better part of our time, yours
         and mine, with a green like this. Maybe some of
         it would rub off.
```

Remley recalls a commercial created by Paul Bernasconi for Casio Easyplay Keyboards with a sheep playing the product. "It was recorded at a radio workshop and it was good enough for air." The commercial has a single voice-over describing how a sheep was left alone with a Casio keyboard. The only other sounds in the ad are the sheep — and the product. The idea derived entirely from the user-friendly product. To all intents and purposes, it was a demonstration commercial conveying a very bizarre image.

TITLE: CASIO EASYPLAY KEYBOARDS

The voice is very matter-of-fact.

VO: The common sheep is generally regarded to be the world's dumbest animal.

For example, no sheep has ever been trained to fetch a stick.

There is no tourist development where sheep jump through flaming hoops.

A sheep cannot ride a unicycle.

Recently, a group of scientists left a sheep alone with a Casio Easyplay Keyboard. After only half an hour, this is what they heard:

SFX: *DISCORDANT KEYBOARD NOTES AND "BAAAAs"...*

VO: Another half an hour later, it was this:

SFX: *KEYBOARD PLAYING "BAA BAA BLACK SHEEP". THE SHEEP IS BLEATING OUT THE TUNE...*

VO: And after only two hours with a Casio Easyplay Keyboard, the animal had progressed to this:

SFX: *"BAA BAA BLACK SHEEP" NOW PLAYED WITH A ROCK BEAT, THE SHEEP IS BLEATING ALONG...*

VO: At this point the sheep refused to perform any further, and demanded from the scientists standard Musicians' Union fees, plus 70% of all recording revenue. So they ate him.

The common sheep is generally regarded to be the world's dumbest animal.

Classic simplicity: a demonstration with a difference — proving you only need a straightforward voice, the actual sound of the product and a great idea. Agency: OMON. Writer: Paul Bernasconi. Production: Paul Goodwin at Hello Testing.

SQUEEZING IN THE MANDATORIES

Newman discusses what to do with a shopping list of mandatories. As he explains, sometimes it's not so much a case of squeezing in the mandatories, it's more a case of squeezing in the idea.

"In print executions, the copy points can be relegated to a smaller typesize and hidden away in a panelled-up corner of the ad. But in a radio script, every line is the same size. So the best answer is to write one script per point. If you lose that battle, then my advice is start the scriptwriting by putting everything you have to mention into a short, utterly unadorned piece of copy. Time it out. *However many seconds you have left tells you precisely how much idea you can afford to have.*"

Sometimes, he says, using or creating a character can be the vehicle you need to carry lots of "guff". "The NRMA was Australia's biggest radio advertiser when we won the account. So radio Brand Properties were the answer because they had so many different products, services and promotions on offer during the year. An ongoing character like 'Wallace Fairweather', the earnest insurance groupie, became their long-running and award-winning character. He provided both continuity and branding — and a conduit for the mandatories."

Hertz looks at the financial sector, too. "If you choose to advertise financial offers, the mandatory caveats can easily make your ad sound like everyone else's. Consider communicating strategy, not just tactics." Many advertisers see radio as a medium for tactical offers, observes Hertz. "But if tactical advertising doesn't also reinforce brand relevance, it's a lost opportunity."

Danielle Sterrie believes there is always a more inventive way of handling the mandatories. She references a financial commercial that made a feature of the mandatory legal copy instead of rattling it off as quickly as humanly possible in one breath. "It stood out a mile."

EVALUATING A RADIO IDEA

How should creatives judge their own scripts? How should creative directors approve or reject radio ideas?

Conrad's focus on judging radio commercials is visual. "A great radio script is visual, it paints pictures. *I've seen it on the radio…*"

Fromowitz believes the brief itself is the first yardstick. "Always begin with a solid brief. Only then do you know what to say in the spot, and how to judge your idea. I would never begin writing a radio spot for which there is no written brief agreed to by the client." Memorability is his next consideration. "We remind ourselves that there are a huge number of spots the listener is exposed to. So our execution must contain a memorable, standout element. The radio spot is of little use if it communicates effectively, but is never remembered."

Fromowitz's next question: is there too much copy? "Emotion is the root of persuasion. It's easy to impair or destroy the emotional elements of a radio spot by including too much copy that appeals to reason. Emotion needs time, and breathing space, to develop fully. A 30-second radio script that is mostly voice- or announcer-read script, with little or no music or sound effects, can handle about 65 words comfortably. Any more can reduce the effectiveness of the commercial." Another taboo: treating listeners as morons by aiming far below the average intelligence level. "It's critical to recognise that this is not directed against the simplicity of the idea, but against mediocrity, blandness and the dogmatic manner of the execution."

Reichenthal applies the "warehouse" test to his work. "When I was in junior high, I worked as a stock boy in a warehouse. They had the radio playing over the PA system all day long. We'd hear the same radio commercials over and over and over again. The good ones were a pleasure to hear. The bad ones … not such a pleasure. I think I evaluate my radio scripts by asking myself, 'If I was still working at that job with the radio playing all day long, would I want to hear this commercial?' "

Edmonds has developed a personal checklist for judging his own copy. Be really honest, he says, and ask yourself three questions:

1. Is this relevant to my product?
2. Will this be interesting to my listeners?
3. Have I heard this before?

He also believes copywriters have to share their scripts with the world. "Either read the script to creative people whose ability you trust. Or make a demo and play it to your wife's father. Or your daughter. Try and pick the most unbiased people you know. There was a girl once in my agency who was so friendly. She loved every script I showed her. I soon stopped showing her anything." If you can't make a script work, or more than two people don't "get" it, says Edmonds, "take a deep breath and kill it. Move on. Walk away..."

HOWE insists that writers present premises first. "I think this probably applies to any medium, really. The best creative ideas, not unlike the best strategy statements, can usually be boiled down to one simple idea that can be explained in one sentence. Truthfully, a bad writer can write a great radio commercial if they have a great premise." *Firips*, he reminds us, had one premise behind it. So did *Real American Heroes*. "As David Droga of Saatchi & Saatchi London says, 'it's all about inspiration.' If there is going to be one inspired premise, and ten not-so-inspired premises, I'm only going to show the client the one. Frankly, inspiration is so rare that I can't remember the last time I saw two equally inspired directions in the same creative presentation..."

Howe believes most clients will see inspiration if it is presented properly. He references a presentation to a cheese company. "One concept was totally appropriate for them, with enough entertainment value to keep the listener's attention. The other was appropriate for the brand, but totally inspired and way outside of their comfort zone. Way outside! But they saw the rightness of it and after addressing a number of their concerns which we had anticipated ahead of time, we convinced them that we had to do it."

Newman also likes his creatives to tell him the kernel of the idea in a single short sentence. "It exposes the naked thought. If your radio commercial starts life with an identifiable idea, it will only get healthier in production. If not, you're gambling. A simple precise idea that takes no longer than a sentence to present can be used as a cutting tool to refine the eventual script, ridding it of lines that don't contribute directly to the central thrust. Getting your idea clearly defined into a sentence is easier to sell to a client than a nuance, or a sound effect, or a piece of dialogue." A clearly defined idea is also easier to defend against changes, he adds. "It keeps everyone on track. That single sentence can easily be dramatised to fill the available airspace rather than the more usual problem, which is trying to fit a complicated thought into a commercial length. As Saki once said, 'In baiting a trap with cheese, always leave room for the mouse…' "

REMLEY workshops his scripts. "I tend to overwrite grossly myself, but I have the luxury of a studio where I can workshop it and hammer things into the length that they should be, and if it takes me a day to make a 30-second commercial, I'll do it. There's no reason why a writer can't do the same thing with a group of friends, or getting the two actors he plans to use to come join him at his kitchen table." What happens at a workshop session? "My way of getting a thing into time is not to slave over it myself and kill off my own children. I get the best minds around me, people I really respect, and between us we kind of referee the thing and get it into shape. I immediately involve the talent I'm going to use, and that might involve a musician as well, and I'll say look, here's where I am. I've got 62 seconds' worth of material here and it needs to be a 45. I want you guys to help me economise, and I want you to be brutal. Where there's something I think is funny it'll be precious to me, but if you tell me it's not funny or you can make it better, I'll take those opinions very much to heart."

Remley adopts a very intuitive writing and production style based on experience. "I always stand back and say, is this thing branded properly? Or is it over-branded — am I causing an irritation factor because this client wants me to deliver the product name four times and in doing so I know I'm going to lose the listener. But I don't apply a set of rules, and I don't try to avoid any techniques. I won't do jingles, and I don't use sound effects or music unless it is absolutely appropriate. It's like the old principle, one plus one equals three; a picture of a Volkswagen and a headline, *Lemon*, but there's a third thing, a third emotion. The only time to use sound effects or music in radio is exactly the same principle; if they don't amplify what the voice is saying, then they shouldn't be there."

IT is almost impossible for many clients to judge a radio idea off the page. And if they don't "get" it, they believe their audience won't either.

For one thing, *written* English and *spoken* English are completely different, which could well make finely crafted dialogue hard to appreciate. For another, the script could look seriously underwritten — and simply begging for more copy to go in!

A cheap demo tape, or an acted presentation, is a better way for them to judge — by hearing rather than reading.

"I insist on clients hearing the idea before seeing it on paper," asserts Van Dijk. "I have been acting and voicing scripts for as long as I have been writing them, and this certainly helps when presenting. Before the script is completed, I will often run the outline idea past the client, describing the premise and tone of voice. They then get to judge the idea without getting fixated with the details. If they like it at that stage, the rest should follow easily."

Hahn endorses the demo tape presentation. "Agencies and clients usually want to see an initial presentation in script form. But I can't tell you how many of my spots and campaigns, particularly the big award winners, would never have been produced if they'd only been presented on paper. Well-produced demos, on the other hand, have an amazing tendency to go on air. Killing a script is mere contraception, while killing a great demo is murder."

WHEN Hill sells her radio ideas to clients, she is unashamedly theatrical. "I always stand up, and do character voices, and get a bit animated. And the clients have as much fun watching me present the script as they do listening to what it's saying. Some people record it simply and present it that way, but I think it's better being yourself across a boardroom table, having fun presenting it. It's great to see clients laugh and enjoy a radio script. When you present television to them, you can see them thinking, oh no, that's not going to work, the logo's up too late. But with radio they tend to sit back and enjoy it."

Hertz agrees. "When you present your spot, act it out for the client before you show a script. Don't just read it, *perform* it. I began to sell more radio ads to clients once I stopped worrying about my dignity."

But performance is merely one part of Hertz's radio concept presentation technique…

HERTZ does radio "storyboards". "It's a communications thing I do to explain to somebody else what I'm going to do. The A4 page is the most dangerous thing that could happen to a radio commercial. Because you have a piece of paper from your agency that has 'Copy' or 'Script' on it, people start creating so that it will fit on that A4 page, which is a strange way to write radio when you think about it. When I wrote the Dovercourt commercial, I wanted to say to the client there's a page with blue and curving letters, and creamy kind of stuff, and what I wanted to get across was that this commercial was going to have texture. And he could *see* that texture. A big part of the creative relationship between clients and agencies is confidence. If the advertiser believes you can do it, he will allow you to do it. Part of writing things down and drawing them is also to say that this guy thinks differently, therefore he must be able to do it differently. If you want to break out of the dialogue trap, get yourself a layout pad."

Dovercourt Volkswagen

VW dealer in Bristol. Wanted to announce their move to a new location.
They called themselves "The Cream", I.e. Cream of the Crop

The cream.... mmmmmmm
la crème de la crème ...of the crop
is fresh...is moving
Dovercourt is the cream *is the* cream....
it rises to the top *the cream is moving*

gently moving cream...

Dovercourt is the cream
The cream is moving it's ready to serve
Dovercourt Volkswagen
at Whitby Road.

"*Creamy*"
Music

Voices as
instruments

What I thought "Moving Cream" would look/sound like.
(And how we presented it to the client)

Tony Hertz storyboards his radio commercials to escape the tyranny of the A4 page.

GREEN - SUNG WORDS
BROWN - RADIO DEEJAY
BLACK - SFX
RED - HEROINE
BLUE - OTHER CHARACTERS

Brooke-Bond "D" Tea   UK 40 seconds.
1 of a campaign of 6

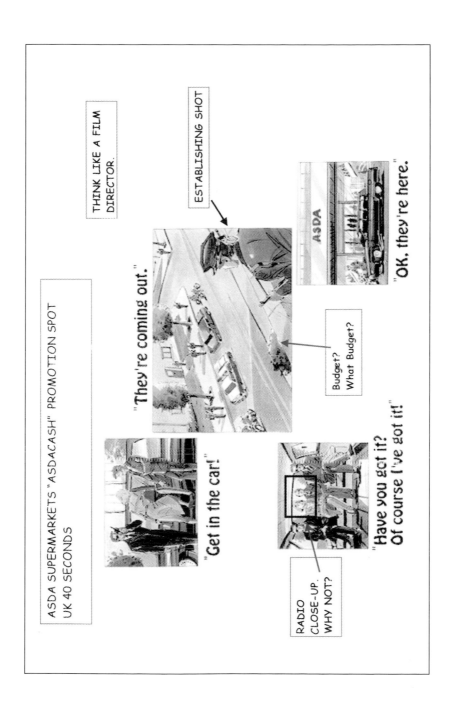

H&M Belgium: 40 seconds

You're walking down the street thinking about nothing in particular and suddenly you see this BRIGHT GREEN SWEATER. And you say to yourself, *I gotta have it.* But it looks so good it must have cost *an arm and a leg.* . .

H&M Poster...   and how we made it work on radio

5

THE MOST CAMPAIGNABLE MEDIUM

I n America, radio advertising's defining moment happened in 1961.

"I heard the Fuller Paint commercials when I was an absolute beginner in the business and I was just overwhelmed by them," recalls Tony Hertz. "They were just so wonderful. There was this guy, Bob Pritikin, who had decided simply to do brown or yellow with sound…"

Every commercial invited the listener to stare with their ears at a different colour, which was then evoked by free-associating words, musical riffs, and subtle sounds. Yellow, for example, referenced taxis. Brown was conjured up through the music of a harpsichord and a monologue about purists. The images conveyed were at once graphic impressions and impressionistic graphics. Ken Nordine's rich voice provided a curious narrative, his voice becoming another instrument in the "chemistry of colour".

Hertz attributes his own achievements to the inspiration derived from hearing that campaign. "In 1997 I was in Auckland at a radio conference, and one of the guests who had been invited was a guy called Jerry Gibbons. It turned out he had been the account man on Fuller Paints. I told him he was responsible for my being in the business because he was the account guy who *didn't* say 'you can't do that on radio…' "

TITLE: FULLER PAINT COMPANY "BROWN"

ANNCR: The Fuller Paint Company invites you to stare with your ears at Brown.

MUSIC: *A HARPSICHORD EVOKES THE ATMOSPHERE OF STAID, TRADITIONAL BROWN...*

ANNCR: Among purists — and you know how many purists there are — Brown was having some difficulty.

Some of the purists wanted Brown to be more...

MUSIC: *A TRILL ON A FLUTE SUGGESTS BRIGHTNESS...*

ANNCR: Others wanted Brown to be more...

MUSIC: *DESCENDING WOODWIND NOTES SUGGEST MYSTERY...*

ANNCR: Still others wanted Brown to be...

MUSIC: *A FRESH CONTRAST... THE MUSIC SWITCHES TO AN INTIMATE JAZZ FEELING. THE BRAND NAME "FULLER PAINT" IS WHISPERED IN TIME TO THE MUSIC AND CONTINUES TO THE END...*

ANNCR: Yeah... A lesser colour might have fallen apart. But Brown met the problem beautifully by becoming more and more subtle.

Brown has become just about as subtle as subtle can get.

That's why today you hear people say: "My, that's a subtle Brown..."

If that's the kind of Brown you want, why want less? Remember to remember the Fuller Paint Company. A century of leadership in the chemistry of colour. Visit your Fuller Colour Centre tomorrow. Or the day after yesterday.

The campaign that defined the possibilities of radio: Fuller Paint from 1961, written by Bob Pritikin, conveyed colours and textures with sound.

Fuller Paint wasn't Robert Pritikin's only significant creation. Later, Hertz reports, he also wrote a book called *Christ Was an Adman.*

BRITAIN'S seminal radio campaign was created in the early 1980s. Engineer Rob Townsend had joined London's Angell Sound in 1983 and remembers the Philips sessions with great affection. "They were very funny. What generally happened was that Mel and Griff would come in without any agency or other creatives present and simply sit opposite each other in the studio and bat ideas off each other." Townsend said the whole session would be recorded, just in case there were other little gems that could be used. "If my memory serves me correctly, the Philips ads were done in one take and generally ad-libbed around the basis of an idea." It remains Britain's most-referenced radio campaign.

GIVEN the high costs of television production, radio's economy of scale is liberating. In fact, for less than the production cost of one television commercial, a whole radio campaign can be created, recorded and run.

These days, a creative's last chance to do a campaign might well be on radio. Clients are more likely to grant creative latitude with radio. Ironically though, the president of London International Advertising Awards Barbara Levy says it is very rare these days to find radio campaigns that build brands. "Laughing Cow cheese and Blue Nun wine were sold from radio commercials. If the client wanted to get into your head, he used radio."

Leveraging the loyalty of radio audiences lets campaigns deliver a variety of executions consistently to the same people. "Even though the consumer has about the same number of choices on radio as on television, radio listeners are roughly two and a half times more loyal," explains Keith Reinhard. "This loyalty characteristic is important, not only because we have a better chance of *reaching the same listener again and again,* but also because our studies show that audiences loyal to a particular vehicle are much more receptive to advertising messages carried by that vehicle."

Mike Fromowitz says radio allows him to structure campaigns of

TITLE: GREAT KEPPEL ISLAND CAMPAIGN

Sound bites of young adults having fun are integrated throughout the commentary. Duration: 60 seconds.

SFX: *SURF WASHING UP ON A BEACH...*

MVO: Great Keppel Island is a TAA holiday island just off the coast of Queensland. A lot of kids go there, but when you ask them how they liked it, you don't get your everyday testimonials.

YOUNG MALE: I'm really whacked.

GIRL: I'm ripped.

SECOND GIRL: I want my mother.

GROGGY MALE: My teeth feel like they're wearing little sweaters.

SECOND GIRL: Operator, please get me my mother.

MVO: So why do kids go to Great Keppel? It could be the water-skiing...

YOUNG MALE: I've never skied before... Hang on, don't go yet!

SFX: *BOAT ENGINE ROARS, SPLASHING, SCREAMING...*

MVO: Or maybe it's things like...

GIRL: I've never gone out in a glass-bottomed boat at night before.

YOUNG LECHER: Trust me...

BOY: How'd you ever get sunburnt there?

YOUNG MALE: Carol, do you want red wine or white wine?

GIRL: Yes.

MVO: You can go to TAA's Great Keppel Island for seven nights from Melbourne for $377, including TAA air fare, accommodation and all meals. Just book through a TAA travel agent or TAA. But you'd better think about it. After a week on Great Keppel Island...

YOUNG MALE: Two dozen oysters, please, in a hurry...

MVO: You're going to really need a holiday.

GIRL: I want my mother.

A great line is all it takes to inspire a great campaign: After a week on Great Keppel Island, you're going to really need a holiday. *One execution from Street Remley's radio campaign for Lionel Hunt at The Campaign Palace Australia. Studio voices were seamlessly blended with effects to suggest location recording.*

greater depth and variety. "Radio allows opportunities for greater frequency, or for more different spots to be run in a campaign." He believes radio commercials have a generally less jarring effect on audiences than television or cinema ads. "Radio allows listeners to do other things as they listen. So your radio spot is probably less irritating to someone who doesn't want to be interrupted by an ad that they're forced to watch on TV or in the cinema."

Radio production costs are low enough to make multiple executions affordable. Audiences are spared the irritation of hearing the same execution repeated at high frequency. Executions can be different purely in terms of duration; the pace of the ad can be slowed without any copy changes. Having a campaign can also allow greater synergy between the creative execution and the media placement: a commercial written for a weekday breakfast audience can be fast, dynamic and intrusive; a different, more relaxed execution can address a Sunday morning audience. Being audience and mood sensitive helps each different audience relate better to the brand.

Garry Abbott believes a radio campaign will increase the audience's attention span. "If you've got a great idea and a great strategy, you can take the strategy and do executions that repeat the idea. You're constantly innovating, but the strategic direction is exactly the same. If you've established a rapport with the audience, they're the ones who will actually expect the next commercial. And each new ad has to exceed the one before."

LIONEL HUNT recalls his favourite radio campaigns at The Campaign Palace. "I did one for Wrangler Jeans with Street Remley, Australia's 'Mr. Radio'. I sent Street all round Australia interviewing rodeo riders about the toughest horse or bull they'd ever ridden. He got some amazing stuff. At the end of each ad, with the interview edited down to 25 seconds, we asked each rider whether the horse or bull was as tough as Wrangler Jeans with the answer, 'Oh, no, nothing's as tough as Wrangler Jeans'."

Another classic was the Great Keppel Island campaign. Again, Hunt hired Street Remley. "We positioned Great Keppel as a young person's 'party island'. The ads were about how wrecked the kids were at the end of the week. The end line was, *After a week on Great Keppel Island, you're going to really need a holiday.*"

Radio is a natural medium for storytelling, and long-running radio campaigns let characters develop into folk heroes. "It's easy to keep characters fresh and entertaining," confirms Michael Newman. And because it's radio, "no exotic location or acrobatic scenario is impossible."

Singapore's longest-running radio campaign was created at MediaCorp Radio for retailer Marks & Spencer. The creative idea came out of the brand; Mr. Marks and Mr. Spencer became the central characters with sharply defined personalities. Conceptually, the campaign was flexible enough to handle everything from food to women's fashion. Over the years, each new execution extended the campaign's reach into public debate.

In Canada, Elspeth Lynn and Lorraine Tao created the Labatt Blue campaign. "The overarching idea was that 'anything can happen out of the blue'. Instead of writing scenarios where this happened, we created a campaign based around a guy who made live calls 'out of the blue'." Like any other medium, say Lynn and Tao, a radio campaign idea is almost always more memorable than one-off executions.

BRITAIN'S Nestlé-Rowntree reportedly spends 8% of its media budget on radio. The brand builders appreciate the intimate one-to-one connection with consumers and the opportunities to construct affordable, long-running campaigns.

Kit Kat has inspired some renowned radio ads from J. Walter Thompson. Having a break from frustrations is a campaignable idea that lends itself to radio. In one execution called *Clothes Shop*, a rather vague woman rings directory assistance for the number of a clothes shop whose name she has forgotten. She gives the long-suffering operator clues like "It's called something-something fashion", "It's near the traffic lights opposite the bakery", and "There was a big ginger cat in the window and it barked", leading to the end voice-over, *Have a break, have a Kit Kat.*

WITH no physical visuals, no pack shot and no logo in the corner, how do radio campaigns achieve branding objectives?

"One-off jokes don't allow for campaigns," says David Droga. "A consumer insight, or a relevant human truth, always provides you with the opportunity to develop an *ownable* campaign."

Ken Bennett sees branding in terms of rewarding the listener. "Great, long-running radio campaigns tend to have a *consistent attitude and tone* that make the audience feel like they're part of the picture and in on the joke. You have to create work that rewards the listener, *which the listener looks forward to*. If you get the audience on your side and consistently reward them for listening, they will be open to your message."

BEHIND THE SCENES AT MOTEL 6

The Motel 6 campaign has won the respect of creatives worldwide, not to mention recognition at the Mercury Awards, the One Show, the Clios, and the New York Art Directors Club. In fact, winning the $100,000 Mercury Award in 1992 enabled Thomas Hripko to start The Radio Spot Dallas, whose motto is "award-winning radio without an award-winning attitude". Like many radio giants in this book, Hripko insists radio should be all about having fun.

Hripko worked at The Richards Group Dallas when he wrote the commercials. "It was a fabulous environment. My client, Hugh Thrasher, was the finest gentleman I've ever met and one of the sharpest at his job. It was a dream gig." Once Hripko left the agency, he was hired to produce, direct "and tweak". All told, Hripko produced over 300 Motel 6 commercials.

"They would send me scripts a day or two before the session and I'd fly up to Alaska to record them. We would play them over the phone for the client when we finished, but there was no one there peering over our shoulders."

The campaign was the brainchild of David Fowler, who wrote the spots for the first six months. Fowler also "discovered" the campaign's presenter, Tom Bodett. Hailing originally from Sturgis, Michigan, Bodett had worked on crab boats, on the fish processing line, and finally started his own company as a housing contractor. His wisecracks and observations on the job site prompted a buddy to suggest he write the stories down. Bodett did, and broadcast them on his local Public Radio Station in Anchorage, Alaska. Fate took a hand when National Public Radio held a meeting in Anchorage, someone heard Bodett, and decided to carry his essays nationally on NPR's *All Things Considered*. Because the radio in Fowler's pickup truck could only receive one station, NPR, he happened to hear Bodett and thought he'd be good for something one day. When Motel 6 came along, Fowler knew exactly who he wanted to use. After some coaxing, Bodett agreed.

HRIPKO attributes the campaign's success to its honesty. "Here was one guy admitting that this product had some flaws. *It was what it was.* Tom Bodett made no promises. Well, only one..."

He also believes the time was right for the campaign. "We were coming into the last half of the 1980s where spending money by the bushelful was blasé. Excess was overdone. Along comes Motel 6. 'No, we don't have fancy artwork, but who can see it when you're sleeping anyway?' Pure, simple, country logic, mixed with a little Depression era thinking. The kind of thing your dad or uncle would say. It appealed to people, because they'd been hearing it all their lives, not just in the context of an ad. To me, the ads were so believable because they're true to that way of thinking. Interestingly, we learned in focus groups that people were embarrassed to admit they stayed at Motel 6. These spots more or less let them 'come out'. It was now okay to stay at Motel 6. Even cool, actually..."

Hripko calls Motel 6 the "easiest and most fun piece of business I ever worked on". He understood the presenter Tom Bodett. "We were both brought up in the Mid West and close to the same age. So it was easy to get him in my head, so to speak. As for his cadence, I knew where he would breathe. I could write spots that followed a rhythm enabling him to do so — without having to pause awkwardly." Bodett listened to the music while he read. "I also wrote the spots that way, so I guess a bit of that rhythm in the words came from the music. Anticipating notes, knowing that when the fiddle hits a certain note you have ten seconds to go."

The campaign was a perfect exercise in aural branding. Hripko believes radio campaigns are branded by:

1. sound,
2. music,
3. voice,
4. tonality.

"Give it some frequency and soon when people hear that note or that voice, they'll know it's your spot."

Every commercial opened with the same line: "Hi, Tom Bodett for Motel 6." The country fiddle was heard behind Bodett's voice. And there was always the consistent, memorable tag line, still remembered to this day: *We'll leave the light on for you.*

Hripko recalls how comfortable the sessions were. "It was just the three of us, including Bob Linder the engineer. He did every session, no matter where we recorded. Truly, it was like the three of us hanging out all day."

Two of Hripko's classics:

```
TOM: Hi. Tom Bodett for Motel 6 with "Tom's Tips for a
     Greener America". Instead of plugging in an electric
     hedge trimmer around the house and then going to
     the gym for a workout, why not pick up a pair of
     manual clippers. They don't use any electricity
     and they're great for your pecs. Just picture it,
     you've got your heart rate up into your training
     zone, getting in a workout and getting your yard
     work done at the same time. Why not? And while
     we're at it, why not do away with the 60 pounds of
     coupons that fall out of Sunday's paper. If everyone
     would just charge less to begin with, we could save
     a whole forest instead of printing coupons. That's
     why you'll never see a coupon for Motel 6. We've
     already got the lowest prices of any national chain.
     So come see us. Enjoy a clean, comfortable room for
     around 25 bucks. More in some places, less in others,
     so not only will you save money, but if you recycle
     all those coupons that are cluttering up your
     refrigerator, you could even make a little, too.
     I'm Tom Bodett for Motel 6, and we'll leave the
     light on for you.
```

TOM: Hi. Tom Bodett for Motel 6 with an idea for the 90s. It's kind of a behaviour modification programme for anyone who wants to uncomplicate their life. Here's how it works. Come spend the night at Motel 6 and discover how to survive comfortably with only the bare essentials. Afterall, material things are just a burden we place on ourselves, creating an endless pursuit to make more, so we can get more. And at Motel 6 you won't find any material things around burden you. No, you get just what you need. A clean, comfortable room, where you can relax, take a hot shower, and put things in perspective. And unlike those trendy Zen stress-relief clinics, a night at Motel 6 doesn't mean taking a second mortgage on the house. No, all this reality will cost you around 25 bucks. More in some places, less in others, but always the lowest prices of any national chain. So get out of the fast lane and come spend the night with us. I'm Swami Tommy for Motel 6 and we'll leave the light on for you.

Hripko won the $100,000 Mercury Award with this satirical take on having a telephone number in a radio commercial. Even the end line, consistent throughout the campaign, was given a twist.

TOM: Hi. Tom Bodett for Motel 6. A lot of you have written in lately and said, "Tom, we'd love to make reservations at Motel 6, but you say the phone number so doggone fast — we don't have a chance to write it down, let alone remember it." Well, the folks at Motel 6 thought a jingle would help you remember it a little better. I told 'em I could just say it slower and you'd get it, but they said no — they want a jingle. I even told 'em I wasn't very good at that sort of thing, but they said that's okay. So, get your pencils ready. Here goes. *(SINGING)* 505 - 891 - 6161.

Aw, let me try this.

(SINGING) 505 - 891 - 6161.

> Told you I wasn't any good at that. Well, hope it
> worked. I'm Tom Bodett for Motel 6 and boy, am I
> embarrassed.

Hripko's commercial titled *Aunt Josephine* won a Clio, as well as Silver at the One Show:

> TOM: Hi, Tom Bodett for Motel 6 with good news for the
> traveller. Well it's time for the biannual trip to
> see Aunt Josephine. She's a wonderful lady, but the
> only problem is her cats. It never fails, the moment
> you step in the door, the big black one, Muffie,
> starts that curling thing around your leg and for
> the rest of your stay, you're doomed to be the
> object of Muffie's desire. It makes it hard to
> concentrate on Aunt Josephine's story about Mildred's
> cousin's husband's neighbour, who just had their
> goiter worked on. But maybe I got a way to get you
> off the hook with Muffie. Motel 6. We'll give you a
> clean, comfortable room for the lowest prices of
> any national chain. Around 25 bucks in most places.
> A lot less in some, a little more in others, but
> always a heck of a deal. And at Motel 6, you'll
> never wake up to find Muffie flipping her tail in
> your face. And personally, that's worth the price
> of the room right there. I'm Tom Bodett for Motel 6
> and we'll leave the light on for you.

What can the advertising industry learn from a campaign like Motel 6? Hripko believes: "Advertising doesn't need to trick to entice. It needs to tell, in a compelling way, why your side is right. Be honest. Don't reel me in with BIG SAVINGS and explain the fine print to me later when I call to complain."

A TACTICAL CAMPAIGN WITH A BIG IDEA

Fast-food radio campaigns are generally hard sell with lots of noise and little in the way of an idea. McDonald's, from Leo Burnett London, provides an outstanding exception.

Explains Adam Furman, Burnett's Head of TV Administration and

TITLE: McDONALD'S OMELETTE McMUFFIN "TOILETRIES"

A 40-second monologue delivered by no-nonsense Jack
Charlton, who played in England's 1966 World Cup-winning
football team and was former manager of the Republic of
Ireland football team. It begins with Jack quoting the
labels of male toiletries with increasing disbelief…

JACK: Intensive facial cleansing cream…

gentle exfoliating mousse for a man's skin…

pore cleaning facial treatments…

pre-shave peppermint oil…

apres-rasage soothing cucumber cream pour homme,
revitalised facial spray, anti-wrinkle gel…

vitamin enriched gentle cleansing lotion for
sensitive skin formulated by dermatologists to meet
a man's specific needs…

What!… Come on, fellas, get a grip and get
yourselves down to McDonald's for a 99p Omelette
McMuffin with bacon and cheese, specially
formulated for *men*.

At participating restaurants, but only for a
limited time.

This tactical radio campaign sold Omelette McMuffins as a real man's breakfast.
Single voices drove home the single proposition. Leo Burnett London.

TITLE: McDONALD's OMELETTE McMUFFIN "TEAS"

A down-to-earth 40-second protest against fancy teas by Liverpool-born actor Ricky Tomlinson, who plays the character "Jim Royle" in the acclaimed BBC series *The Royle Family.*

RICKY: Peppermint tea…

Camomile tea…

Lemon Verbena…

Lapsang Soouchong, Ooolong, goolygong…

Black Cohosh? Red raspberry leaf? White willow bark?

Dong Quai? Eucalyptus leaf…

Passionfruit and orange, jasmin orange pekoe, rose petal orange pekoe, rose hip…

Even rose and flippin' violet…

For crying out loud, men… Get a proper start to the day! McDonald's 99p Omelette McMuffin with bacon and cheese, at participating restaurants for a limited time…

And while you're at it, wash it down with a good honest cup of McDonald's tea… Lovely!

a passionate radio advocate, "The strategy behind the campaign was that men should eschew the dubious delights of unusual toiletry and tea products, and find comfort in reliable products such as the Omelette McMuffin."

Scripting and casting answered the strategy perfectly. Who better to lead the attack against men's toiletries than football hero Jack Charlton, who played in England's 1966 World Cup-winning team and was the former manager of the Republic of Ireland football team. Charlton hails from the northeast of England and is known for his plain-speaking, no-nonsense approach. Meanwhile, putting down fancy teas was Liverpool-born actor Ricky Tomlinson, who first came to prominence in the UK Channel 4 sitcom *Brookside* and won tremendous acclaim as "Jim Royle" in the BBC series *The Royle Family*. The characters he plays are very down-to-earth and traditional. A third ad in the campaign heaped scorn on New Age energy treatments and self-realisation.

Both *Toiletries* and *Teas* were shortlisted for the Retail & Finance category of Britain's Aerial Awards 2001, which *Toiletries* won. (Significantly, another McDonald's commercial from Leo Burnett London called *Wedding* had won the same category prize in 2000.) *Toiletries* also won the Best Casting Award and was voted the most outstanding radio commercial of 2001.

In the UK, says Furman, McDonald's radio advertising targets the 16 to 34 age group. The Omelette McMuffin campaign was broadcast only in breakfast radio, from 5.30 to 10am. "During this period, the radio stations achieve their highest audience and will reach more people than other media. The media will be bought for high frequency and coverage. Trafficlink and Newslink spots will be bought, too, where one spot is bought around the news and traffic and reaches 200 stations simultaneously. Research has shown that there is a high degree of recall and retention for commercials featured in these slots."

Furman says the Omelette McMuffin campaign was a good example of breakfast advertising because it spoke *directly* to the listener. "The scripts were so strong, and the voices so right for them, that any further additions were rendered unnecessary. Music and effects would have diluted their impact. Radio, in direct contrast to TV, is a very personal and intimate medium and it is important not to bombard and overwhelm the audience." Obviously, there are occasions when effects and music can be used, says Furman, but only where they will enhance the understanding of the commercial. "For example, if you want to establish a specific environment for a commercial, a good shortcut is to use the appropriate sound effects." Furman believes sound effects are overused when there is less confidence in the script and there may be pressure to ensure that the idea stands out. "I think largely though, that people are cautious in overusing sound effects."

Aural branding is key to a strong radio campaign. Furman suggests a variety of ways to achieve it:

1. Use the same voice-over for the end line.
2. Make the campaign entertaining. "If it stands out, it is more likely to be remembered."
3. Employ sonic brand triggers, including jingles and musical devices that link the commercials. "They can breed familiarity with the brand," but adds a warning, "and possibly contempt from the listener."
4. Repetitive airplay, to establish familiarity with the commercials.

INTEGRATING RADIO INTO A WORLD-FAMOUS TV CAMPAIGN

One of the world's most successful, longest-running television campaigns funded by a public authority through the same ad agency has been on air since 1989. It has been a critically acclaimed creative success, winning Best of Show at America's One Show, and awarded by Britain's D&AD and other leading festivals.

In Australia, the Victorian State Government established the Transport Accident Commission to operate an insurance scheme funded by premiums levied through vehicle registration fees. All road users are automatically insured against injuries as the result of road accidents anywhere in the State, whether they are at fault or not. TAC's objective was to keep the incidence and cost of road accidents as low as possible. In 1989, the State road toll peaked at

A car slams into the back of a semi-trailer. The blood-smeared young male driver is alive, breathing his girlfriend's name: *Julie*. There is no reply. The events leading up to the crash, and its aftermath, are then recreated in harrowing detail…

We see a flashback to her father's 53rd birthday cake and the young couple at his party. Cut back to the rescue team trying to extricate them from the car. We flashback again as Julie wishes her father happy birthday.

Her father's voice: *I'll never see her again… I'll never hear her voice … hear her laugh…*

In another flashback, the father waves goodbye to his daughter and her boyfriend as they leave the party. *Take care of my baby girl*, he tells the young man. The boyfriend says he will.

The father's voice continues: *I'll never see her get married … cuddle her children…*

Julie asks her boyfriend if he'd like her to drive. He says no, he's only had a few drinks. Then the distraught father is at the accident scene, restrained by rescue workers, screaming his daughter's name and sinking to his knees.

His voice continues: *I'll never forget having to choose a coffin … for my beautiful baby…*

Super: *If you drink, then drive, you're a bloody idiot.*

One of the highly effective, highly awarded television commercials created over 13 years by Grey Worldwide Melbourne for the Transport Accident Commission. This commercial titled Never *won Gold at America's One Show.*

776 deaths. In 1990 the TAC campaign contributed to a 29% drop in road fatalities, and a reduction of 49% followed in 1992. By 1999, the State road toll stood at 383.

Over 13 years, and after 60 television executions, the TAC campaign has helped save 3,514 lives and achieved financial savings of US$4 billion in claims and costs to the community. The campaign's tonality is documentary. The camera is an observer of reality. Viewers are not lectured. They are allowed to work things out for themselves. But without the compelling images, how has radio contributed to the campaign?

At Grey Worldwide Melbourne, creative director Nigel Dawson traces radio's role: "Radio is the perfect medium for changing people's driving behaviour. After all, much of the time they are listening to radio they are also behind the wheel." In the first few years of the TAC campaign, Dawson says radio was used to virtually run the TV commercials without the pictures. "A traumatic, emotive TV commercial was played at night. The next day, the viewer would hear a narrative of that commercial on radio. Much of the dialogue was simply lifted from the TV. Grabs of conversation, the sound of the crashes. Just as the TV campaign was basically a series of dramatised documentaries, so too was the radio — no embellishments, no hyperbole, rarely any adjectives. It was impossible not to fill in the pictures for oneself and thus get a numbing reminder of bad driving behaviour. It was impossible for the listener not to put himself into the narrative and realise how easily *that could be me.*"

What held all these disparate commercials together? "David Kirkcaldie's voice, the 'Voice of Death', became one of the most recognisable voices on radio. His deep, breathy voice was solemn without being preachy, and could tell chilling stories without a hint of melodrama." The voice became one of the most instantly identifiable branding devices. "The name TAC was never mentioned because David *became* TAC. When he opened his mouth, listeners knew who was bringing them the message. It had immediate strength and credibility." As Dawson reflects, *"Everybody wants to brand their radio campaigns, and sometimes you have to look no further than a voice..."*

However, in recent years the "so-called shock-horror" style of TV has been augmented by more educative commercials. "The TAC campaign is now built on the pillars of Emotion, Education and Enforcement. And as TV has evolved, so too has radio. In the last few years we have looked for campaigns that continue to reflect TAC's established tone of realism, but which contain radio ideas in their own right."

One such commercial featured a speedometer. "You cannot see a gradually rising speedometer needle on radio. But you can use a monotonal voice to recite the speeds as the driver talks to his passenger or listens to music. Just as picture and sound conspire to create drama on television, so two sounds can do the same on radio. In this case, the conversation is the 'sound', the speed recitation the 'picture'." The ads won Campaign of the Year in Australia's Golden Stylus radio awards.

Novice drivers were also targeted by radio, without pointing the finger. The "HELP" campaign was based on the letters "L" and "P": the letter "L" appears on the logo of a Learner driver's plate, and "P" on a Probationary driver's sign on the windscreen. "One campaign wanted to tell Learner drivers to get practice in all conditions. You only have to keep your ears open to hear the different sounds that dominate in different driving conditions. The wipers swish in the rain. Cicadas chirrup at night. Trams, car horns, crossings create a cacophony in the city. It's fertile ground for good radio. All we had to do was turn the one verb "practise" into the sound of the wiper blade, the cicadas and the city noise. The campaign stood out on air and got across a simple, very prosaic message with great impact." It, too, won Campaign of the Year at the Golden Stylus awards.

Dawson describes how a horrifying graphic on television was transferred into an equally powerful radio campaign. "The TV campaign called *Pinball* showed what happens to a passenger in the front seat of a vehicle if they are unrestrained. The passenger indeed acted like a pinball, bouncing off the windscreen, side window and eventually smashing into his driver. But how do you do it on radio? A simple description would not do a sound medium justice. Instead, we decided to take the *Pinball* thought, but replace the clanging pinball sounds with *single word descriptors* of how the bouncing around breaks your body — head, rib, tibia, spine, and so on. It was very telling, very chilling, and an idea that only works on radio."

While TAC television commercials are researched, radio executions are not specifically tested. "It all comes down to gut feel, and how the radio complements the main TV campaign. There is an ongoing tracking study that is undertaken every three months among about 600 people, primarily to check recall and attitudes. Generally speaking, radio commercials are recalled by about 25–30% of those surveyed, rising to close to 50% among certain groups such as young men at whom the commercials are targeted. Not surprisingly, radio does not impact with anything like as much strength as the TV, but TAC radio does appear to have an impact that is generally substantially higher than 'most' radio advertising."

Dawson believes radio has added new strength to the famous TAC TV campaign over the past four or five years. "We avoid spurious gimmicks, maintain the in-your-face realism, but have exploited many of the opportunities afforded by an aural medium."

TITLE: TRANSPORT ACCIDENT COMMISSION "SPEEDOMETER 1"

In this campaign, a monotonal voice recites the speedometer readings as a counterpoint to people's conversations or activities in cars.

SFX: *INTERIOR OF DRIVING CAR THROUGHOUT.*

VOICE: *113...*

DAD: So how was the netball today?

VOICE: *112...*

GIRL: We lost.

DAD: Oh...

VOICE: *113...*

GIRL: Dad, how fast are you going?

VOICE: *114...*

DAD: Oh, it's alright, Jess...

VOICE: *115...*

DAD: A few kilometres over, doesn't matter.

GIRL: Why not?

VOICE: *117...*

DAD: Well, we've got a good, safe car...

VOICE: *118...*

DAD: No problems.

VOICE: *120...*

GIRL: I've got some pocket money —

VOICE: *121...*

SFX: A *SCREAM OF BRAKES, FOLLOWED BY A COLLISION.*

VO: Don't fool yourself. Speed kills.

*Creating horrific pictures on radio: Grey Worldwide Melbourne for the
Transport Accident Commission.*

TITLE: TRANSPORT ACCIDENT COMMISSION "SPEEDOMETER 2"

SFX: *INTERIOR OF CAR DRIVING THROUGHOUT.*
OPERA IS PLAYING ON THE CAR RADIO...

VOICE: *94...*

WOMAN: *(SINGING ALONG WITH RADIO)* Dah-de-dah...

VOICE: *95... 97... 102... 107...*

WOMAN: *(SINGING)* Dum-dah-dee...

VOICE: *111...*

WOMAN: *(SINGING NOW LOUDER)* Dahhhh...deee...

VOICE: *113...*

SFX: *CAR HORN OF APPROACHING VEHICLE...*

WOMAN: *(SUDDENLY)* Oh my God — oh no —

SFX: *SQUEAL OF BRAKES, FOLLOWED BY DEAFENING*
COLLISION...

VO: Don't fool yourself. Speed kills.

TITLE: TRANSPORT ACCIDENT COMMISSION "PRACTISE – CITY DRIVING"

In this commercial, the verb "Practise" is integrated into the sounds of car horns. The pitch of the voice was altered to match the various horn sounds.

SFX: *WE ARE DRIVING THROUGH BUSY CITY STREETS.*
CAR HORNS BLARE.

GRADUALLY WE BECOME AWARE THAT EACH "BEEP-BEEP" SOUND CONTAINS A MONOTONAL VOICE SAYING THE WORD "PRAC – TISE"…

"BEEP-BEEP" BECOMES "PRAC – TISE"…
"BAH-BAH" BECOMES "PRAC – TISE"…
"HONK-HONK" BECOMES "PRAC – TISE"…

EVEN A SQUEAL OF BRAKES AND A PEDESTRIAN CROSSING WARNING ALARM BECOME "PRAC – TISE"…

VO: Learners need at least a hundred and twenty hours' practice in all conditions, including city driving.

Are *you* roadworthy?

A series of 30-seconders turned driving sounds into audio mnemonics, reminding Learner drivers they needed practice in all driving conditions. Grey Worldwide Melbourne for the Transport Accident Commission.

**TITLE: TRANSPORT ACCIDENT COMMISSION "PRACTISE —
DRIVING IN THE WET"**

The key verb "Practise" is integrated into the sound of
windscreen wipers in wet driving conditions.

SFX: *WE ARE IN A CAR DRIVING THROUGH RAIN.
WE HEAR THE RHYTHMIC SWISH OF THE WINDSCREEN
WIPERS.*

*THE VERB "PRACTISE" IS HEARD AS A CHANT THROUGH THE
SWISHING SOUND, SOFTLY AT FIRST, THEN GROWING
LOUDER...*

*"PRAC – TISE, PRAC – TISE, PRAC – TISE,
"PRAC – TISE, PRAC – TISE, PRAC – TISE,
"PRAC – TISE, PRAC – TISE, PRAC – TISE,
"PRAC – TISE, PRAC – TISE, PRAC – TISE..."*

FADE FOR:

VO: Learners need at least a hundred and twenty hours'
practice in all conditions, including the wet.

Are *you* roadworthy?

```
              TITLE: TRANSPORT ACCIDENT COMMISSION "BODY"

   SFX:        A HORRIFYING CAR SMASH IS HEARD IN SLOW
               MOTION.

               A SERIES OF SICKENING METALLIC CRUNCHES ARE
               HEARD THROUGHOUT, SYNCHRONISED WITH THE V.O.,
               AND WE CAN PICTURE A BODY BEING TOSSED ABOUT
               IN THE CAR LIKE A PINBALL...

   FEMALE VO:  Head...

               Rib, rib, rib...

               Lung...

               Brain...

               Nose...

               Cheek...

               Brain...

               Knee...

               Spleen...

               Tibia...

               Spine...

   ANNCR:      Without a seat belt, your body is a pinball.
               Belt up, or suffer the pain.
```

These two 30-second radio commercials convey what happens to someone in a car smash who isn't wearing a seat belt. A series of single word descriptors delivered by a matter-of-fact voice communicate horrifying images. Grey Worldwide Melbourne for the Transport Accident Commission.

TITLE: TRANSPORT ACCIDENT COMMISSION "CABIN"

SFX: *A HORRIFYING CAR SMASH IS HEARD IN SLOW MOTION.*

A SERIES OF SICKENING METALLIC CRUNCHES ARE HEARD THROUGHOUT, SYNCHRONISED WITH THE V.O., CONVEYING WHAT HAPPENS TO A BODY BEING TOSSED ABOUT IN THE CAR LIKE A PINBALL...

MALE VO: Windscreen...

Steering wheel...

Dash...

Roof, door, roof...

Door...

Gear stick...

Head rest...

Passenger...

ANNCR: Without a seat belt, your body is a pinball that can also severely injure others in the car.

Belt up, or suffer the pain.

6

VOICES AND VICES

"The most important thing in any radio ad is casting." John Immesoete believes the right actor makes a spot come alive. "Good voice-over people are very special actors. Their voices are truly instruments. Cast, cast, cast, until you've got the perfect person." He recalls the initial setbacks in recording his *Real American Heroes* campaign. "We cast all around the country and recorded the first spots with at least eight different announcers. They weren't funny. We thought we were going to lose the campaign until we got the right guy, Pete Stacker. He not only understood what we were going for, he was able to improve upon it and deliver. His talent saved the campaign."

"If you cast well," says Ken Bennett, "the director should only have to give the talent minor steering changes here and there. If you cast the wrong person, you end up doing 35 takes."

But how should you choose your voices? And how do you know when you've found the right voice?

VOICE CASTING

"No matter how clever the radio ad, if it sounds like someone is reading a script you will lose your audience." David Droga avoids voice-over artists who are familiar. "Actors are usually better than voice-over experts."

"Voice-overs — I dislike the word, I loathe the breed and I hate the sound they make," avows

Tony Hertz. "Radio is supposed to be a personal medium, offering companionship and entertainment to human people, who listen for the most part, one at a time. The voice-over is the complete contradiction of this."

Hertz bemoans the stereotypical voice-over read. "In the typical radio ad, when somebody talks to the audience — that is, you and me — they hardly ever sound like anyone we would ever meet. No real person would ever try to sell me something, or tell me an address, with that unique singsong inflection, that deeply impersonal set of intonations, which characterise the MVO or FVO. Why do they talk like that? Because they've trained themselves to deliver what they think agencies and clients want to hear. Because agencies have come to believe that a smooth read is what they want to hear, and they actually write scripts to that end. And, saddest of all, because both groups have forgotten that radio ads should be like radio itself — real people talking to other real people. In a bizarre, lemming-like evolutionary spiral, the voice-over, who doesn't exist in real life, has become a persona which hundreds of performers play every day."

Scripts, says Hertz, are a contributing factor. "Write the way a real person would talk to someone sitting directly in front of him or her. Someone he likes and respects. Then, read what you've written out loud, in front of that someone. I am convinced that, no matter what you have to sell, there is a reasonable, human way of saying it. If your writing is right, even the most audio-narcissistic voice-over can't damage it too much."

Hertz's advice on casting: "Write a one-sentence description of everyone in the commercial, including the announcer. Give them names, flesh them out a bit. A dialogue featuring MVO 1 talking to MVO 2 doesn't give actors anything to hang a performance on, which means it won't give the listener much either."

Casting, he says, isn't about voices. "It's about finding performers to bring to life the characters you've created. Actors' CVs with a list of roles they've played will tell you more than their mostly awful voice tapes. So can their agents, if you ask the right questions."

IAN REICHENTHAL casts as many people as he can for each role, often casting right up until the day before the recording session — and sometimes on the day itself. "If you've done your homework in casting, then your job at the recording session is easy. You can give minimal direction. If you haven't done your homework in casting, then your job at the recording session is tougher. You have to give a lot more direction." The casting session is also a litmus test for the script: "Was something less funny, or less clear, or less 'anything' than you imagined…?"

Ralph Van Dijk's advice: "Look for interesting people and *take risks*. Judge their acting ability before judging their voice quality."

Andy Lerner prefers more natural-sounding actors "as opposed to those who sound like they're performing."

Michael Conrad recommends using real actors from local theatres, while Nigel Dawson seeks experienced actors who are smart and prepared to ad-lib: "One thing I have learnt is to be very cautious of voices from 'off the street'. Most radio commercials require good acting performances from people who can assimilate three or four simultaneous instructions. People off the street may have new or unusual voices, but that is worth nothing if they cannot perform."

"ONE thing we don't do is cast 'voices'," explains Christine Coyle. "The people we cast may have an interesting sound, but they use it to create a *fully realised character*, not a disembodied voice. We're lucky being in Hollywood — our access to good actors is almost unlimited." Over the years, The Famous Radio Ranch has developed a company of players. "But it grows larger and larger as we discover new talent. Sometimes we write with a particular talent or character in mind. If we're casting after the spot has been written we try to determine who will make the character a living, breathing thing."

Adam Furman begins by reading the creative brief, which highlights what idea is central to the campaign, then studies the script. "I then make lists of appropriate actors and voice-over artists. I always try and look out for new voices as I think that it is the producer's job to push the boundaries and challenge the status quo. It is too easy to select voices from the many voice-over agencies' CDs." Furman places great value on ensemble acting. For example, a John West commercial that parodied disaster movies was recorded like a radio play. The actors were all in the studio together. "The important thing was to create the right atmosphere, involve the actors, and explain to them what we were trying to achieve at the outset. We cast the best voices available, and to give it an authentic feel I cast actors rather than specific voice-over talent. As quality actors, they readily understood the nature of the script and took direction well."

Mike Fromowitz never relies on voice-casting tapes in his final decision-making process. "I like to get together with the talent at a casting session. It's important that you believe the talent you've chosen to do the job can cut it, that their range is wide enough to give you several unique interpretations, and that they're willing to work with you, not against you." Actors are great, he says, "because they *feel* their way through a script. It's not just words to them. The best of them will want to continue to do more takes until they feel they've given their best."

Mike Edmonds agrees. "I've been doing radio for 20 years and can still be surprised by a voice-over talent I wouldn't have chosen from just their demo CD." Edmonds sends scripts to talent agencies. "Have them send it on to the talent, and get the shortlisted actors to ring you up and read the script over the phone." He also recommends casting sessions, as though you were making a TV commercial. "It's amazing how infrequently this happens. Ask a studio for a favour, or a special casting rate, and actually put some voices down."

Stage actors are accustomed to researching their characters, discerning their traits, mastering their accents and factoring in the times in which they lived. Radio commercials invite a similar discipline. As Linda Locke says, it is a question of treating radio with more respect. "If somebody has to play a Chinese businessman, a *towkay*, I'd encourage them to go to a karaoke bar the night before and check out how they behave, how they talk, whether they have any voice mannerisms we could borrow."

"WE went through a period where I had written a very high percentage of what we did, and I had a little repertory company of probably 20 actors," recalls Street Remley. "And just out of love of the business, Leanne Vine, Bobby Dennis and other people in the studio including myself would also do voice work. Now the pendulum has swung and 70% of our work is agency-written and 30%

is what I have written, but still there are reliable people I will always use when I'm improvising." One reason why Remley stayed in Adelaide was the city's acting talent. "There's all kind of back alley theatre, repertory groups, amateur theatre groups. Adelaide grows new generations of actors every day, but there's very high attrition. As soon as they get good, they go off to Melbourne or Sydney." One of Remley's "discoveries" was Geoffrey Rush, Academy Award-winning star of the movie *Shine* and an Oscar nominee for his roles in *Shakespeare in Love* and *Quills*. "Geoffrey was an Adelaide boy and we used him a lot, then he moved to Melbourne. He has a wonderfully warm, chocolatey voice, he has texture and timbre, and he's a perfectionist. He would do 20 takes of a one-line voice-over. He would strive for the absolute nuance. He's a great guy, straight as an arrow, and a good friend."

Bob Dennis believes each part of a commercial presents different casting challenges. "Stage actors are very good at playing parts, especially if they have somebody to bounce off, but get them to read a voice-over and some don't know where they are." He recalls one embarrassing incident. "I used to go to a lot of theatre to source new talent because you don't want to use the same people on every commercial, otherwise every commercial will sound the same. I found this guy who was a superb actor and we tried him in some bit parts acting with someone else and he was wonderful, he knew exactly what was needed. Then we tried him on a descriptive narrative, and he couldn't do it." Dennis considers that radio people tend to be better at voice-overs. "The voice-over is the informational part, or the sign-off, and it's as important as the rest of the commercial." Dennis believes agency people like to use voices they know. "They feel insecure if they have to try and use somebody else. And if they've got a tight budget, there isn't the money for an hour and a half using someone new who can't give them the performance they want."

ACCENTS, too, are important. Most multinational agencies prefer Western accents for international campaigns. In a recent study by the National University of Singapore, the Australian accent emerged as the most appealing and persuasive in Australia and Singapore, while in Myanmar (Burma) the British accent won the day. Curiously,

Australians voted the British accent tops for comprehension, while Singaporeans voted the Myanmar accent as easiest to understand.

"Radio is more grassroots than television," observes Fromowitz. "Whether you're in Singapore, Toronto, San Francisco, Hong Kong, Sydney or Jakarta, one of the reasons that listeners are loyal to their local radio station is precisely because it is a local station. Commercials on these stations reflect a hometown quality by tying in with community happenings, using regional geographic names and having a voice talent or a station announcer whose voice and style are known to the local community, making the product more compatible with the listening audience."

Hertz has witnessed considerable changes in accent preferences both in Britain and America. "For the longest time, the only accent that was acceptable in advertising was what the BBC calls 'RP', Received Pronunciation, which is kind of middle class, educated and non-regionalised. In America, for a long, long time, you would never hear a Southerner saying anything intelligent on radio because 'South equalled Ignorant'. Then retired football players became TV sports commentators. They sat next to beautifully voiced commentators and did what is called the 'colour'. It suddenly became possible for people who didn't sound 'beautiful' to be broadcasters." The same thing has happened in the UK, reports Hertz. "Now it's Estuary English, basically the accent from the southeast corner of the UK, slightly London but not cockney, but not polished either." In Birmingham, which Hertz says has "the ugliest of English accents", the last thing local advertisers do is use local accents. "It makes the ad sound patronising." Hertz's own accent sounds American to British ears, and vice versa.

"SOMEONE once said if you want a commercial that doesn't sound like a commercial, go to Flint Webster." David Flint specialises in casting for radio. "A lot of the people telling the actor and the engineer what to do don't have a clue themselves. I try to get into their heads, to hear how they're motivated and where they're coming from. Are they after comedy, or satire, or something more serious?" It's not always possible to judge from the script, says Flint. Some things can be interpreted several ways. "The voice has got to be right emotionally, socially, and mentally match up to the product whether it's one line or the whole commercial." Flint has even cast a comedienne to inject fun and happiness into voice-overs for a museum. "People needed to like it, and a straight voice-over would have been too boring." More often than not, he will cast real people to create a commercial that sounds like real life, not like everyone else's commercial. One example was a scene where a Chinese waiter was reading back the order in a restaurant. "They'd wanted an actor speaking in a Chinese accent and I found that a little rude. I found a guy in a Chinese shop who was a real talker. He wouldn't do it at first because he was very shy. I left him the script and in the end he agreed. A lot of the words you couldn't quite understand, but that's life…"

David Alberts prefers real voices, too: "I'd rather someone who is less clear but more real, than someone who can do the perfect read first time. So many of the same voice-over guys are used on either side of your own ad."

"I DON'T want familiar and correct," argues Austin Howe. "I want unexpected and dangerous. Most times, if you *don't* have the possibility of failure with your actors going into a session, you don't really have the chance for success, for cutting through on air."

Howe believes in eccentric casting. "I once heard Spielberg respond to the question, 'What is the key to making great movies?' by saying, 'Eccentric casting.' That sums up my philosophy. I loved the Joe Sedelmaier model: go to bus stops in Iowa and Indiana and recruit funny-looking people. I just look for funny-sounding people. I have personally helped launch the voice-over careers of directory assistance operators, concierges, hair stylists, psychologists, stand-up comics, engineers, and more than a few bored copywriters." Howe describes this as one of the benefits of not being a radio commercial "factory": "I have the luxury of time to cast the net way out there. On any given day, I'm casting actors from San Francisco, Toronto, London, Chicago, New York, Seattle, Portland, Denver, Paris and Los Angeles."

Almost everyone in the States, he says, goes to ICM (International Creative Management) for their radio actors. "While they definitely represent some talented people, I purposely listen to their auditions last, primarily because when we were at our busiest I would listen to their auditions first because I knew they would have lots of 'capable' people. But I don't want to do commercials that sound like commercials, unless the concept for the spot is to sound like a commercial." As a result, the casting approval process becomes more arduous. "Experienced actors know how to win an audition by 'nailing it'. That is, doing what feels familiar and correct. But as a general rule I don't cast slick, I don't cast perfect, I don't cast the expected."

Mostly, Howe wants the "rogue element" — the wild card, the actor or non-actor "who brings some interesting, chewy character, life experience, quirk, nervous tics, to the commercial. And I want the person to be genuine. Authentic. Not a person 'doing' a voice, but a guy with an interesting voice *being* that guy." For Figaro's Pizza, Howe cast a non-actor called Domenico, fresh off the boat from Rome, who can barely speak a word of English. "We found him through a translation service."

Some advertising agencies, he says, go through casting agents, listen to dozens of audition CDs, and then send it all to him to sort out and make recommendations. "I would rather find new talent and use fresh actors in every spot. It's part of my daily routine to listen to new voices. I'm always listening. I hear stuff in people's voices, stuff that they themselves sometimes don't hear…"

GETTING A PERFORMANCE

"The best way to get a performance that works on radio is to go out and record real people." Failing that, says Steve Owen, use actors not voice-overs. "Listen to how real people speak. It isn't how you first think it is. Your brain filters out all the double words, the pauses, the erms and ums. Listen to how the pitch and pace of people's voices change when they are under stress. It's not about how many words you use, it's about how they're delivered." Owen recommends a book called *Directing Actors* by Judith Weston.

"When briefing actors on delivery, don't tell them how to read your script," Edmonds advises. "Tell them why you wrote it the way you did, and then see what they can bring to it. Getting a great performance from a good actor is incredibly easy."

"If you've done your job in casting, and *you know what you want*, getting great performances shouldn't be too hard," agrees Lerner. "Knowing what you want is really important, so you're not changing your direction after each take and confusing the actor. I try to keep the actor as relaxed as possible, to have fun, and give them some freedom to find what it is you need. I try to talk to them in as realistic and normal way as is possible. Once I get what we need, I try to experiment a bit and see if there are other, funnier ways to go through improvisation or new copy."

John Culverwell says if you know what you want, and if you take the time to understand the intent and emotion behind the words, *no more than five takes should be necessary*. "Casting is everything. First make sure you cast the right voice for the job, perhaps through auditions. Knowing what you want is also critical. So many times creatives do not really understand what they want and over-produce voices."

Michael Newman also believes radio is often over-directed. "Don't ask the voice talent to read that line with 'more of a raised eyebrow'. And I can't **stress** too much that you **should not** give the voice talent *too* many **key** words to **stress**."

"STRESS is an ugly and unrelaxed phenomenon," explains Rob Townsend. "The voice should be treated like a musical instrument. In our everyday conversation, the musical notes we put together are very wide-ranging and complex, and the use of this musicality in commercials is paramount to delivering the message." Rather than stressing a particular word, Townsend suggests a more effective option: "A small rise in musical note on the particular word will lift it out from the other words around it. It also produces a better sound for the listener."

Townsend argues that the musicality of voice-overs should reflect the natural musicality of everyday conversation. "Why should we change that perspective? We should understand that voice-over convention should actually be based on very naturalistic reads. I encourage my voice-overs to think about what a word means, and help convey that meaning in the way they colour it and add musical texture. I have been in sessions where the voice-over has failed to grasp the meaning of the thing they are reading. It comes over as if they were just joining some words together — very structured and clinical — and in my view, this unrelaxed style of read will not sit comfortably with the listener. As soon as the voice-over opens his or her mouth you know, almost immediately, whether it is going to work or not." If the voice-over hits the wrong tune in the words, Townsend says that can affect the attitude in the voice and hence the ultimate message being conveyed. "How many times have you been in a situation where you have said something to someone and they have taken offence at what you said? It is not what you have said, but the *way* you said it. The recipient got the wrong message. You will be amazed how often this is done in the commercial framework. Again, it is all linked to the rules of natural speech. It is a basic premise, but so overlooked."

Townsend believes the degree of musicality, and the subtle use of rhythm and colour, should be tempered to suit the script. "A voice-over for, say, a dramatic film or book or TV series would still use musicality, but it would not be so pronounced. I like the idea that a dramatic read should leave the listener with somewhere to go. The voice-over is simply there to entice and tease. It's what I call the suppressed dramatic read. Less is more, the voice shouldn't give it all away in the delivery."

There are voicing conventions which audiences accept, Townsend says, quoting the analogy of a newsreader. "We are accepting of the way he or she communicates the news to us. But if you analyse it, they adopt a very complex pattern of rising, falling, and what I call the 'mid-held cadence'. You'd think there was something wrong with them if they communicated with you in the same way in everyday conversation, but for newsreading it is highly desirable and if they didn't follow those set patterns we would think it most peculiar. The same is true for commercials."

While he does not suggest that every commercial should be delivered with high degrees of musicality and colour, Townsend believes voice artists should be able to take them into account. "There is a big difference to using an actor as a voice-over as opposed to an actor-and-voice-over combined. An actor, especially a respected one, may not inherently understand the musicality of commercials, and as a result it can be a difficult climb to get the performance. Sometimes they can't achieve it and the read is rather flat and uninteresting."

One solution he suggests is to offer the actor a line read. "However, the line read itself has to be correct. It is no good, say, a creative giving a line read that bears no resemblance to what is needed. I will often hop in here and give the line read myself. Sometimes I will convert the actual line we may be having trouble with into musical notes, for example, *da da da daa*. I feel this helps the actor to understand the musicality of the particular line."

Townsend believes actors should always be given the subtexts behind the characters they play, even the subtext behind the end voice-over. "Even if someone is reading the end line, they should have a listen to what has gone before. It will aid their understanding and delivery. After all, the end line is designed to be the succinct wrap-up of the whole commercial."

Sometimes a voice-over will ask for the script in advance. "This is fine if they want to consider its suitability, but *not* if they want to practise," warns Townsend. "Often they will become rigidly stuck on one particular style of read which may not be the style required, and to get them out of it can be a long haul."

Getting a performance is one thing, Townsend reminds us, but getting it within the studio time booked and budgeted for is another matter entirely.

"I always advise creatives and producers to be aware of this. Spending all the time getting the perfect read will mean nothing if you only have five minutes left to lay up effects and music and mix them, with another client banging on the door at the top of the hour. Believe me, this kind of thing does happen…"

BRENT HAHN believes in laying the groundwork first. "Hire the right actors by holding a casting session. It takes time and costs money, but it's worth it. A casting session is also the preferable forum in which to find out that your script is 20 seconds too long and largely unpronounceable. Plus, you get to practise directing your spot."

Hahn reminds us that scripts should be double-spaced, "so the talent has room to add notes and changes. When actors have to make notes in the margins, they screw up more. And then they get all stressed out." In the actual recording session, Hahn keeps in constant communication with the talent between takes. "Nothing erodes the talent's energy and confidence faster than a drawn-out conversation on the other side of the glass — especially if they can read lips. As part of your feedback, tell the talent what bits you liked as well as the bits you didn't. But don't overwhelm them with changes; work on fixing one or two things at a time." Let the talent hear a playback early in the process. "You might be amazed at how quickly the talent will then make adjustments." Hahn keeps a DAT running at all times. "A lot of good stuff happens between takes."

ONCE, the great Orson Welles was booked to record television voice-overs for Findus foods. Fortunately, the engineer kept a tape running throughout and captured for posterity how advertising agency people should *not* direct talent.

WELLES: "We know a remote farm in Lincolnshire where Mrs. Buckley lives. Every July, peas grow there…"

AGENCY MAN: I'd start it just half a second later.

WELLES: Don't you really want to say "July" over the snow, isn't that the fun of it?

AGENCY MAN: If you could say it when that shot disappears, it'll —

WELLES: It's so nice that you see a snow-covered field and say "every July, peas grow there".

HE STARTS AGAIN…

WELLES: "We know a remote farm in Lincolnshire where Mrs. Buckley lives. Every July, peas grow there…" We aren't even on the fields, you see? We're talking about them growing and she's picked them.

AGENCY MAN: *(MUMBLING)*

WELLES: What? I don't understand you. What must be over before "July"?

AGENCY MAN: When we get out of that snowy field.

WELLES: Well I was out, we were onto a big dish of peas when I said "In July..."

AGENCY MAN: I'm sorry.

WELLES: Yes, always. I'm always past that.

AGENCY MAN: You are?

WELLES: Yes. That's about where I say "In July".

2ND AGENCY MAN: Could you emphasise "In", "*In* July"?

WELLES: Why? That doesn't make any sense. Sorry. There's no known way of saying an English sentence in which you begin a sentence with "In" and emphasise it. Get me a jury and show me how you can say "*In* July" and I'll go down on you. It's just idiotic, if you'll forgive my saying so. It's just stupid. "*In* July"... love to know how you emphasise "In" in "In July". Impossible, meaningless.

AGENCY MAN: I think all they were thinking about was that they didn't want to —

WELLES: He wasn't thinking... There's too much directing around here.

MOVING ON TO THE FISH FINGERS SCRIPT...

WELLES: "We know a certain fiord in Norway near where the cod gather in great shoals..."

AGENCY MAN: A fraction more on that "shoals" thing, you roll it around very nicely.

WELLES: Yes, roll it round and I'll have no more time. You don't know what I'm up against, because it's full of things that are only correct because they're grammatical, but they're tough on the ear. This is a very wearying one, it's unpleasant to read... Unrewarding...

HE CONTINUES...

WELLES: "Because Findus freeze the cod at sea
               and then add a crumb-crisp coating…"
               That's tough, "crumb-crisp coating". It's
               because of the way it's written, you
               need to break it up, it's not as
               conversationally written.

AGENCY MAN: Take "crumb" out.

WELLES: Good.

THEN CAME FINDUS BEEF BURGERS:

WELLES: Here, under protest, is Beef Burgers…
               "We know a little place in the American
               Far West where Charlie Briggs chops up
               the finest prairie-fed beef…"

AGENCY MAN: You missed the first "beef" completely.

WELLES: What do you mean, missed it?

AGENCY MAN: You're emphasising "prairie-fed".

WELLES: But you can't emphasise "beef", that's
               like his wanting me to emphasise "In"
               before "In July". Come on, fellas, you're
               losing your heads. I wouldn't direct
               any living actor like this in
               Shakespeare. It's impossible.

AND FINALLY…

WELLES: The right reading for this is the one
               I'm giving it. I spend 20 times more for
               you people than any other commercial
               I've ever made. You're such pests. Now,
               what is it you want, in the depths of
               your ignorance? What is it you want?
               Whatever it is you want, I can't deliver
               it.

AGENCY MAN: That was absolutely fine, it really was.

WELLES: No money is worth it…

STUDIO DOOR OPENS AND SLAMS.

FROMOWITZ allows the talent to "dive right in" and read the script without receiving any direction from him whatsoever. "Sometimes you'll find their delivery unexpected, different than what you had in mind. But when you have an open mind, you may just get that magic moment." Fromowitz only talks over the script after they have tried their own interpretation first. "I won't read the script, but I will try to give them mental pictures to which they can attach words, much like a director does with talent in films. If I think emphasis is needed to bring out a major selling point or to enhance an expression, then I may read a line or two."

In Toronto, Elspeth Lynn and Lorraine Tao brief actors on the idea of the spot, but leave the door open for improvisation. "We'll generally have a very clear idea of how we hear the spot performed and will direct the talent in this way. Often, because we've cast great actors, they will put a spin on it that is even funnier. Improv can be your best friend with great actors."

Dawson also values spontaneity. "If it is something very difficult, or as sometimes happens with the Transport Accident Commission, something that demands the telling of a very personal experience, I'll ask the producer to give the outline script to the actor before the session so they can think about it. But usually it is much fresher and more spontaneous if the first time they see the script is the moment they walk into the studio." Dawson always attends the recording and will almost inevitably change a few words during the session. "Quite often words that sounded fine in one's own head sound slightly wrong in somebody else's mouth. A radio script has to be an organic thing that should be allowed to take shape as it is recorded." He encourages input from actors and engineers. "Often I realise there are things that can be left out to give the script more space and thus greater strength."

He adds a cautionary note: "There will be times when the actor was the wrong choice, or you couldn't get the performance you were after. Fine — abandon the session and start again." But the fault could also lie with the script. "It can be that some scripts are not possible to perform satisfactorily. I'd encourage every radio writer to try putting on the cans and performing some of their own work in the booth to see how it sounds. If they can't do it, it is unlikely that an actor will be able to either."

VETERAN Australian voice-over Jim Berinson articulates his love affair with sound. As a child he "broadcast" by attaching the wires of a telephone handset to the pickup terminals of a radiogram. He began his radio career as a singer in the days when "live" audiences attended the studio.

Berinson pioneered the soft sell read in Australia, "a normal chat, as you would talk to one another". When he started in radio, the 25-second commercials of that era often employed two male announcers reading line for line, "as though they were completely unaware of each other. A double-serve of knowledge, done with a loud-hailer style of delivery. Were they all deaf in those days?"

The first line of the commercial, he says, should always be clearly communicated. "If people miss it, they'll tune out. As long as you do the first line right, you can always pick up pace later on. You have to grab attention."

Berinson is a perfectionist. His tradecraft includes the ability to texture his voice and repunctuate scripts as he reads them. He is a self-confessed mimic and enjoys crafting his own characters.

The great radio commercials, he says, have one thing in common. "Simplicity — a simple message told in such a way that it creates interest and gives new information. Bad tracks underestimate people's intelligence, are overwritten and overproduced."

PHILIP WEBSTER experiments with talent. If the script calls for them to be in bed, he records them lying on the floor. "When one lies on the floor one speaks differently, one's projection is different." Conversations over breakfast are treated literally. He sets up a breakfast table, with toast to be buttered. Sitting down loosens up the actors, he adds. "A lot of engineers say you don't need to do that, Protools can do it for us, but the point is that when actors are doing real things, when they're moving and talking, their energy is correct, their intonations are more natural, than standing rigidly in front of a microphone." He places great importance on having fun in the session. "I have a terrific working relationship with writers and actors. The actors know when they come here they're going to enjoy working, they're not just going to be standing in front of a microphone doing the straight announcer thing."

Before each session, Webster has the agency scripts retyped in double spacing, taking out the bold text and instructions, and ensuring that the last three digits of telephone numbers don't disappear onto the next line. Webster believes intelligent talent can put in their own punctuation, their own stresses and colours on words as required. When he was working in London, the late Arthur Lowe taught him about colours in the voice. "Lowe liked to be not just an actor but a fine voice person, too. He didn't like looking at a script with underlines on things because he was doing that naturally anyway."

If he is recording sports personalities, Webster will use lapel microphones. "I don't put them in the studio. I put them in the control room with me. The tape will be rolling when they come in. While I chat to them and get to know them, I'll just pin the neck mic on them. They forget all about it. They'll do a run through, and pretty well in take one you've got them, being natural, being themselves, unaffected. They're not seeing a big mic stuck in front of them."

One of Webster's clients, Emma Hill, describes how he put the talent together in a small cupboard to create an intimate scene for Just Jeans. "They were supposed to be making love, but when the boy tried to remove the girl's jeans, she swore at him: 'Don't touch my ——— jeans…' The cupboard kept them really close together. Her head was banging against the wall. They were good friends, and they'd acted together a lot, and I didn't need to tell them how to do it. The microphone was up in the roof. The cupboard gave it a sense of intimacy, a sense of realism, like we were spying on them." As Hill reminds us, "When you write a script, you've got to give it up eventually to another person to tell the story for you. And you expect it to take on a bit more of a life…"

THOMAS HRIPKO concentrates on cadence.

Writers start with an advantage if they understand their actors. "If you're the writer, write the script in their voice. Listen to their cadence and write to it. It'll be the easiest thing they've ever read, and consequently, the performance you heard in your head." But he adds a corollary: "You must read your scripts *aloud* after you've written them. It's funny how something sounds one way in your head and totally different once it's read aloud."

If you weren't the writer, Hripko says you can assist actors interpret the script by helping them with the cadence. "I try to picture sentences as hills and valleys, then tell them at the end of sentence two — start walking up the hill."

No matter what, says Hripko, have fun. "If it's fun, it'll be good."

TOWNSEND believes that actors should use microphones as audio cameras. "I had a script wherein a boy and a girl had to kiss. Why bother to put the kiss effects in later? It was two people having a romp on a sofa so I got them to do it for real, then added some extra foley work where necessary."

Townsend ensures voice projection is appropriate for each "shot" in the commercial. "If you are recording voices to drop into a scene, ensure that they project at a level that matches the scene. I recorded someone who had to battle against wind and rain so he projected accordingly. I premixed some effects and played them into him through cans."

LES FRANCIS paints pictures for the talent. "I might say, look, in this commercial you're 6'3" and 250 pounds, so that's the size you are, and the other talent with you are much shorter than that, and they're three feet away so you don't have to shout at them, or they're 30 feet away so you do." He suggests dynamics, using film director's jargon. "I'll tell them where they are — in a bar, in a lounge room, and I'll say the whole thing is a medium close-up, it's only shot from the waist up, so think of that visually and how loud you think you should be according to that perspective. I might say, look, on that line we're going to zoom in on you so it becomes a full-face close-up, so that becomes intimate, then after that we zoom out again so you can get louder again. It's amazing how the talent pick up on it immediately. I'm giving them an accurate picture of what we need to *see* in this radio commercial." If the talent is meant to be sitting down in the commercial, or lying in bed, Francis will record them sitting or lying down "because the diaphragm goes into a different position and the talent will perform better because they are in the position they should be."

Francis avoids telling talent how to read individual lines. "It's better when the talent find their own way. They don't want to be offended by being told how to read something. It's a last-ditch option." A lot of very good writers can't "read" scripts, he says, but they insist on reading it to the talent. "They read it three times faster than we want it, there's no articulation whatsoever, no performance, no nothing, and it's awful. And the extraordinary thing is, if the talent read it that way you'd boot them out and go and book somebody else." Francis often has agency scripts retyped before the recording session. "We've all seen radio scripts come in jam-packed with sound effects and instructions for engineers, like a global road map. I'll have the text retyped, so the talent doesn't have to scan over sound effects instructions. I'll have it typed in a larger font with double spacing, triple spacing if the script allows, so the talent can write their own comments within the script." He also deletes talent instructions like "Serious" or "Friendly". "It's another word they have to read and it interrupts the momentum of the script. If the talent see an instruction they'll follow it, and if you tell them not to do it any more, it will still be there. The talent just need the words they have to read."

He also believes engineers should leave their finger on the talkback button when there is a discussion going on in the control room. "There's nothing more frustrating for the talent than standing behind the glass and seeing a big conversation going on. They have no idea whether it's them that everyone is talking about. The talent should be constantly involved, so they know that a new piece of direction is the by-product of that last five minutes of conversation and where it's come from. They shouldn't feel left out. They may also have good ideas. If you've got to workshop it, include the talent. But there should never be five people giving directions to the talent at the same time." The only time Francis will take his finger off the button is if the agency is talking about replacing the talent.

DIRECT for a film performance, says Howe, instead of a sitcom or commercial performance. And respect the actor's craft. "I try to help them do what they do even better. I like lots of white space, illogical, incomplete sentences and roughness."

Howe is the actor's advocate during the session. "I always try and greet them when they come in, introduce them to the other players, tell them who each player will be. Sometimes I give them a script. I make sure they're cosy with a beverage or whatever. I also like to get the paperwork out of the way up front. It's not a huge deal, but when the session is over I want them to be able to make a graceful exit." It is not coddling them, he explains, rather it is "just out of respect and appreciation".

Before the talent arrives, Howe will have briefed the client and agency what to expect. "I'll tell them I'm going to work with the actors a bit, get them warmed up, so don't worry about pronunciation just yet. At this point I don't even let them have a talkback button, but they can listen."

Howe works in the booth with the actors. Usually he has written notes that give the context of the spot. "I like to have them 'back up into' the spot, to live in the moments right *before* the action in the spot actually happens."

In the case of a single-voice narrative, he might be looking for a straight read from someone who wants to add an 'elbow' to help the listener get the humour. "When they don't need any help, I'll have the actor read an obituary, or think about something morbid, or some ridiculously happy thing. Whatever works. Often I'll hover around the talent, to get them off guard. Obviously I have to have their trust first, but then I will stand behind them, or invade their space, or distract them, just to get a different, more visceral read..."

DENNIS has worked on both sides of the microphone. "When somebody else is giving you directions, it teaches you to be very precise when it's your turn to direct. A big problem is when people say, give me this kind of inflection, you just parrot what they're doing. It restricts the performance, instead of letting an actor contribute and make it better." Dennis says a far better solution is to *tell the talent what the listener's emotional response should be*: read this and make me cry, read this and make me laugh. "But don't give them too much information, just try it out."

Many agency producers and clients insist that breaths sound "messy" and should be eliminated in the final track. Sometimes voice-overs will be told to read the same take endlessly, in one breath, rather than taking a breath as they read. Dennis disagrees. "I think breaths in commercials are quite good, otherwise it sounds like a computer voice. A lot of people have breathing problems, and microphones are so sensitive. But you don't have to cut out the breaths — you can just lower the level of the breath. Or ask them to turn off mic a bit, which softens the breath. In the days of tape editing, we used to cut the middle out of breaths to soften them. It's a problem that's always been there." Breath control, he says, should not become central to your concentration. "The important thing is the performance, and not whether your breathing is loud."

VAN DIJK combines naturalistic performances with a sense of perspective.

"I have in my head how each character should sound and each line should be read — but that's my fallback. My objective is to achieve a naturalistic performance, so my talent needs to interpret the script in their own way. I describe where they are, the sort of character they are, what they do for a living, and even picture someone they know who is similar. Often this means changing the script or dialogue slightly, but that will only improve the overall performance."

Then Van Dijk works on perspective. "In radio acting, performances often sound self-conscious and are rarely underplayed. Actors over-enunciate and the perspective is pretty much limited to 'on-mic' only." Because radio is an intimate medium, Van Dijk argues that it needs subtlety to draw in the listener. "In natural conversation people move, scratch, turn and cough. Sometimes these sounds make all the difference when you're trying to achieve a believable performance."

Van Dijk encourages the talent to learn their script so they are free to move around the studio. "As well as their individual mics, I also like to use a couple of ambient mics (stereo pairs). The talent is then free to approach, turn, bend down and … act!"

REMLEY believes in improvising. "I do my best with dialogue, and I do my best to make it as natural as I can, but I rely on the actors. I turn them loose on it. Generally I don't let them keep the script in front of them very long. If there's a lot of product information obviously they have to have something to refer to, but generally that's not the case in stuff that I'm involved with. Once they understand the situation — two guys on a bus, one guy's problem is he's out of beer at home and his guests are all waiting for him to get back, and something funny happens — as soon as they understand that, I say good, now you both know who you are, and you know how the thing has got to end, you know the final line I've written. You guys get me there — but we've been doing it in 40 seconds, we have to do it in 28 seconds. The actors love it, and they're excellent at it. There are so many things that an actor can say with tone of voice that don't require extra words." It takes a lot of editing, says Remley, because invariably one of the actors will forget the thread and make a mess of it. "I just end up refereeing it and making careful notes when they do it well…"

Once the actors start work, with or without a script, Remley says you should start policing yourself as a writer. "It becomes very apparent to you when you hear something you've written that you think why did I ever put those three sentences in there, they're not needed, I could do that with three *words*. It's getting into the habit of being your own best Copy Chief."

MORE on that subject from Hertz: "Quincy Jones was talking about Frank Sinatra's ability to 'sell' a song. *'He made it his own,'* was the phrase Quincy used. Sinatra got so into the words that he would sing them as though he had written them himself, or as though he had personally lived the experiences the lyrics spoke of."

The same applies to radio commercials. "First, it takes an immaculately crafted script that conveys a story worth telling, written in human language for a believable character, and with enough breathing space to enable that character to develop. The second requirement is someone to play the character, an actor capable of making the audience believe the story. *Someone who not only completely understands the message, but also has the talent and presence to make the script his own.* Requirement number three is that the writer has the confidence to make or allow script changes right then and there — words, stresses, even whole sentences in the script — in order to better define the character. Actors, too, should be encouraged to leave the security of the prepared script. One of the things I say to actors, if you've got a better way of saying what I've written and you don't say it, I'm going to hate you. I want you to take chances with it. You can throw the script away as long as what comes out is what I want to say. It's only when copywriters realise that their radio copy exists to create character that we can loosen up, and think fast enough, to let go and make it happen."

Dialogue commercials, Hertz reminds us, should be recorded as ensemble pieces to capture *moments*. "In his book *About Acting*, Peter Barkworth points out that in real conversation you rarely know what the other person is going to say, so your answers don't just sound spontaneous, they actually are." Radio dialogue should sound like genuine natural responses, not a recited list of answers. Writers have to make sure there's a relationship between the characters, and a reason for the conversation. "Listen for whether the actors are acting the part, or just the script. The characters should be making real contact with each other, not just taking it in turns to speak."

In other words, acting is *reacting*.

Radio needs as much directing as television, says Hertz, and it is vital that one person with a vision of the spot be in control. "Recordings at which six people all give directions will never result in great ads. It doesn't matter whether the director is from a production house or the agency, as long as there is only *one*." Hertz believes reading lines yourself to the actors is counterproductive. "If you give them the inflection you want, they'll give it back to you, but you won't get the best from them. It's better to tell them how the character would feel in the situation, and let them find a way to express it. If that doesn't work, it's more likely that the problem is in the writing. So don't get locked into the script. You must be prepared to change the words, instantly — to better suit the character, to help an actor, *to make a moment more true*. Or even just to try something different." He directs in the studio with the performers. "It's lonely behind the mic. I tend to listen to playbacks and give notes in the studio rather than from the control room."

CAN THE CANS

"There are scores of actors — gifted players capable of performing the subtlest nuances of character — who become robots the moment they don headphones in Soho," says Hertz. "On autopilot, they do their well-paid version of voice-over and leave. Over the years, I've had to spend hours in sessions talking actors out of voice-over mode so they could do what they're already good at." With cans, Hertz says voice-overs become so fixated with the sound, tone and music of their own voice that they want to make it as beautiful as possible — instead of speaking in a normal way. Their attention is distracted from performance and what they are trying to communicate.

Hertz's solution is to remove the headphones. "If you watch a radio play being recorded, you don't see actors wearing headphones. They talk to each other. And because radio is a physical medium, actors work better standing up. A surprising number of them, and many sound engineers, seem not to know this." Hertz asks his actors to take their headphones off, "and just stand up and talk to me. And the difference is amazing. I even go into the studio and stand in front of them and say, talk to me..." Hertz describes how dialogue commercials are generally recorded in London: "The convention these days is to go into some incredibly expensive studio with lots of zinc, and wood, and *cappucchino*, where the actors sit down next to each other facing the glass and put headphones on and then try to act." Hertz believes copywriters and producers are putting artificial barriers between themselves and the greatest pool of acting talent in the world. "If you're acting in the theatre, you generally have somebody to talk to. Even if you're doing a monologue, you have an audience. But what you don't have is a big sheet of glass and people behind that glass whom you can see are muttering to each other. It's quite false..."

When Hertz conducts workshops for agency people, they have to write commercials to his briefs, then act them out themselves in a studio and make their own sound effects. "One of the purposes of this is, I want them to know how lonely it is in that box when you've people staring at you, and a piece of paper in front of you, and a lot riding on it. A lot of the people sitting there at recording studios get so wrapped up in the system they forget there is a vulnerable human being on the other side of the glass who is an actor, and therefore by definition more insecure than almost anybody else in the world."

WEBSTER always hides the headphones. "You should think about what you're saying and be true to yourself. Someone doing an end tag doesn't have to listen to himself. A hand behind the ear forces the words up so they can hear a resonance." For exterior recordings on the studio balcony, a talkback system is rigged up so the actors can hear control room instructions — without headphones.

Dennis also believes that better performances are achieved without wearing cans, even when the voice is reading to music. "It's a good idea to play the music to the voice talent to let them get the feel of the mood, whether it's a relaxed mood or a romantic mood or whatever, but then take the music away and let them concentrate on the performance. On radio, you're after a feeling, not specific cut points. The engineer can cut and position the voice anyway if he wants it to fall in a particular spot." Wearing cans, Dennis says, is an old school radio thing. "Radio people are so used to wearing cans because they wear them on air, they're like a security blanket. Whereas if you use stage actors they tend not to like wearing cans at all."

Francis discourages headphones. "Hearing your own voice over the cans in your own head is different from hearing yourself through speakers. A different physiological process happens. When talent hear themselves, they tend to direct themselves. So when you ask them to change nuance or cadence, they think they're doing it in their head, but because they're listening to themselves they aren't externalising it. It happens in their head, but not out in the control room." If voice-overs insist on wearing cans, Francis asks them to take at least one side off so they can hear themselves semi-acoustically in the room and get a better idea of the dynamic.

CHARACTER VOICES

The greatest character voice the world has ever heard was Mel Blanc, the legendary radio actor who voiced 848 Warner Bros. Cartoons, supplying as many as 14 different voices for one cartoon! Blanc was Bugs Bunny, Porky Pig, Elmer Fudd, Woody Woodpecker, Daffy Duck, Yosemite Sam, Henery Hawk, Foghorn Leghorn, Pepe Le Pew, Speedy Gonzales, Tweety and Sylvester, Roadrunner and Wile E. Coyote. Blanc even named Bugs and "in his mind" heard the rabbit speaking with a Brooklyn accent. Significantly, Blanc was a stickler for clarity. *He believed that if a character voice wasn't absolutely intelligible, it was useless.*

Blanc described voice men as needing versatility and an elastic voice box; in his case, one teaspoon of salt and one of baking soda mixed in a glass of extremely hot tap water and gargled promptly ensured the elasticity was maintained. Another prerequisite: the kind of ears that allowed them to consistently reproduce the same timbres, tones and textures.

Surely though, voice characterisations are unnecessary when scripts merely call for "Dad", "Mum" and "Son", or "Man" and "Woman"?

Hertz writes a one-sentence description of the characters in all his commercials, *including the announcer.* "A voice is what somebody sounds like, but there has to be a 'somebody' attached to it. It drives me nuts when people refer to the actors simply as voices, because as soon as they do that, they rob themselves of that actor's ability to play characters. I hate voice-overs, that pattern of rising and falling inflections that only exists in advertising. If there is an announcement to be made and that announcer is speaking on behalf of the company, then I want the recipient of that announcement to feel something about that company. The biggest part of communications is what the listener brings to it, not what the sender sends."

Townsend calls character reads a different ball game. "It could be argued that it's easier for an actor to hide behind a character read. In a funny sort of way, it gives them greater confidence. I have worked with people in the past who spent their careers 'in character' and successfully voiced commercials 'in character'. But give them a straight read, take them away from their characters to being themselves, and it is amazing how often they fail to perform."

He recommends giving actors in character-styled commercials a bit of freedom to ad-lib where necessary. "In a two-hander, for example, do not stick rigidly to Voice 1, then Voice 2, then Voice 1 again. Allow them to overlap, interject, things we do naturally. If playing character, I get voice-overs to stand when delivering. It gives them more freedom to breathe and helps their performance. It also allows them to use the room. If they need to enter a room in the script, get them to do it. If they need to be behind a door, get them to be behind a door. If they need to be on the telephone, connect a telephone to the desk and record it on the phone. If the performance is set outside, get them to record outside if at all possible. If not, record them standing up, but directionally into the mics so as not to pick up any of the natural ambience of the room. Then, when you're mixing, equalise the voices to blend into the effect. You can even add a little bounce on the voices as if the voices are being reflected off a wall or similar."

CELEBRITY voices, real or imitated, have long been popular on radio and television tracks. On one hand, the audience may well recognise a famous voice and it may well do some good. On the other, you could ask whether the audience is going to relate more to the voice than they are to the message? Opinion is divided. As Barbara Levy observes: "Why would Michael Douglas' voice sell the product when you know he doesn't use it?"

Imitating famous voices is an even more popular device in radio commercials. When it is done merely to "get attention" or "sound different", it is pointless and distracting. However, Sydney's Young & Looby Advertising had "James Mason" in his role of Humbert Humbert buying Bradford insulation in a bid to cool Lolita's midsummer passion. His house, it seemed, was already too hot...

New Voices For Old

Lionel Hunt often uses singers because they have perfect phrasing and nobody knows their speaking voices. "Singers doing voice-overs was my little secret for quite some time. Using non-professional voices is another good idea. There's nothing worse than actors that sound like they are acting."

Lynn and Tao cast for voices they've never heard before, voices with character. "Listening to casting tapes is generally very depressing. After a while you start to doubt whether the idea works at all. Then finally, someone who 'gets it' performs it in a way that makes you laugh out loud and then you relax."

"All I'm interested in is the right tone and attitude in the voice, the right social outlook from that person, and intelligence," explains Flint. "But for a lot of other people it's a challenge to make commercials. If I go into the street and cast someone, my partner Phil will give it a good try to make it work. We're not scared. But I've found that if engineers cast, they tend to cast people that they're either comfortable with in the studio, or they know they can push a certain way. If you're sitting all day in a studio with a writer, you won't put in an actor who is 'hard work'…"

Mark Rivett also advocates trying people other than actors. "With a little coaxing, friends and workmates can be hidden gems. A friend's 4-year-old daughter won the Australian Golden Stylus Award for best talent a few years back." Time is a real enemy in producing great radio, he adds. "Always make sure you allow enough time to produce the best results. Know your voice talent, and what they are capable of, then push them way beyond it."

"The timbre of the human voice is pure emotion on radio, but too often its power is lost through overfamiliarity," cautions Newman. "Ad after ad, it's the same handful of voices. What if every print ad you saw used the same few typefaces?" Newman is always looking for the head-turning voice. "Someone no one has heard on radio before. That can be far more ear-catching than a reel full of sound effects."

Brad Power tries new talent. He goes along to every new class graduating from the National Institute of Dramatic Art, Australia's equivalent of RADA, where Mel Gibson learned his craft. His priority is finding "people who are into it like I am. I want people who want to make it a good ad. I use actors who understand what we're trying to achieve. If you're directing radio, you're crazy if you don't ask the talent what they think. It might be something we haven't thought of. All the people we use act as comedians too, so they can often make a great contribution. Writers should be encouraged to take on board the options given to them by actors and engineers — a lot of these people have been doing it longer than the creatives, and make a lot more radio ads than the creatives."

FOR many years, Webster always woke up to a different radio station. "I would follow the ads, hear what each station was doing to them. When I was stuck in traffic I'd hop around listening to the commercials and you could hear a sameness of energy coming out. When something is a little bit different, when they're talking *to* you not at you, you tend to listen a little bit more. Even subliminally, subconsciously, you'll hear the difference." A lot of voices, he contends, don't have bodies or souls. "And they're talking *past* you. You can hear them concentrating on the script, not enjoying what's coming to hand. A lot of writers or producers think they need to make their ads louder and louder, and you don't have to do that." Webster argues the case for naturalness in voices, sound and production. "We're proud of the fact that our work doesn't all sound the same. Everything is different. The listener, the person who's going to go and buy something, is entertained."

HOW *NOT* TO GET A GREAT PERFORMANCE FROM TALENT

From Austin Howe,
President/Creative Director, Radioland Portland, Oregon

1. If there is no one at the agency who has any real experience directing talent, don't hire a capable director for your spots. That could cost extra, and this is, after all, only radio. Surely the writer can do it. Or the junior producer. Never mind that they don't have any experience except for maybe watching incompetent colleagues rattle otherwise talented and professional actors.

2. Be sure and show up with "Client-Approved Scripts" and treat them as if they were the Holy Bible. Make sure every word is adhered to, and give the impression that a horrible plague may be unleashed if it is deviated from for even the most inspired ad-lib. However, you should also be sure not to time out the scripts ahead of time, so that now your talent has to fit :75 of copy into :60.

3. Start the session by telling them you're looking for "kind of an Ed Grover read". Reference other actors or voice-over talent whenever possible. This will help them realise from the get-go that they were not really your first choice for the spot. They will become quickly disengaged (along with their creativity, spontaneity and confidence) from the process and keep them from giving you that annoying

extra effort that makes for a great performance. Don't give them a (well thought-out) preamble of the context of the spot and then let them bring their own interpretation to the script before you start giving more specific direction. Being professional actors with more acting talent than you, they might come up with something far better than you had in your head.

4. Make sure you have lots and lots of people in the control room and let them all have access to the talkback button.

5. Start nitpicking (and let your client start nitpicking) right from the first take. You want to get the actors addled right from the beginning, and give them a sense that you are nervous about this whole thing and you're pretty sure that they're going to screw you and your entire career right here in this session. Don't worry about developing the character at this point. Just focus on minor things like hitting the word "In" in "In July peas grow there".

6. Make sure no one is really in charge, and it always helps if the creative director is off-site and hands-on, meaning that everyone has to wait until you track him down so he can completely change everything you've been working on for the past hour and a half. Whatever you do, don't stand up to your creative director and say something to the effect of, "Hey, bud, if you want to make huge changes, get your butt down here to the factory floor. Please."

7. Don't praise the actor or actress when they do a good take. Leave them alone and wondering if they're about to get canned, as client and agency people confer for long periods between every take. Or, equally as effective, give them fake praise just as you are about to tell them to do it completely differently.

8. Never experiment with switching roles, or having the actors "back up into" the story and pretend for a bit. (This takes valuable time away from making sure the legal copy is pronounced clearly.) Don't go into the booth with the talent and work with them there. Then you might actually make a human connection with them (you and them against the din of all those evil suit types in the control room) and inadvertently coax them into a better performance.

9. Always have them on mic. In the studio. You can put them outside, or on a golf course, or in a kitchen, later (with sound effects). Never actually go to the trouble of actually taking a DAT and boom mic (or mics) and set up outside, or on a golf course, or in a kitchen. That's a lot of trouble for radio, and besides, that recording engineer you work with doesn't like to do radio that way. And we all know that his whole aim in life is to get your radio campaign in D&AD.

10. Once you have a great take, and one backup, "just in case" keep having them read the same bit over and over again. Get your money's worth. After all, union regulations say that you have them for a full 90 minutes.

11. Always leave the talent in the booth, while you call for approvals. That way, they can hear your client talk about them on speakerphone, saying things like, "He sounds kind of effeminate and stupid. And he needs to emphasise 'In' in 'In July…'"

12. Never tell the talent that you will send them a CD of the spot. This will make them think that you are proud of it and you think that he or she should be, too. Plus, it's an additional expense. If you do actually send a CD to their agent within a few days of the session, they might remember that and give you a better performance next time. (And we don't want that.)

7
RECORDING BETTER RADIO

Mandy Wheeler, director of Mandy Wheeler Sound Productions, once described the production process as "where we ask the audience to come along with us, where we ask them to enter into the fantasy, to believe in the story, to come with us to this place that we are asking them to paint in their imagination."

Production is very important, says Steve Henry. "It is in music, and possibly even more so in comedy or dialogue. The arts of timing, performance and editing are very underrated."

By leaving space in his scripts, Michael Newman ensures that if someone has a nuance or gag that helps, he can use it. "Ideally, a radio ad should leave the studio 10% better than the script that went in. So there must always be room for your voice talent to express their talent. Most writers are fast talkers, in every sense. So get a stopwatch. In fact, get a full-stopwatch."

John Immesoete agrees. "Before you get in the studio, make sure your script is as tight as possible. It will probably change when you start recording, but it's better to build on a strong foundation." His only taboo is sticking to the letter of the script because that is the way it was approved. "Be ready to make changes on the fly. That's a radio advantage. You can change something almost as quickly as you can think something up. Make the most of your time and explore options. It's a privilege and luxury that only radio really affords." Record the approved version, he suggests, then try to record something better. "Clients can be reasonable people. It's hard to get in trouble for trying to do something better."

"Producing great radio is a creative talent like any other," cautions Steve Elrick. "So go to a production company that's proven they are hot, otherwise you will end up doing the direction and the production yourself and will invariably be disappointed with the results. You wouldn't direct and camera-operate your own TV spots, so why do your radio that injustice?"

"It should be fun making radio, and it should be fun listening to it," reflects Bob Dennis. "Over the years we've put in a lot of hard work, and had a lot of fun, too. As the world gets faster, people don't have the time to craft a radio commercial. They'll spend the time on a television soundtrack, but not for radio. It's 'let's get in and get out'. Yet a lot of the top people in advertising in America and Australia cut their teeth on radio. Radio teaches you how to economise on words, how to tell a story, how to use sound. As a writer, you're showing us what you're made of, how your imagination works, there's nothing else to back you up."

Dennis says that when people listen to a radio commercial, they're actually looking into your mind. If we agree, it makes production an even more challenging journey.

PRE-PRODUCTION

"The most successful agencies doing radio are treating radio more seriously than some of their competitors. They are having pre-production meetings and they are using people who are professionals in radio to take their ideas and make them come alive," Adrian Reith, Radioville director, once observed.

"The whole idea is to treat a radio job with the same importance as TV," explains Brad Power, who introduced pre-production at Sydney's STELLARadio. He paints a familiar scenario: "The agency shows up at the studio. They might have emailed a list of sound effects, but that's all. The engineer hasn't seen the script and hasn't had anything to do with the casting. The only person who has had the script for any length of time is the client, and they have changes coming through on the phone while we record…"

Power encourages creatives to call him as soon as they have an idea. "We can take your ideas and give you a creative treatment like you would get from a television director to develop the idea further." He references a script he once received from an agency: "It had a note at the top that read, 'This radio ad opens on somebody at a kitchen table thinking that it's Tuesday'. Just because you've written it on a script doesn't mean your listener knows it. You've got to treat yourself as the listener and ask does it make sense? Tuesday has to be written into the script."

Mike Edmonds cautions against walking into the studio "cold". "I always try to discuss a script with the producer or engineer first. Discuss talent and sound effects. And how much time to book in the studio."

As a director and engineer, Les Francis considers it important to talk to the writer before the job begins "because the writer and I have to work together". He believes his biggest contribution to the production, on the technical and engineering side, will be bringing a sense of perspective or what he calls "aural depth". "There's nothing more boring to me than a commercial where there's a lovely scene going on, some nice dialogue, but it's totally one-dimensional. It doesn't live. I don't believe they're anywhere else than a voice booth somewhere in the world." His other role will be devil's advocate, or script editor.

Linda Locke is one agency leader who thoroughly endorses the need for pre-production. "If you think about the film world, when I send a script in to a production company a director and a producer will sit down and look at it. And I fully and absolutely expect that they are going to come back with a treatment, a style, an approach. They are going to add something to that piece that will lift it from where it was, and help us tell that story in a way that we haven't even begun to think about. That is very rarely the case in radio here. We've used producers in the UK, for example, and when we send the script out to them they will come back and even suggest changes to the copy, and tell us how they want to build the sense of theatre. They will contribute as much to the script as a film director would."

Nigel Dawson concurs. "I get as excited about having a good radio idea as I do about an idea in any other medium, possibly more so.

And to make sure the end result matches the track playing in my head, it is important to pre-produce the spot in much the same way as you would a TV commercial." Dawson says he is fortunate that Melbourne boasts a number of skilled radio producers. "One can discuss the nuances of a script and the casting requirements with people like David Flint and Les Molnar."

For his part, David Flint often finds himself cast in the role of copy-editor. Sometimes scripts come in that don't quite work. "I will say to people, you're writing this for a certain social group, but these are just not the words these people would use. What I suggest is that we leave it a little bit open, and we'll get a person who *is* this type of person and let them do it in their own words, and that's how we can shift it."

THE ENGINEER IS EVERYTHING

"When producing TV and movies, the director is critical," argues Immesoete. "When producing radio, the engineer is critical. A good engineer can make your job easier and bring your spot to life in many subtle ways. A good engineer has highly trained ears and is adept at helping direct talent. I make sure before I enter a studio that I've got the right engineer. You learn who's good through experience and by asking around."

"Get a good *conceptual* sound engineer who is on the same wavelength as you," advises Calvin Soh.

"The production process is really make or break for radio," acknowledges Rob Martin Murphy, "and the best spots I've done have been thanks to big contributions from the engineer — not only with effects and mixing, but even script changes and getting the talent to play different parts. I find if you go into the studio willing to be open and experiment, the results seem to be better than you ever imagined."

"I brief the sound engineer or designer on the kind of atmosphere or emotion I want the listener to feel during and after hearing the commercial," says Cary Rueda. "It's much like music scoring; you have to identify *what you want the audience to feel*."

Freshness is Philip Webster's priority. "We have 8-minute ad breaks, and something that's fresh will break through." Significantly,

Webster still does all his work on analog. "I don't relate artistically the same way if I'm using Protools or Fairlight. And because everything else on air is digital, our stuff tends to cut through a little bit more. Young people who have grown up with digital sound will be more aware of a warm, natural analog sound." Interestingly, he adds, big classical orchestras in Europe have now reverted to analog recording because digital was not letting them sound natural.

"Trust your judgement and your engineer," advises Rob Townsend whose passion for sound began when he first tinkered with tape recorders at the age of eight. "Try to arrange a pre-production meeting to iron out any possible problems. You would be amazed how awkward it is sometimes to get the creatives to go with an idea from the engineer. My job is not to make bad radio commercials. I would like to think that I am there to assist in the creative process, not work against it. Too often creatives think they know more about sound engineering than the sound engineer himself — for example, dictating levels that despite my protests are obviously wrong, only for them to come back again and make the changes I suggested in the first place. I hold my hands up in the air and say that I am not a writer and generally would not start rewriting the creatives' script."

TRADE SECRET 1: MICROPHONES

Microphones are part of the creative armoury. Different microphones help to enhance different voice tones and textures. Some capture richness and warmth, others pick up more "tops" in a voice, delivering more sharpness and presence. Great radio creatives understand how the choice of a particular mic contributes to the way their tracks will stand out on air.

In the old days of radio drama, round single-sided carbon microphones meant that actors had to push their colleagues aside in order to get in close enough to say their line. Then came the 44, a diamond-shaped ribbon microphone that was double-sided. Fade-outs were achieved by walking in a circle around to the dead side. Because it had a ribbon, distortion could occur on plosive Ps and Bs. Next on the scene was the cardioid mic with a heart-shaped field, adjustable with a key or a coin, followed by Neumanns and the C12, regarded by many as almost too sensitive for acting. The figure "8" field allowed the microphone to be worked on both sides.

Today, opinion is divided between the traditional diaphragm and valve microphones like the Neumann, and a new era of shotgun mics.

Neumann U87. The large diaphragm Neumann U87 is arguably the world's most widely used studio microphone, famous for its warmth. Earlier models, affectionately known as 47s and 67s, have become jealously guarded collector's items.

At Angell Sound London, Rob Townsend uses the Neumann U47 or U87 for straightforward recording. "The 47 is not made any more so I treasure the two I have." If he were recording a commentator at a soccer match, he would select a ribbon or lip mic.

At Singapore's Opuz, Paul Tan has three types of Neumann — the U67, U87 and the KMR81. His rare Neumann U67 is renowned for its warm characteristics. "It is a tube EF86 microphone made in the early 1960s, prior to the reunification of East Germany with the West. I use the U67 to achieve intimate recordings as well as recordings which require the voice talent or sound source to be loud. The U67's frequency response is practically linear for frontal sound pickup. It is good for plosives, letters starting with Ps and Bs. A large number of US rap artistes use it."

"For good voice-overs, lead vocals and group vocals, Neumann is still the Mercedes-Benz of microphones," attests Peter Clark. "The old U67, the valve one, is very valuable now."

Street Remley uses Neumann. "We use shotgun mics a little more now than we used to, but I still prefer the warmth of a Neumann."

At Sonovision, John Culverwell's favourite mic is the Neumann U87, while at London's Eardrum Ralph Van Dijk calls the U87 "hard to beat. It's very versatile, with cardioid, omni and figure '8' configurations. It's also very sensitive, picks up room ambience and helps to give a very realistic sense of place."

The Neumann U87 is Dennis' choice. "It's the world standard in microphones. It has clarity and a wonderful sound — a warmth and crispness as well, which is almost a contradiction." Microphone positioning is critical, he says. "You can spend a lot of time setting up the talent. If they get too close the sound can be muffled. When you start using actors who haven't recorded for radio before, you're constantly moving them and telling them not to look at the mic. If you're using two Neumanns, for example, and one person is standing exactly right, but the second person is working too close or too far away, it sounds like they're in two different places." Even in an air-conditioned studio, atmospheric conditions make a difference to where Dennis stands his talent. "Whether it's a hot, dry day or a humid day or a wet day makes a difference to the air in the studio. If there's moisture on the microphone, especially the Neumann U87, and if you've done enough recording, you can actually hear the difference."

At Singapore's Four Media Company, Kenn Delbridge prefers the Neumann UA87A because he works a lot with TV mixes as well as radio. "It's an expensive microphone for premium voice recording in music and narration. Microphones like the Electrovoice RE20 are popular in the US, but the UA87A's frequency range is 20–20,000 Hz."

Rennie Gomes at Singapore's Yellow Box Studios chooses microphones appropriate to the individual characteristics of each voice. Yellow Box tracks have found recognition at Britain's D&AD awards. For a straight read, Gomes uses the Neumann U87, the Rode NT or even a GT valve mic. "These mics have large diaphragms, great for capturing the warmth and depth of a voice."

Neumann KMR81. Because a lot of voice-over artists work very close in to the microphone, Tan often opts for the Neumann KMR81. "Its microphone capsule is located inside an interference tube which makes it acoustically open, but also has a high acoustic impedance. It is a very directional microphone with a high degree of 'rejection' at its sides. It's largely used for location recordings and isolating instrument sections when recording orchestras. Voice-over artists can also work the KMR81 in closer proximity without worrying too much about popping." Tan prefers the Neumann KMR81 to the Sennheiser shotgun microphones. "The Sennheiser tends to sound a bit too harsh for my liking. It has a bit too much cut around the 1–3kHz range, too much top-end and not enough roundness, so some recordings sound too 'poky'."

Manley Tube Reference Cardioid. Tan also uses the Manley Reference Cardioid from high-end Manley Laboratories. The all-tube triode design has a thick gauge, 6-micron gold sputtered 1-inch diaphragm which "provides a rich tonal balance and liquid character that lets me score a bit more testosterone in the recordings. Apart from the warmness of the microphone, there is also an extreme openness to it, and it allows me to capture the 'air' around the microphone."

Microtech Gefell. At The Radio Spot Dallas, Thomas Hripko uses the Microtech Gefell UMT 70S condenser microphone in addition to the Neumann U87. He describes the UMT 70S as "awesome — pretty darn close to a U87 in an A/B test, and a tick brighter. The low end is strong and clean. Sometimes, a U87 seems a bit muddy on the lows."

Sennheiser. At Toronto's Louder, Clive Desmond records just about all voices using shotgun mics. "Great voice actors require little or no equalisation or compression. I've recorded some of the heaviest voice actors in the business and the one thing I've noticed was how little acoustic surgery we had to apply to their voices. Actors like Alan Bleviss, Bill Fiore, Dottie Schott, Tony Rossato, Don Lafontaine, Mary Elaine Monti, Patty Dworkin, Fred Napoli, Kenneth Welsh and the late Fred Gwynn just sound great right out of the box. Their natural, God-given acoustics go beyond anything we could do to enhance them."

"I have lots of favourite esoteric microphones," confesses Brent Hahn, "but for me, the Sennheiser 416 works fine for most things. It has long been a favourite for voice-over, sound effects and foley work in LA, and has now become a standard throughout the States. Natural-sounding it is definitely not; the low and high frequencies are hyped for a definite in-your-face presence. It is, however, easily overloaded; it doesn't like being shouted into and its extremely directional pickup pattern gives the talent very little freedom of movement. Its sensitivity in the high frequencies makes it a poor choice for recording such things as wind chimes and jangling keys. It's also tough to record someone on a 416 and later create a convincing phone-filter effect." For natural-sounding dialogue, Hahn selects the Neumann U87. "It's my first choice when voices need to blend convincingly into an outdoor ambience. The U87 can take a lot of level, so it's my mic of choice for shouting, bullhorns and the like.

But it can be finicky about the preamp it's plugged into. Sent straight into a cheap mixing board, a U87 can sound pathetically thin and nasal."

Like Hahn, Brad Power uses the Sennheiser 416. "It's a semi-shotgun microphone, very directional. They give a bright, punchy sound. For sound effects or group things we use Neumann U87s. When we go out on location, we have an older model Sony DAT machine that came with a Sony stereo mic, which is great to get those big, wide stereo sounds, with a real sense of space and area."

At the Famous Radio Ranch, Christine Coyle opts for the Sennheiser MD421. Peter Clark describes the Sennheiser MKH418 as a short, gun-like mic that comes with a good long puff shield. "It's a good directional condenser mic for dialogue." Meanwhile, Gomes chooses the Sennheiser ME66 for a live, outdoor feel.

Webster believes that because certain voices respond better to certain mics, the studio has to offer many possibilities. "We have Sennheiser shotguns that give a very sharp sort of sound. We've got the Neumann TLM17 and U87s, for a much rounder, warmer sound." Webster might use a Sennheiser on one voice and a Neumann on another, because those mics were right for those voices. In many studios, he says, the mics are permanently set up and hardly ever move from that one spot. "I move things around, I leave doors open, I'll change the mics, I set up things specially for each new session."

Electrovoice. Clark endorses the Electrovoice RE15: "I love it, and use it on everything from strings and brass to guitar amps and even voice-overs. It's a rugged dynamic mic with a very nice flat response. They're America's answer to Neumann, except they're a dynamic microphone not a condenser microphone."

Townsend uses an Electrovoice RE50 if the voice is supposed to be a reporter.

Shure. The Shure SM57 and SM58 also get Hahn's vote. "They're identical, with the 58 having a built-in pop filter. Rock bands, emcees, standup comics and the like often use these inexpensive mics. Unlike the Sennheiser and Neumann, they're internally shockproofed for handheld use. If you want that genuine through-the-PA-system sound, the 57 or 58 is the way to go. As a bonus, they phone-filter beautifully."

When recording more than one VO artist in a confined space, Gomes opts for a Shure SM57 or 58. "They are more directional and the engineer can isolate each voice for better mixing later." Gomes prefers to record all voice-overs together. "This fosters greater interaction and sense of timing. It allows ideas about scripts to arise."

Webster recalls doing radio commercials for a Melbourne electrical retailer with the great American entertainer Sammy Davis Jr. "Sammy showed me a briefcase that he carried around. It was full of Shure microphones. There were probably a dozen of them in there, gold, silver, platinum, jewelled, all different, and he explained how each one gave a different feel in the clubs and restaurants where he was singing."

AKG. For adding "toppiness" and presence on air, Gomes' favourite is the AKG414. If the script demands the voice sound more on location than in-your-face, he uses less dynamic mics.

Latvian Blue. Webster has eight different types of microphones, and has recently discovered the new mid-range microphones from Latvia called Blue (an acronym for Baltic Latvian Universal Electronics): Blue Mouse — a small microphone so-named because it has little "ears" on it, Blue Dragonfly and Blueberry. "They have a nice clarity and put a nice bite on the voice, but the warmth is still there."

Francis shares Webster's enthusiasm for the Blue microphones. "The Blueberry is the best mic I've ever worked with. It already has the equalisation that I would normally put on a mic, so rather than me cranking the e.q., which is 'false' really, I'd rather have the mic do the work for me. It has a very broad mid-range that's particularly good for female voices, which don't have much mid-range anyhow and some I know don't have any."

Microphone preamplifiers. Hahn welcomes the emergence of the new, extremely high quality and expensive microphone preamplifiers. "These preamps can make an enormous difference in the overall sound of a spot. They'll make your voice recordings cleaner, clearer and subjectively 'bigger', meaning you can mix your music and effects louder." Hahn's favourite mic preamps are the Avalon M5, Focusrite Red, Grace, and Massenburg.

Tan uses the Focusrite 430 Producers' Pack. As he explains, the signal path of a microphone should be minimised by using good quality preamplifiers, cables and connectors. "My Focusrite 430 receives the analog signal and converts it into direct digital. Sometimes I provide the necessary phantom power, but it is always better to use the phantom power supply that comes with some microphones as this ensures impedance matching. Nowadays I never use the phantom power supply from consoles unless all my microphone preamps are down and out! The reason is that the microphone preamp is a dedicated unit which enables me to achieve less noise and a shorter signal path, resulting in an excellent signal-to-noise ratio and a clean, clear, punchy sound."

TRADE SECRET 2: ACOUSTICS

Studio acoustics are also tools of the radio trade. It helps creatives if they know the basics and appreciate how acoustics underscore atmosphere.

Once, radio station and recording studios had curved walls to deflect sound and avoid any problems caused by direct "bouncing". The risk was that when sound bounced straight off one wall onto another, the microphone would pick up an echo. Control room windows were also angled; invariably, actors faced the control room when they performed and a huge sheet of glass acted as an echo surface. As Tan observes, "You'd be surprised how even a music stand's acoustic reflections can be picked up by a microphone."

In noisy Asian cities, the ultimate studio is "a room suspended from within a room", in which low frequency is kept to a minimum. "The room has to be absolutely 'dead' — absolutely no acoustic standing waves," says Tan. "To achieve this, the entire studio floor has to be 'floated' over another floor, mainly using heavy industrial springs or absorbers. Secondly, if the room is small and square — a common problem in places like Singapore, Hong Kong and Tokyo where land space is limited and costly — you have to break up the corners by introducing some form of irregularity to prevent sound waves from reflecting and bouncing around too much. Thirdly, sound absorbent materials should be used for these corners as well as the entire studio." The most commonly used materials include cheap eggshell crates, Gypsum boards and Rockwool.

Times are changing. Dennis, for example, prefers to have a certain amount of "life" in a studio. "The trend, years ago, was to make a studio quite dead. Nowadays it's gone the other way, to more of a natural sound. I've been in studios where people have spent a fortune soundproofing them, only to put in mirrors or hard surfaces just to make them sound a little bit 'live'."

TRADE SECRET 3: AMBIENT SOUND

Ironically, studios were once designed to keep out unwanted sounds like traffic. Nowadays, more and more engineers are going outside in search of the very things that were once taboo. Dialogue is recorded outdoors, with actors raising their voices to be heard over passing background noises — just as real people do in real life.

"Don't be chained to the studio," says Van Dijk. "Some of my favourite ads were recorded on location. Whenever you hear scenes from feature films on the radio, they sound completely different. The sounds and perspectives are clearer because they are usually recorded outside a studio. As well as improving the actor's performance, location recordings can provide you with some wonderful and surprising *'indirect'* sounds — things you wouldn't think of adding in a studio are there in the background and help paint a very clear picture for the listener."

"It's very easy to think that radio has always got to be clean and clear," debates Power, "but radio can be a bit dirty, a bit real." He points to what he calls another cliché: "The old line-followed-by-sound-effect-followed-by-line-followed-by-sound-effect. It was a case of let's go to the CD and use the same sound effect we use every time, whereas now we try to get the DAT recorder and go out on location. We did a job where we were supposedly in a cab, so we acted it out like a drama in my car as we drove along. We also did a job about an aboriginal tracker, so we went down to the local park. A couple of times he went off mic, a couple of times he yelled a bit and it got a bit distorted, but it was real and the client loved it. Not everyone speaks clearly out there in radio land!"

"Try recording things out of the studio," agrees Mark Rivett. "Go 'on location', record things 'live', or use foley techniques as we do in films."

Gomes also advocates location recording. At the very least he takes a DAT recorder and mic to record atmosphere tracks. "No effort should be spared in giving a proper sense of realism. Street sounds have to sound local. Some stock traffic sound effects sound really different, really foreign."

Townsend shares a similar strategy. "For reality, record outside or on location if it can be arranged. If that's not possible, make use of the studio environment. In our studios, we have a small corridor between the control room and the studio. Quite often I'll record in the corridor because it gives a slightly livelier sound. I once recorded someone in a rather dark and dingy room that we had at the old studios in Floral Street, just to make use of the atmosphere."

FLINT WEBSTER'S entire building serves as a studio. "We have three studios, they're all like lounge rooms, very comfortable, and they're not focused on the technology," explains Flint. "Throughout our building there are microphone points for various situations. If the situation is in a kitchen, we record in a kitchen. You can turn the taps on and it doesn't sound like you're in a studio. If your hands are in the sink, your voice bounces off the wall in front of you and it's very,

The balcony scene at Flint Webster Melbourne.
From left, David Flint and Philip Webster briefing talent.

very real. We can put the mics out on the balcony and you'd hear if it were a bit windy. You'd certainly hear cars and birds, and we don't have any control over them. So when a dog barks or a bird twitters it's natural, it's not placed conveniently where the engineer wants it."

Flint also likes going out into the street and making the idea work naturally. "We did a commercial for advertising in the Yellow Pages. We took a comic actress out into the street in Melbourne. The idea was that this person was talking to people, trying to drum up business on her own, without an ad in the Yellow Pages. She just walked up to strangers and said, 'Oh excuse me, you do look terrible, you look like you need a facelift.' And of course you'd get some not very nice answers. One lady said, 'I don't speak English,' and our actress said, 'Oh I think you do,' and the lady said, 'Oh no I don't.' The agency had originally wanted to act it out, and we said give us a chance, we'd like to go down the street on this one, and we ended up doing about ten commercials in the series."

In another campaign for a brand of country cookies, people in the street were asked to make the cackling bird call of an Australian kookaburra.

For retailer Jeans West, the campaign idea was an "interviewer" who rode around on a tram insulting people's taste in clothes. The agency writer accompanied the actor and the recording engineer, writing lines on the fly. "We cast this brash young guy, and he'd say to people, 'Hey, where did you get your clothes, mate? They look terrible…'" According to Flint, the secret with it was the casting. "If I'd picked a voice-over to do it, the power of their voice would intimidate people. Whereas an actor, who can be a little bit silly or sympathetic or arrogant, got a rise out of people one way or another." Flint used two microphones. "These days some mics isolate so well they make other sounds drop out. We couldn't hear the cars and we wanted it to sound like it was in the street. So one mic was pointed at the road, and the other at the person speaking."

SFX

"For us, less is more." Coyle uses minimal sound effects. "We have found there is a tendency for inexperienced writers to rely on sound effects to compensate for lack of genuine creative. We have a terrific

TITLE: ORANGE "ANSWER FAX"

SFX: *WE HEAR A PHONE NUMBER BEING DIALLED...*

THE NUMBER IS RINGING...

AND OUR CALL IS ANSWERED BY A FAX MACHINE. SUDDENLY, THE FAMILIAR HIGH-PITCHED TONE OF THE FAX MACHINE BEGINS TO CHANGE...

IT BECOMES MORE SHRILL...

THEN INTERMITTENT...

AND THEN ALMOST MUSICAL...

UNTIL AT LAST IT BECOMES...

AN EXOTIC BIRD CALL.

TROPICAL RESORT SOUNDS AND BIRDSONGS CONTINUE UNDER...

MVO: With Orange Answer Fax, you can be confident of receiving the very latest information even when you're out of the office.

Faxes can be sent directly to your Orange phone and stored, ready to be printed off at any fax machine when and where it suits you.

Phone 0800 079 three thousand, and make any space your office space with Orange.

Who said retail radio commercials for telecoms clients had to be dull? This commercial had a brilliantly simple idea based on a sound effect that conveyed the core proposition. 40 seconds proved the perfect length, allowing the idea to breathe with plenty of time for product sell. Created by Vince Chasteauneuf and Paul Kemp at WCRS London.

engineer and we consider him a sound design partner." The most challenging sound effect Coyle has had to create was the sound of a high colonic irrigation at an expensive spa. "We ran a garden hose at high volume against a downspout."

Townsend only uses sound effects if they assist paint the overall picture. "There is nothing worse than putting sound effects into an ad just for the thrill of it. If you have to foley in effects, blend them into the scene either with additional atmosphere effects or the careful use of reverb."

Gomes reminds us that sound effects and music are not novelties. "They are there to tell the story, not impede it." Nothing is sacred, he says. Some tracks work better "cold" with no music, no sound effects. "If an effect or a piece of music gets in the way, either bring it down, replace it or take it out completely."

Years ago, many radio commercials started with gongs, fanfares or ringing bells, in order to catch attention. Today, sound effects are seen in a vastly different light.

Tony Hertz describes them as radio's typography. "They should be part of the scene, and in the proper perspective, helping to make the picture but not drawing attention to themselves. But," he warns, "sound effects alone are rarely effective in creating scenes. Try a well-chosen word *to add context*."

IN the old days of radio drama, studios had a large box with different doors, door handles and buzzers that could be opened, bolted and locked, along with gravel trays for actors to walk in while reading their lines. The sound effects man might shake a metal colander filled with rice above a metal dish; as the grains of rice fell through, they replicated perfectly the sound of rain on a tin roof.

"I've always dreamed of having a foley unit," admits Dennis. "Back in the days of analog, you used to make a lot of the sound effects yourself. With things getting a lot quicker, and sound effects libraries a lot bigger, they've probably got what you want anyway." Once, for a swimming pool commercial, Dennis had to create the sound of a plaster mould being removed from a woman's ear. It couldn't be just a "pop" sound, he knew. It had to have more substance. In the end, he recorded the first "plop" of dog food dropping from a can onto a

TITLE: ATLANTIS POOLS "EAR"

Very offbeat 60-second husband-and-wife-in-bed dialogue, centred on a very singular proposition.

WIFE: *(WEARILY)* George, I've got to get some sleep.

GEORGE: Hold still.

WIFE: I can't hear you, George.

GEORGE: Of course you can't hear me, I just filled up your ear with plaster of Paris.

WIFE: Can't hear you, George.

GEORGE: Your ear is full of plaster of Paris.

WIFE: Uh?

GEORGE: If we want Atlantis Pools to build us a pool shaped like your ear, we have to give them the shape of your ear.

WIFE: Uh?

GEORGE: Your ear is the perfect prototype for a swimming pool. That should be set by now. Hold still.

SFX: *PLASTER MOULD REMOVED FROM EAR.*

WIFE: Oh!

GEORGE: Look at that fabulous detail.

WIFE: *(SARCASTIC)* Fabulous.

GEORGE: See the pointy bit?

WIFE: What?

GEORGE: Diving board goes there.

WIFE: Where?

GEORGE: And the ear lobe —

WIFE: Ear lobe?

GEORGE: That's where the patio will be. And here, where you had your ear pierced, guess what goes there?

WIFE: What goes there, George?

GEORGE: Barbecue pit!

> WIFE: Oh my God... *(CONVERSATION CONTINUES UNDER...)*
>
> MVO: Atlantis Pools can build almost any shape pool you want. And Atlantis will pay a hard cash penalty if your pool's not finished when promised. Drive out to the Atlantis display centre at 9 Springvale Road, Springvale, seven days a week.
>
> GEORGE: Sorry, love, I took the mould from the wrong ear.
>
> WIFE: Get away from me, George...
>
> GEORGE: We can't use your left ear, we have a right-hand backyard.
>
> WIFE: Don't touch me, George...

Bob Dennis eventually used dog food plopping from a can to replicate wet plaster of Paris being removed from a woman's ear in this Street Remley classic.

plate. Another classic: the 3-second sound of an elephant sitting on an air conditioner. "The sound effect didn't exist anywhere. We tried so many different things, and the end sound was a combination of elements. A stick being rubbed along a corrugated iron fence suggested metal being stretched. As the air conditioner was squashed, we recorded the springs inside an old door handle under stress. For the metal being compressed, we cut up a Coke can with shears..."

Unusual sound effects make the listener's imagination work a lot harder, he says. "There are a lot of sounds that you cannot get from a sound effects library. And it depends how much time you're willing to put in to create your own. Car horns and refrigerator doors are two problem effects. Modern car horns don't sound aggressive, modern fridges don't have the 'clunk' of old ones. If you record a modern fridge door opening, you don't know what it is. So we'd add a double sound of the door opening with rattling bottles, so you'd basically know it was a fridge without having to explain what you're doing." Likewise, car engines are difficult to reproduce on radio. "Does a BMW sound any different on radio to a Mercedes-Benz or a Peugeot?"

One of Dennis' toughest challenges was to create the effect of someone driving out of a drive-in movie with the speaker still attached to the car window. "It's not a sound effect that you will find anywhere! Your imagination goes to work and you ask, what would it sound like? I spent four hours just trying to make this one, 3-second sound. The guy in the car was having an argument with his girlfriend and he says 'Let's go home then!', forgetting all about the movie that is playing on the speaker that's hooked onto the window. So he starts up the car and begins to drive off, and you hear this stretching sound as the cord gets taut, then the window smashes as the speaker falls out." There was nothing in the script to tell the audience what was happening. The sound effect had to tell the story without verbal description. "It was difficult, and we did it back in the days when you only had a 4-track machine. There were so many effects needed to create that one scene."

FRANCIS discusses other sound effects that present problems for the engineer. "If someone is sitting in a chair, the only way the listener can know that is if I pick a chair that's noisy. I might even put a microphone down next to the chair to get the leather sound. But there are some sound effects that in their real form don't work on air. Some sound effects actually need a visual backup. An example is scissors. If someone is doing a 'cut-price sale' and says the commercial calls for scissors, I'd never use scissors but garden shears. They're bigger. Scissors have a very sharp rise time, so on radio they just go click-click-click. On television you can use them because you can see the scissors and the mind says 'that's a pair of scissors', but on radio you don't have the visual so you need to make the sound larger." *Francis often slows down sound effects, or pitches them down, so they sound "thicker".*

The weirdest sound effects Francis ever created were for a radio campaign that launched Swan Lager into the West Coast American market. Scripted by Scott Whybin, the concept positioned Swan Lager as the beer from the driest continent on earth, Australia. In the commercials, Australian naturalist Harry Butler described the creatures able to survive the harsh, dry conditions, whereas all humans had to do was crack open a can of Swan Lager. "The sounds of flying foxes, birds and insects were obtained from the national archives. The essence of each sound effect was real, but Scott wanted a human element added. One effect called for a bird-eating spider so we added a human slurp and swallow. Another was a real flying fox, mixed in with a Saab jet recorded at Adelaide airport and the *whop-whop-whop* sound of bat wings." When the commercials ran in Los Angeles, they proved so popular that a name-the-sound-effect competition extended the campaign's impact.

EMMA HILL passionately trusts sound effects to drive the whole story. "It's all part of coming up with a good concept. The sound effect can do the job of telling people what's going on. But if you also have to have someone explaining what's going on, then it's not a simple idea." She once used the sound of a doorbell followed by footsteps running through a house. The footsteps grew closer and closer throughout the commercial. The voice-over only came in right at the end and delivered the proposition of buying a bigger home from builder AV Jennings.

But if people only hear radio rather than listen to it, can a purely sound effects-driven concept work?

"Radio isn't a background medium when you've got your listeners captive in a car," explains Hill. "A lot of retailers also have radio blaring out in their stores. It's very difficult to get the attention of people working in offices with the radio on quite low — they're not allowed to have it up very loud," she admits. "But I don't worry about it. It's like when you present a television script to clients and it doesn't have any dialogue, just sounds. Nine times out of ten they'll say, but what about the people in the kitchen? How will they know what the ad was about? You can't get everybody, people are going to be in situations where they're not going to be captured, but with radio if your ad is also going to be played in the morning drivetime you know you'll get them then."

"WE like to do as much reality as we can," says Flint. Once for a wife-beating commercial, the gruesome fleshy sound was achieved by beating a side of lamb with a belt. "If there's a plate breaking in the script, we break plates. We try not to take all the sounds off discs."

Hill recalls a commercial for *The Age* newspaper: "It was about the Federal Budget and what it would mean for you — it would cost you an arm and a leg, so the commercial was a guy having his arms and legs sawn off. Philip Webster actually got a side of lamb into the studio and recorded it dropping onto the floor because he couldn't find quite the right sound elsewhere."

The question is, can the average listener tell the difference and do they care? "What makes great radio stand out is when it's not in the studio, it's when it's somewhere else, *it's when it's a real moment*," argues Hill. "Then you've achieved a lot more than the other ads, which are just information being yelled down a microphone that washes over the listener."

8

THE FINAL MIX

The final mix — or the final muddle? Just as print and television ideas can be submerged beneath a plethora of technique and technology, radio commercials also run the risk of being loved to death.

Tony Hertz says radio should have rhythm and flow, like film. "Good radio should have a 'look'. Check this out by closing your eyes while you listen and asking, is it pleasing to the ear? If it's stereo, close your eyes again. Have they simply shoved everything left and right? Or is there a 'picture' with depth, scope and colour?" But, he warns, you shouldn't hear anything in stereo that you can't hear on a small, mono radio.

Everything should be governed by the idea, says Mike Fromowitz. "You must let the idea determine whether the commercial should be minimalist or detailed with sound effects. Remember, radio is theatre of the mind." When constructing the sound of a commercial, he also takes into consideration the specific target audience being addressed and the specific stations on which it will run.

"When it comes to mixing," say Elspeth Lynn and Lorraine Tao, "*we're listening for the idea to come through.*"

Lionel Hunt is not into techno-wizardry. He puts his trust in the human voice and the spoken word.

Bob Dennis agrees. "I've seen a lot of people make *Ben Hur* productions out of something that should really have been so simple. Some of the most effective commercials I've ever heard have been just a voice, and it's been down to the performance of the actor that was used."

In Paul Tan's view, today's digital technology has created a tendency to overindulge in editing.

And too often the mix is all *too* final, says Lane Atkins. "A muddy mess; three or more separate tracks blended together to make one. Most clients want to fill every void with more and more copy." The key to a proper mix, he believes, is the consideration of all the elements from conception onwards. "Only with enough planning, and a strong account service executive, will adequate time be allowed in the script for the music and effects to occur."

Brent Hahn eschews the fancy studios that provide "geisha treatment for the entourage". Hahn has one all-digital Protools suite with KRK monitoring and outboard gear from Lexicon, TC Electronics, Mark of the Unicorn, Sony, Eventide, Focusrite, and Avalon, as well as synthesisers and samplers from Yamaha and E-mu. He can also provide a complete digital remote-recording rig for recording celebrities and athletes in locations as diverse as limousines, trailers and even shower stalls. However, he quips: "Our client's favourite piece of equipment is the Frost-Free Kenmore, with the Nintendo running a distant second."

VOICE LEVELS

"Most mixes start with the voice," explains Kenn Delbridge. "It needs to be heard clearly. Starting with the assumption that the voice track will be as loud as possible throughout the mix, everything else tends to get added in relation to the voice, literally keeping the levels at the maximum allowed — 20dB (decibels) for digital or 0dB (the centre of the VU scale) for analog, which is technically the same." Delbridge discusses subjectivity. "The unknown variable is the client. Some will ask me to crank the voice up in the mix, even if it would then be overpowering. But since the mix is already at the limit, the effect of increasing the voice is turning the rest of the elements down."

Rob Townsend says careful miking from the outset will help the final mix. "If you want the voices to blend into an outside-styled effect, for example, do not record them with too much bass. In real life, bass is generally suppressed when recording outside."

Rennie Gomes starts his mixes with the voice. "Equalise it to make sure it is nice and strong and dominates the mix. Then you can envelop the voice with atmosphere, using equalisation and reverberation."

Sometimes creatives want to combine too many different voice takes to make up one selected take. In some situations, this may be inevitable. But as Tan warns: "The voice takes must have been recorded in a similar situation — for example, in the same room, using the same microphone, and maintaining the same distance from it. Most importantly, you have to keep a sharp ear out for minute differences in tonal quality of the voice and delivery."

"De-breathing" to save airtime is another of Tan's concerns. "It may result in commercials sounding unnatural. To 'over-doctor' radio or TV commercials can sometimes be disastrous because the listeners' attention is disrupted from the intended message. This holds especially true for radio, because ultimately the radio ad will be a stand-alone item, unlike a television commercial where you have moving images as well. So before I embark on a final mix, I must have the entire edited voice track sounding as natural and smooth as possible."

BUT what kind of voices cut through best on radio — deep voices or lighter, "toppier" voices?

"The trouble is, everyone falls in love with the big deep growl," says Peter Clark. "You don't need that extra resonance at the bottom end — it sounds good on the studio speakers, but on air it will sound like a dog barking. And as soon as a bit of compression gets on it, it will make it even worse." Clark says you have to discipline yourself to roll some of the bottoms off it, otherwise the voice will be so big it will just make speakers everywhere rattle. "You can't have every part of the spectrum cutting through. If you want the cut through and clarity then you go for the edge in the voice, which is higher up around the mid-area. Leave that intact, and get rid of some of the bottom — rather than boost the top and try to leave the bottom full. That will only get you into trouble because if you push the top end too hard, you'll still have the big, boomy bottom end that is going to rattle speakers. Even if you roll *all* the bottom out of it, a big, powerful deep voice will cut through anyway — on a small speaker it's going to cut through like a buzz saw."

Dennis recalls that once all radio voices were rich, deep and booming — "down in their boots," he calls them. In terms of clarity though, what is the ideal? "Today the radio voice is more towards the natural voice, the chatty voice, and commercials have changed along those lines, too. It's more of a voice that people can associate with, it's not talking at you but *with* you and *to* you."

How Many Layers Of Sound Will Realistically Work?

"You can listen to a Pink Floyd CD a hundred times, and every time you'll hear something new. Which is fine for Pink Floyd, but this is advertising," observes Hahn. "Assume people are going to hear your radio spot once and only once. Also assume they can only perceive one thing at a time. Which means *the main job of mixing is actually sequencing — creating a perfectly timed sequence of sounds and silences*. Once that's accomplished, you can backfill your mix with as many layers as you like. But," he cautions, "just don't let those layers distract the listener from your sequence."

All too often, multiple sound effects are shoe-horned into a radio track. Sadly, in the final mix, nothing stands out, nothing breathes, and the idea is completely overpowered.

Ralph Van Dijk's solution at Eardrum: He first edits the voice tracks as though nothing else is going to be added. Then he builds up the picture by adding subtle effects, little by little. "There's a fine line between producing a multi-layered ad that is still interesting after the fourth time of hearing, and bombarding the listener with so much detail that it obscures the message. It takes experience to know when enough is enough."

When he was in the producer's chair, Antony Redman applied the same judgement he would use with any other medium. "Usually that means if it's not necessary, get rid of it. Something I tend to hear a lot in radio is wall-to-wall dialogue. No one seems to believe in letting things breathe anymore. Sometimes the use of natural pauses and breaks in action and conversation can be very effective. They might call it dead air in the radio world, but it works."

"You should only use those sounds that are truly adding something to the atmosphere you're trying to create." Linda Locke is convinced less is always more. She advocates a process of elimination. "If you don't miss it, you didn't need it in the first place."

Concurs Thomas Hripko, "In the physical sense, you're trying to create the environment. I just close my eyes and imagine what it would be like to be there. What would I hear? Where would it be coming from? But I don't spend hours on the subtleties and nuances of place. Chances are, they'll get lost over air anyway."

"You're only as good as the broadcast quality," says Garry Abbott. Anything more than three layers of sound, including the voice, is overly ambitious. "We're not all listening to radio in a studio."

BRAD POWER reflects: "Sometimes you've got a nice street sound, it makes total sense, and then someone might say why don't we put in a dog barking away in the distance? And sure, let's put in a dog barking. Sometimes I'll say why do you want to put in a dog barking? What is it going to achieve? It's much easier I've found, to put in ideas and then start taking them out as you go along in the mix." There are also issues about compression, says Power. "The dynamic range, quiet bits, loud bits, isn't so achievable when it gets on air."

"It's what you leave out, not what you put in," says David Alberts. Referencing his agency's Red Cross campaign: "There were a lot of other ambient noises, but they were distracting. In fact, it was the pauses that caused the drama. There are so many ads and station promos on air, you're in a very cluttered world, and less is definitely more."

"I don't think a lot of layers are necessary. I like to do things simply and if you do put them in, you always end up taking them out," agrees Emma Hill.

Where does Philip Webster draw the line? "Everything has to be relevant to what you're trying to get across. These days, because of the energy that digital FM radio offers, less is more. A pause in the voice still creates attention and makes us listen a little closer."

"LESS is more," avows Les Francis. "You only need the sound effects that are integral to the plot. If a commercial is taking place in someone's lounge room, you might have some air conditioning running and a radio in the background and then someone might say, why don't we have some birds? And I'll say, but we're inside, why do you want birds? And they'll say, well, the window could be open. But that is asking a lot of the listener. If we do put the birds in, the listener will be confused. Where am I? Am I inside or outside? Don't give the listener too much to think about. If you're inside, you're inside. You could have a clock, for example, but only things that augment the fact that you're inside. If you listen to it and you *believe* you're in a lounge room, you don't need any more."

Francis shares his logical approach to the layering of sound: "We've recorded the dialogue, we've cut it all, we love what's happening, so then we ask, where are we? We're in a restaurant. So the first question is, how expensive is this restaurant? The script will dictate that. If it's a couple of young kids talking, it's probably a bistro at best or it's a fast-food restaurant. But if it's a couple of adults, you'll know by the language and performance that they're a certain demographic, either blue collar or white collar. You might put them in a more expensive restaurant. Usually if you hear music and silverware, it's an expensive restaurant. I did a commercial with Street Remley where we had four men talking in a Japanese restaurant. Usually Japanese restaurants have a fairly subdued atmosphere, so we had the talent speaking rather quietly, hunched over, because that's what you do in Japanese restaurants."

The placement of effects is critical to the layering process. "Street Remley and I try and avoid what we call the 'pat' placing of effects, which is absolutely in the gaps between dialogue. In our minds, it's like 'cue the effect'. We always sneak an effect out from the end of one word, maybe through a gap and into the beginning of the next word, rather than just 'in the hole'. Sometimes you might want to underscore a word, so you put the effect there. It's an aural way of actually making the word louder in the listener's mind."

He contours sound effects around the voice, and cautions against effects in the mid-range of the aural spectrum, which is where the voice works. "If there's an effect that we really want to be loud around the voice, I'll drop out the 'middle' of the effect so the 'bottom' and 'top' can sit around the voice. That way we still hear the volume and get the relationship we want between the voice and the effect." By creating different equalisation or tone for different sounds, they can break through rather than hide each other. "Everything is almost as 'loud' as each other, without having to pull things down."

"EVERYTHING should have its weight at the right place," affirms Hertz. *"You have to leave room for things to happen, so when you mix you don't have to drag things down and bump things up.* There's no point loading all sorts of stuff into a commercial if you're not going to hear it." Atmosphere tracks are one case in point, says Hertz. "If they think about it, when people write SFX: ATMOSPHERE SHOP, what they really mean is SFX: ATMOSPHERE TRAFFIC, because the basic atmosphere of most of our urban lives is the street outside where we are. So what I tend to do in that case is to take a street sound and run it very, very low in the background so it doesn't draw attention to itself."

In fact, Hertz says *it is not really a question of mixing; it is how the commercial is written and structured*: "Orchestral recordings are still done 'live'. Because of the way the composer wrote the piece, and the way it is conducted, you don't have to go back and remix it."

He talks about the value of the *pause*: "If you don't allow yourself pauses, voice-overs will sound like voice-overs instead of real people because voice-overs don't pause. Real people have to think about what they're going to say next, and then they say it, whereas people in commercials know instantly what to say."

Because radio works on frequency of exposure, Hertz believes commercials should contain *rewards* for listeners. If you give your whole commercial away the first time, he argues, no one's going to listen to it the second time. "I like to find a balance where it's clear, but I don't care if they don't get every single word the first time. The audience should know who paid for it, but you've got to mix it so there's something left to hear. If you listen to it a number of other times, you're going to get a lot of stuff out of it — not necessarily more information, *but more colours*."

STREET REMLEY talks about placement of sound and adding perspective to the visual picture being created in the listener's mind. "It's very hard work and you just have to do it and not fool yourself into saying 'that's good enough'. A lot of scripts are very dependent on it."

Remley references a commercial by Euro RSCG Partnership Singapore for Fuji Floppy Disks. Two old folks conversed on their farmhouse verandah. The squeak of rocking chairs was close up, the crickets and frogs were further away, as was the intermittent owl. "A lot of what was being said by the old folks was conveyed by the sound of the rocking chairs. By experimenting with effects, we created the distance and ambience of a hot night in the Deep South. Some effects cancel each other out so you have to get rid of what you originally thought, like a bed of cicadas. If you can't hear the owl, you blow the cicadas."

John Culverwell has no hard and fast rule on layering. "It depends totally on the script — as many effects as are needed to create a realistic, believable backdrop."

Dennis believes there is no formula for a good mix. "You develop gut feelings through experience. When you've been through enough recording sessions, you kind of 'know'. It's your ear, or the engineer's ear. You have to treat each element individually, but the voice is always the hero. You position sounds and balance them. You can make a sound like a crow sound further away by adding some equalisation to it — in layman's terms, the bass and treble. You dial the bass out of it, thin it out, and it will sound more distant. When an engineer is doing an effects track, he plays with sounds levels, with equalisation. Each element is an individual element, even though it goes to make up the overall sound. To edit tape in analog days was a craft, an art. These days with digital workstations, editing is still a craft; it's just a different craft." Dennis compares working without digital as like trying to find a thatcher to build a roof.

CLARK looks at equalisation and compression techniques from a visual point of view. "If you've got a picture frame, the more things you want to put in the frame, the further back they have to go and the smaller they become. If you just want to see a vase, it will be right up in front of you and that's all you'll see. But if you want to see anything around the vase, the vase has to become smaller. It's the same with sound. If you need to hear the dialogue in your face, then the other things are going to suffer. But you can equalise short-length effects — door handles, bells, impact-type sounds — in such a way that they are a bit smaller and sharper, don't intrude into the voice, but still cut through from the background. You make them smaller by rolling the bass off them and sharpening them up in the upper-mid area. Sometimes, depending on the sort of sounds they are, you can sharpen them in the top end as well so they become little. Little sounds like glockenspiels and xylophones always cut through orchestras like a knife."

Once they become small, spiky, penetrating sounds, says Clark, you don't need to turn them up in terms of VU (volume). They could be well below zero decibels, but they will still cut through from the background. "You'll be able to hear your key effects, but they're not fighting with the dialogue." The same technique works for background voices, explains Clark. "Roll off all the bottoms, without even boosting the tops, and that will automatically give you an effect of them being smaller and 'toppier'."

As a rule of thumb, says Clark, "After the dialogue, you're battling to get beyond another two layers and really have everything heard. The residual noise in the listening environment — travelling in a car, or having a tap running at home in the kitchen — will kill many of the subtleties that people try to achieve in their backgrounds."

Clark believes the work of orchestral and jazz composer Henry Mancini has relevance for radio commercials, especially music tracks. Mancini pioneered "doubling", explains Clark. "Instead of having one alto flute playing a haunting melody, he'd get four playing the same melody — not playing harmonies, but all four playing in unison. So the sound was huge. He'd do that with other instrumentation, too, getting the same instrument to play the same notes on another track, or getting additional players in to play the same notes on the same instrument, always in unison." Doubling, tripling and quadrupling is now common practice to add texture to solo vocals and vocal groups, says Clark. In the soundtrack of the movie *Is Paris Burning?*, four grand pianos playing chords in unison provided the motif for the German Army. "Four grand pianos are a lot of acoustic weight," observes Clark. "They say that a grand piano is the equivalent of four musicians playing single-note instruments like a clarinet, a trumpet, a trombone. So with four grand pianos, you'd have the power of sixteen musicians."

DOES THE END VO NEED MUSIC?

Many commercials suffer from the knee-jerk desire to put library music under voice-overs. Producers and clients think the solo voice-over sounds "cold".

"Is it being used for what it can add, or simply as background wallpaper?" challenges Hertz. "Whether it's an original track or something from Rent-A-Song, music should feel as though it's been made for the commercial. When you hear speaking over the music, ideally the voice should sound as though it's part of the musical arrangement."

"Some people think the commercial's not busy enough so they slap on some library music as well, to fill in the gaps," comments Danielle Sterrie. "If you're unlucky you get the choice of library music that the producer likes and not what's appropriate to what the script is saying. You can get it really, really wrong."

"I'm not a big jingle fan," says Emma Hill. "Some clients like to put their music tag on the end, just to let people know it's their commercial. It's 'their part' of their ad. I don't think playing a jingle under the voice-over copy makes it any more memorable — if anything, it doesn't. There's so much music on radio anyway…"

JUDGING THE MIX

Neil French discusses how many layers of sound you should mix together: "As many as it takes. Depends on the brief and the script. But check through the small speakers, of course, never through the big jobs. When I was chairman of judges at Clio, I hired a bus and went on a tour of Chicago with the rest of the judges, with all the radio entrants playing over the speakers on the bus. Anything that cut through and got people's attention away from the Michael Jordan steakhouse and Al Capone's laundry was a finalist!"

Mark Rivett agrees. "Dub your mix onto a CD, and take it out for a ride in your car in peak hour traffic with all the windows wound down. If your ad stands out and still gets noticed, it's a good mix."

Clive Desmond defines his role. "I'm a track director, so it's my job to create clarity rather than muddle. To ensure our spots cut, we compress the hell out of everything." Music, he adds, is more often than not mixed way too low, "to the point of the ridiculous." He mixes with an Auratone speaker, which provides a professional narrow-band mixdown reference for small speaker comparisons.

Delbridge also uses Auratone speakers to simulate what a radio mix will sound like in a worse case, real world scenario. They allow him to judge how far he can push the mix.

Clark adds: "They've been the popular mini-monitor in music studios for decades now. They're a very good yardstick. If something sounds excessive on Auratones, you're in trouble."

Because radio sets differ widely, from low-end to high-end audiophile types, Tan uses a combination of speakers in his control room. "Accurate, flat frequency response monitoring speakers will cover the audiophile equipment; a medium set of hi-fi speakers and a low-end set of radio or car speakers cover the rest".

Cary Rueda asks for a cassette so he can hear the finished product outside the studio before he presents it to the client. "It's so easy to get insular and fall in love with your own work within the confines of a soundproof studio. But you must listen to it in the real world, in the car, or the office, or at home. Watch TV, listen to music, then stop and play the commercial..."

"No one else will be listening to your commercial in a recording studio," so Paul Fishlock suggests playing the ad to someone who wasn't involved in the session.

Nigel Dawson leaves the studio after the recording. "I believe that no writer should be around while the track is being mixed. It is vital that you hear the result with fresh ears, having allowed the engineer to add his own interpretation. It is exactly the same as a TV commercial edit. No team should sit through that." If Dawson finds the first mix is too full, he will peel away sounds for simplicity and audibility. Like Fishlock, he will play it to somebody who has not worked on the production.

Webster turns his back on the speaker, places his fingers in his ears, and listens to the mix with his eyes closed. "Can I hear all the words?" is the first test he applies, "although that's always not important these days. People are going to hear the commercial maybe a dozen times along the way. It's not like seeing a movie once. If it's a complicated commercial, I'll get someone who hasn't been involved in the mix to listen to it and see if it all makes sense."

Similarly, Francis leans back, shuts his eyes and sees if he can hear everything. "Often, if I've been in the one room listening to something for six hours, I'll patch it through to another room, say the dub room, and it's amazing what you hear or don't hear in a different room."

Hertz often mixes through a transistor radio wired to the mixing desk. "I know if it works through that, it will work through anything."

Can You Control The Way Your Commercial Will Sound On Air?

Remley talks about the way radio stations compress commercials for transmission. "Compression gives everything a uniformity of level so it isn't jarring or jumping out of the radio, so in the process of building a commercial *you have to compensate for what you know is going to happen when it gets to the stations*. We tend to make sound very 'live' because the compression that stations use will subdue and squash sound. If you don't have a biting edge to the equalisation, the commercial will sound muffled on air and all the hard work of the mix will be lost. We mix with a lot of mid-range, but not top end because that makes voices sibilant. Some engineers like to add bottom end, which very rarely gets through the radio speaker. I'm more in favour of mid-range — it keeps sounds crisp, and voices crisp, without 'spitting'."

For that reason, explains Remley, the mixes that are right when they leave his studio often alarm clients and agencies. "They'll come back and say the music or the effects are too loud for the voice. We know that they aren't, because by the time the radio station is done with them, they're going to be pushed down a lot by compression. It's a constant battle we fight and sometimes we do a mix only for the client's ear."

Trade Secret: Compression. Clark elaborates: "Broadcasting stations have to have peak limiters and compressors to control the modulation of their programmes so they aren't overloaded. They're a necessary evil, but you can do some of that processing work on your signal before your commercial goes to the station. There are two different graphs: one is called compression, a gentler process where the soft parts of the signal are brought up, and the loud parts are squashed down. That often leaves a fairly small dynamic range of maybe only 3- or 4dB. This is all very fine for the deejay's dialogue and pop songs, which have already been compressed anyway, so a little bit more doesn't seem to hurt them. But if you set up a particular balance on a commercial and you want it to be heard a certain way, you could be in for a disappointment depending on which station you hear it and how hard their on-air chain compresses the signal. I've done jobs where the client says 'No, the background's too loud, turn it right down under the voice.' Okay, fine, but go and listen to it on air. When it's broadcast, the background will come up and 'pump' — it will go up and down, up and down, between the voice-over. You're actually better off compressing your voice reasonably and bringing the music or effects up around it, so when it goes to the station there's a less radical effect on it from the compressor." In other words, the voice-over is treated almost like a vocal track.

Trade Secret: Limiting. The other half of the equation is limiting, which Clark says is more severe. "It's more linear so it just chops things off. It doesn't matter how loud your track gets over a certain threshold, that gain is held back." One of the benefits of equalising, says Clark, is that while the sharp, spiky sounds will be pushed down a little bit, they will still cut through. "They don't have to be loud in terms of VU. If they're below zero dB they'll still cut through, because they won't be touched by compression."

WHILE it may sound like technospeak, argues Tan, creatives ignore it at their peril. A cutting edge idea needs a cutting edge sound if it's going to stand out from the pack. "Digital broadcasting is commonplace nowadays and a comparison between analog and digital metering can vary greatly. Analog metering is more forgiving for very fast transients, whereas in digital metering these quick transients can be extremely sensitive. Therefore maximising bit rates, studio compression and equalisation plays a very important role. If, for example, the dynamic range of your mix varies too greatly, you may not gain a greater 'loudness' factor on air. But if you over-compress your mix, it will sound like something is masking it. Equalisation is where a lot of 'presence' and 'cut' can be brought out in the mix, especially in the voice."

Tan identifies another potential problem area for creatives: the compatibility of mono and stereo mixes. "Some mixes might sound great in stereo, but seem to shrink on mono speakers — in fact, some elements might disappear altogether. This is due to phase cancellation and incompatibility of the audio signals."

As Tan says, "Some people choose to be involved only in the creative process instead of the techie stuff. Some people say these differential techie factors constitute only a negligible portion of the commercial, but if one were to look at the big picture, these differences become significantly audible, even to the layman."

9

WORLD RADIO

Tony Hertz, whose cultural roots lie on both sides of the Atlantic, reviews the difference between American and British radio commercials. After what he describes as a "near terminal dose" of American radio ads, Hertz concludes: "Americans actually kind of like being sold to, but the Brits don't. Most US advertising — radio and TV — is out-and-out hard, medium or soft sell, with little attempt to entertain or seduce. Even in the form of 'real life' dialogue, characters in American spots converse with each other in a way that would sound hopelessly corny in Britain:

A: You oughta try Crunchie Crispies, Ken.

B: I don't see why I should try Crunchie Crispies, Don.

A: Are you kidding, Ken? Crunchie Crispies contain 35% tetracyclene dioxide!

B: 35% tetracyclene dioxide in Crunchie Crispies, Don?

To British ears, it simply wouldn't sound like real conversation. But over there, it doesn't seem to matter because it's advertising, not entertainment, which doesn't make it better, or for that matter worse, just American. And having overheard a conversation between my sister-in-law and her mother about a brand of bagels, it may even have been understated!"

Hertz believes accents are another defining factor. "I don't want to get into class politics, but to my ears the fundamental difference between the US and Britain is that in America the accent spread is horizontal, while in Britain it's vertical. Say you went to Cincinnati and recorded the CEO of Procter & Gamble reading some copy, and then had a foreman in the company's shipping department read the same thing. A listener who didn't know either person would be hard-pressed to tell who had what job, even if one of them had a regional accent. If you did the same thing in Britain, you'd be able to tell instantly who had the higher position. So what does that mean in terms of radio ads? Only that American spots are populated by characters with attractive voices who are actually harder to picture as characters because their social positions are less obvious. In that sense, British spots are more interesting because class forms part of the comedy, even when it's not referred to. In other words, much British comedy is expressed by who the character *is*, while for the most part American comedy is based purely on what a character *says*."

The crucial question, asks Hertz, is which is the more mind-numbing: "Hours of American radio ads — earnest, sincere, unaccented salesmanship? Or hours of British spots — deeply sociological, desperately trying to be funny and not selling?"

AT the London International Advertising Awards, Danielle Sterrie listens to each of the 2,000 radio entries submitted every year from the UK, the US, Asia, Australia and South Africa. "You hear some real dross, but ultimately you hear some fantastic work is still being created. Every year I feel that radio is very underrated. It's still regarded as the poor cousin in the world of advertising which is so sad because if you get it right, you can do so much more with radio. It can have so much more impact and cost a fraction of a TV commercial that is trying to create the same effect." In her view, the countries consistently doing the best radio commercials are Australia, South Africa, the US and Canada.

Tham Khai Meng, Ogilvy & Mather's regional creative director for Asia, is also well-placed to give an overview of global radio creativity. Tham was a member of the first non-English language jury at D&AD

in 2002 chaired by Marcello Serpa, with Michael Conrad, John Hegarty, Donald Gunn and Mohammed Khan. He also judged radio at the Clio awards and recalls: "Bud Light's *Real American Heroes* had such a great, brilliant idea it won the Grand Clio. It conjured up images in your head. It used humour, and was beautifully and economically done, whereas radio in Asia still doesn't use ideas. It's all about penetration of noise with no iota of an idea. People haven't really thought about using radio as an interesting, cutting edge medium." Tham says young Asian creatives should develop their aural sensory perceptions. "Pretend you're blind, or write a commercial with a blind person. These are the people who use their aural capacities as we use our eyes. You still need an idea behind a great radio script…"

A WRITER'S perspective: John Kyriakou has worked as a creative director in Australia, the UK, Singapore and Canada. "I found neither TV nor print presented dramatic differences from country to country. But when a radio brief came to me, the sooner I could pass it on, the better — usually to a creative team who grew up in the market! *Radio is the one medium that allows you to explore the true culture of a community.*"

Language nuances and idiosyncrasies, local culture, local concerns, humour, music and situations should all be exploited to make radio advertising effective because they are what makes radio effective as a medium.

"Hence, writing for radio is less universal — and more difficult," Kyriakou reflects. "Understanding and appreciating a culture goes a lot deeper than throwing an 'eh?' on the end of a script in Canada, or a 'lah' on the end of a sentence in Singapore."

As a medium, radio does not change from country to country. "Radio is still about engaging through listening. It's still about stories. But a story written for Toronto, Canada, won't work in Melbourne, Australia. A story written for a Top 40 station in the UK won't work on a morning talk show in Singapore."

Kyriakou's advice: "When you move to a new country, listen to the radio. It gives you a great sense of local issues and personalities, of the way people think and feel in the same place where you live and work."

WHEN the BBC was founded, its lofty credo was "Nation shall speak peace unto nation". After 80 years, it is interesting for marketing communications specialists to review how various radio markets speak unto themselves.

AUSTRALIA

In arguably the world's second oldest commercial radio market, 245 Australian stations generated advertising revenue of US$370 million in the year 2000–2001. Radio was the only advertising medium that increased its share of advertising expenditure, earning over 8% of Australia's total adspend. On average, Australian radio listeners spend three hours a day listening. Industry studies have shown that radio outreaches any other medium from 5.30am to 6pm; in fact, one in five food and grocery shoppers listen to radio within the two hours prior to setting foot in a supermarket.

Twelve networks own 80% of the stations. The Australian Radio Network, jointly operated by Clear Channel Communications of the US and APN (an acronym for Australian Provincial Newspapers), broadcasts to more than 3.5 million listeners each week. APN News & Media, an Asia-Pacific media company, is Australasia's largest radio broadcaster with investments in 12 Australian metropolitan stations and 55 radio stations in New Zealand, and interests in newspapers, educational publishing and pay television. APN's largest shareholder is Independent News & Media plc of Dublin.

The Austereo group operates the Today Network and the Triple M Network, with two FM stations in Sydney and Melbourne, as well as stations in Brisbane, Adelaide, Perth, Canberra and Newcastle.

Interestingly, Britain's Daily Mail Group has emerged as a major player in Australian commercial radio. Commencing operations from its Adelaide headquarters in October 1996, DMG Radio Australia is now the largest network in the country with 62 metropolitan and regional stations. It has accumulated more licences than any other Australian broadcaster, mainly by acquiring existing stations in regional areas.

Legendary Australian adman John Singleton owns two AM stations in Sydney, 873 2GB and 1170 2CH. In the ACNielsen radio ratings survey, May 2002, 2GB was the number one rating talk station in that city.

TITLE: AUSTRALIAN CONSOLIDATED PRESS "BEER GUT"

Straight from a romantic novel (well, almost), an Aussie girl remembers her first encounter with an Aussie bloke. Translation: thongs are cheap slippers you hold on with your big and second toes, Stubbies is a brand of shorts favoured by labourers and usually worn low on the hips, Bundy is short for Bundaberg Rum, and a sheilah is a woman.

SFX:	*SOFT, ROMANTIC MUSIC UNDER.*
AUSSIE GIRL:	It was the way his beer gut wobbled under his singlet that first caught my eye…
	His rubber thongs clip-clopped as he glided to the bar, an alluring inch of bum crack peeping from his navy blue Stubbies.
	I'll never forget Robbo's first words… "A Bundy and Coke for the sheilah, thanks."
	He shared so much with me that night, including the pizza he'd had earlier in the evening…
SFX:	*MUSIC ENDS.*
FVO:	It's hard for Aussie girls to find a great single man, but in *CLEO* there's 50 of them. Australia's 50 most eligible bachelors in February *CLEO*.

Relevance is everything on radio. In this economically scripted 30, Australian women's magazine CLEO addressed the innermost fears — and dreams — of every Australian woman. Agency: The Campaign Palace Sydney.

TITLE: VIRGIN COLA

A young English voice, a "bit of a lad", streetwise and cheeky, underscores the brand's British anti-establishment origins and values. Duration: 45 seconds.

SFX: *A REGULAR MUSIC BEAT IS HEARD UNDER THROUGHOUT...*

VO: Tell you what, you've got to be really careful when you advertise this Virgin Cola stuff.

SFX: *CAN OF COLA BEING OPENED.*

VO: I mean, as promotional ambassador, I can't just say, "Excuse me, sir, have you had a Virgin today?"

SFX: *SOUND OF SOMEONE BEING PUNCHED.*

VO: See, it's riddled with innuendo.

I can't just waddle onto a beach and say, *(THROUGH LOUD HAILER, SEAGULLS IN BACKGROUND)* "Hey, hands up who wants a Virgin," or do a radio advert that says, *(MOCK VOICE-OVER DELIVERY)* "Hurry to your cola emporium — there's a fresh Virgin waiting." There'd be an outcry!

SFX: *SCREAM IN THE BACKGROUND FOLLOWED BY SPED-UP TELEPHONE BABBLE.*

VO: The moral custodians would be whining on the phone before you could say, "Throw me another Virgin. This one's empty, John." So I'll keep it nice and uncontroversial. Virgin Cola is brown, fizzy and out there.

The power of a radio monologue, with a healthy dose of irreverence.
Virgin Cola from Grey Worldwide Melbourne.

Over the next three years, the Australian Government's "Black Spots" programme will extend the industry's coverage to an additional 360,000 Australians in areas with poor or no commercial radio reception.

As they are in America, regional stations are the backbone of the industry and deejays still have to go to the "bush" to serve their apprenticeship. Nowadays, country radio is hubbed from major centres. One Sydney-based talkback radio star John Laws is heard on 70 stations around Australia. Thanks to new technology, his specially pre-recorded local inserts are seamlessly integrated into his national broadcast. So sophisticated has this become that at the Australian Film Television and Radio School, the syllabus for the Graduate Diploma of Commercial Radio Broadcasting actually includes a subject called "Panelling the John Laws Show".

Joan Warner, chief executive officer of Commercial Radio Australia, the industry federation, believes that an increasingly competitive media environment has meant that agencies, stations and clients now focus heavily on creative that cuts through. "We are so committed to the development and improvement of radio creativity that we have launched a creative archive on our website and joined forces with AWARD, the Australasian Writers and Art Directors Association — the creative authority in Asia-Pacific — to encourage and nurture radio creativity."

Cost effective production values, she says, allow radio to create images for brands that take listeners on a journey that may not be within any major client's budget.

Gazing into the crystal ball, Warner predicts that digital radio could change the way Australian listeners interact with their radios. "We are looking at testing a range of value-ads as part of our Sydney-based digital trials, including text, graphics, rewind radio, stills and interactivity. New programming formats are also challenging the current thought process on what audiences want…"

CANADA

Canada is the second largest country in the world after Russia, and encompasses six time zones. Radio, according to Canadian creative director Carl Jones now based at BBDO Mexico, spans the vast distances. "In my opinion, some of the best radio in the world comes from Canada because sometimes campaigns are created solely for radio."

Some 1,400 radio stations serve Canada. The CBC (Canadian Broadcasting Corporation) is a public radio service like Britain's BBC, with a station in every market. The rest are private. AM stations are mostly talk format, FM stations mostly music. With rare exceptions, radio advertising is primarily a support medium to television and print. As Paul Ruta of D'Arcy Toronto observes, "So many spots always end with, 'See newspaper for details'. It implies the tragically secondary status suffered by radio advertising. You never see a newspaper ad that ends with, 'Hear radio for persuasion'..."

Toronto stations serve a catchment of ten million people with very specific programming. While English predominates, stations broadcast in French, Italian, Mandarin, Greek and even Urdu.

Because Canada has two national languages, English and French, campaigns are often created in English then translated into French. Jones believes creativity is often compromised. "Language has many subtleties and sometimes these cannot be translated."

Ruta references his experience as a creative director in Asia. "French in Canada, like Mandarin in Singapore, is as much about a cultural difference as a linguistic one. It's more than words; it's ideas. A straight translation is a wasted opportunity. We sit down with the French writers, take them through the brief, the objectives, how we approach it in English, then leave the rest up to them."

At Toronto agency Zig, separate concepts are generally created for each language because radio is relatively inexpensive to produce. Unlike TV, Elspeth Lynn and Lorraine Tao rarely receive a brief for radio that requires both English and French versions of the same script.

Ad literacy is high, and radio advertising in Canada can afford to be subtle in terms of strategy and execution. Listening attitudes are not passive and humour is generally the order of the day.

Interestingly, Canadian radio has a Canadian content ruling, nicknamed the "Can Con". A minimum 40% of all music broadcast must be written or performed by Canadians, or recorded in Canada.

As Ruta reflects, "This was a truly heinous ruling when it was first imposed in the early 1970s, because there was so little for programmers to choose from: Gordon Lightfoot, Anne Murray and The Guess Who." Over the years though, Ruta believes it has nurtured a national music industry and the quality of Canadian music today is nothing to be embarrassed about.

CHINA AND SINGAPORE

"A great creative idea in Chinese is the same as a great creative idea in English — it would be single-minded," reports Lim Sau Hoong, CEO and executive creative director of 10AM Communications Singapore. Lim's agency creates Chinese-language campaigns for use in China and across Asia, and she frequently judges Chinese award shows. "First you have to think from the nature of the medium itself. You can't see it, you can't read it, you can only listen to it. So the use of the medium should be based on the audio form. Sometimes it can be a clever use of language, a jingle, a conversation, humour or an emotionally touching story. Language shouldn't be a barrier. A good idea is a good idea. Chinese radio, English radio, it's the same."

Lim's passion for radio was nurtured when she was a Mandarin deejay on Singapore radio in her student days. She learned how imagination can be tapped on radio: "When you are sitting in the studio all alone, you know your audience can be anywhere. You imagine they are there, facing you, and you have to make your voice and content appealing to them." Later she attended a Street Remley radio workshop in Tasmania.

As a spoken language, Chinese relies on different tones to communicate the meaning of a word. Mandarin, for example, has four tones and the sound *ma* can mean a mother or a horse, depending on the tone value used. "For Chinese, pronunciation and clarity are very important, and you need the voice to be mixed more upfront. Clients prefer more authoritative male voices. Female voices are not very popular in Mandarin." Lim often involves theatrical people and casts from all over Asia. She once went to Taiwan to get the right voice for a 5-year-old boy. The Beijing *Ren Yi* performance school is another source of talent.

Mandarin, however, is very formal. In Singapore, where the

correct use of Mandarin is officially encouraged, even one or two words of dialect are out of the question. "Language in commercials has to reflect the spoken language and a lot of Singaporeans don't speak in proper Beijing Mandarin," Lim reflects. "So if your characters are speaking proper Mandarin they don't really appeal to the consumers. In Hong Kong, where Cantonese is spoken, they can write what they speak."

Music, however, offers surprising scope. A lot of Western music has crossed over into Chinese culture. Lim has used Schubert in her commercials and even Indian music on one occasion. "Music and sound effects should complement the idea itself and not just be put there for the sake of putting them there." To demonstrate how a Carrier air conditioner could switch itself on and off automatically, Lim used notes played on a cello. "A cello is so Western, but doesn't have an *ang moh* (Western) feel."

Her work reflects theatre of the mind and humour. "You want to hear conversation, you don't want to see the faces, you want to have room for imagination, and radio does this well." Her award-winning commercial for the Conrad Hotel Singapore's Chinese restaurant was written at Ogilvy & Mather with Chua Li Ling. "The Empress Dowager was scolding a high-pitched eunuch. He was sent in search of the best Chinese food. It was very bizarre."

Using music and the voice of a young girl, Lim created an intriguing commercial for Scotts Emulsion. The girl's lyrics began:

"My clothes are too small, I can't wear them, what happened…?

"My toys are too small, I can't play with them, what happened…?"

The idea was that the girl was growing up on Scotts Emulsion. "It was very subtle. The little girl was very cute. You didn't have to see her face." As Lim says about radio, "Close your eyes, listen, hear to believe … it's stronger. Your imagination can go wild…"

HONG KONG

"Ninety-nine percent of Hong Kong radio ads are in Chinese," advises

KC Tsang, former executive creative director of BBDO Hong Kong and now a partner in Chan Tsang Wong & Mee Advertising Firm, a new agency run entirely by creatives. "Almost all Hong Kong creatives do not have any experience in writing radio ads for Westerners."

Radio advertising, he says, is not well-developed in terms of creative technique, production quality, audience mentality and appreciation. The use of sound effects, popular in Western radio commercials, would not gain attention in Hong Kong. "The listening environment for Hong Kongers is normally chaotic. Humour is about the only thing that can make a radio ad work here. I guess it is people's instinct to listen to jokes. Unfortunately, writing jokes is not easy at all, so you can hear a lot of formularised jokes on Hong Kong radio."

Tsang advocates keeping radio ads short and focused. "Start with a strong device, have one theme throughout the ad, leave an image in the audience's mind, and end with a memorable device." Tsang's award-winning work for telecom company Sunday includes an hilarious radio campaign in which people talked rubbish to each other. "The idea was that Sunday's IDD price was so low that you could afford to talk rubbish, real rubbish, with anyone you know, think you know, or don't know…"

INDIA

Until the invasion of television, radio was the soul of the nation, reports Ravi Deshpande, chairman and creative director of the Lemon agency, Mumbai (Bombay). Deshpande is also consultant chief creative officer for Euro RSCG India and the Middle East. "People listened to cricket and hockey broadcasts, political speeches, movie songs and drama. The image that springs to mind is a small transistor attached to the ear of each and every person during a cricket match." Yet, he says, radio as a medium has not evolved over time.

With 195 broadcasting centres, 283 transmitters covering 97% of the population, and 100 million sets in use, radio is big business. The government-controlled All-India Radio was once the only medium that reached deep into every corner of the country, and only recently have privatised FM stations entered the scene. Licences for 108 stations were granted initially to 16 Indian-owned companies; foreign players are effectively barred from the medium.

A mix of programmes is transmitted in the national language, Hindi, as well as regional languages: news, current affairs, songs from Indian movies, countdown pop shows, *bhajans* (mythological and religious songs), Indian classical, Hindi pop, and sponsored programmes covering financial, farming and cooking tips. News and Indian movie songs have the highest listenership. One of the longest running radio dramas, *Hawa Mahal*, still airs while news programmes still follow the traditional format: a single newsreader presents the headlines, then elaborates on each story, followed by sports news and weather forecasts. FM stations broadcast Hindi and Western pop to more sophisticated urban audiences.

"Radio commercials in India were predominantly jingle-based, or were hard sell ads where the anchor repeated the brand name after every second sentence." Nowadays, says Deshpande, more dialogue-based commercials are produced. "There are a few humorous dialogue commercials that reflect real life, and enough that are simplistic."

Deshpande describes his own radio creative style as flexible, but admits he does tend to write humour. He prefers to tell most of the story with sound, without too many words, "just like in TV commercials where you make the visuals tell most of the story. I wrote a radio spot for a music system that offered powerful sound. The commercial was just the sound of a building crashing, followed by a voice-over that said 'Philips Powerhouse, 600 watts of sound'."

Malaysia

The big three networks — AMP (Airtime Management & Programming), RTM (Radio Television Malaysia) and THR (Time Highway Radio) — operate 33 FM stations broadcasting in English, Bahasa Malaysia, Mandarin, Cantonese and Tamil, with nine other stations airing on ASTRO satellite television. Radio currently accounts for 4% of the national adspend in a multicultural market of 22 million people. AMP's ERA FM, a Bahasa Malaysia station, has the biggest audience; AMP's HITZ FM is the most popular English language station. AMP's executive director Borhanuddin Osman reports that his network has 60% market share, cybercasts, and points to interactive media as the way forward.

With the rise of American-style formatting, Malaysian radio offers inexpensive opportunities to target tightly segmented audiences. One creative director, Cary Rueda at Dentsu Young & Rubicam, calls it a sleeping giant whose glory days have yet to come.

"Unfortunately, most marketing people don't believe that subtlety sells," Rueda laments. "With no visuals to guide the consumer, that insecurity gets worse with radio. The airwaves are dominated by in-your-face reminder ads, replete with phone numbers and price tags mentioned twice within 30 seconds. The primal fear of clients is not being understood, or being misunderstood."

Rueda perceives radio as daunting. "The only restrictions are the ones you yourself create. Radio can be hard-hitting, the jab right in the gut, especially for public service or political ads. A few years ago we did a radio commercial for a women's aid organisation. It just played on the sounds of a normal household — a TV set, an electric fan, a crying baby. The voice-over talked about the normal day-to-day activities in a household, while the sounds became darker and more ironic. A few weeks after its airing our client called us almost in tears, thanking us because the commercial actually prompted a few women to walk out and leave their abusive husbands. It felt good to be able to actually do some good and to think, 'it's only advertising'."

At Leo Burnett Malaysia, executive creative director Yasmin Ahmad says humorous commercials work best in Malaysia. "Malaysians may laugh at things other people don't, but they like to laugh just like anyone else. Sad to say, jingles work too, but I believe that just because you have to sing about a product doesn't mean you have to do it in a stupid and uninteresting way." Her preference is for the storytelling genre, but she is guided by the brand's essence. "I start by thinking of ordinary situations, then I put them out of their context."

At Naga DDB, creative director Ted Lim believes campaigns like *Real American Heroes* — using humour, music and sound effects — work every time, everywhere. "Commercial art imitating life," is how

TITLE: UNITED OVERSEAS BANK VISA CARD "PAWN PROMO"

A typical Chinese pawnbroker delivered this 40-second monologue.

ANNCR: The following is a paid announcement.

SFX: *TAPPING ON MICROPHONE.*

AH LONG: Hello? Hello? Okay.

Hi, my name is Ah Long from Ah Long Pawnshop. Do you need cash fast? Do you have something emergency to pay for? I can help you. For a limited time only, I will give you extra value on diamond lings, Lolex, even Seiko watch. So come, okay? And please-ah … don't listen to that UOB Bank. They say if you apply for a new UOB Visa Card, you get ten thousand cash advance at zero interest for seven months. Come on, lah. You think really can? UOB, you all must be crazy. Anyway, don't forget. Ah Long Pawnshop. My address is number 8, Jalan Pu — *(CUT OFF)*

A Chinese pawnbroker complains about the United Overseas Bank's special interest-free cash advance to new Visa Card applicants. Agency: Naga DDB Malaysia.

he describes his agency's campaign for United Overseas Bank's Visa Cards. The first spot is a monologue by a Chinese pawnshop owner complaining about the bank's interest-free cash advance. The second, sung like a Bollywood movie soundtrack, is an Indian moneylender with a similar grudge. Lim says copywriters should listen to what's been done and try not to do the same. They should also be aware of life around them. "Go sit in a crowded restaurant, or go to a *pasar malam* (night market), and eavesdrop. Keep your ears close to the ground." He advocates an open approach to production, and encourages others to contribute ideas. "Go into production with something in mind, but try not to dictate. Let the talent and studio do their thing. The outcome may change your mind."

"Radio commercials should have a singular message and the brand should be prominent," believes Tony Lee, chief executive officer of Batey Ads Malaysia. "Radio is a fleeting medium and the audience is invariably doing something else when they receive the message. Lengthy monologue radio commercials will not be effective, nor will complicated plots. Radio is an excellent medium to build brand awareness and because it is relatively inexpensive, it can do this rapidly. The brand should speak in the tone and manner that is relevant without losing sight of the brand essence portrayed in other media. Very often you find a brand sounding different on radio in an attempt to stand out or entertain. By the same token, running a TV soundtrack on radio is a waste of money." While Lee cautions against copying the West, he condemns the use of *Manglish* — "Malaysian English" — a local phenomenon that mixes English, Malay and Chinese dialects. "Humour works if it is scripted and executed well, but invariably we are deluded with slapstick humour and *Manglish*-style spots. A deep Indian accent is heard, followed by a lost voice in broken English with a sprinkling of Hokkien dialect, and another accent taking the mickey. Then here's the brand, and to top it off, here's that deep Indian voice again. That is pretty much the premise and format, and I can only describe it as irritating. The intention is to humour me, but not everyone can tell a joke properly..."

Borhanuddin, a former adman with JWT, O&M, Lintas and Dentsu Young & Rubicam, echoes Lee's call for simplicity. "A good radio

TITLE: NIKE "ANACONDA"

A compelling, matter-of-fact voice with jungle atmosphere throughout. Duration: 40 seconds.

SFX: *ESTABLISH AND SUSTAIN JUNGLE ATMOSPHERE...*

MVO: If you are attacked by an anaconda, do not run.

Lie flat on the ground.

Put your arms against your sides, your legs against one another.

The snake will nudge and climb over your body.

Do not panic.

After it has examined you, the anaconda will suck your legs into its body.

Lie still.

When the reptile has reached your neck, and you can see the white of its eyes, remember one thing...

You could have escaped, if you had been wearing...

SFX: *BACKGROUND FADES OUT FOR LAST WORD...*

MVO: Nikes.

Grim humour for Nike by Dentsu Young & Rubicam Malaysia won international awards.

commercial can just be a single voice. It shouldn't have too many elements, just one or two, but not crowded. Let the listener imagine with the theatre of the mind."

Rueda confirms that TV is still regarded as the most effective medium in Malaysia to get immediate awareness for mass-market products, with radio used as strong support. High-involvement products like automobiles or specialised services like management consultancies, he says, can use radio; anything that requires more information or scrutiny would need more than just radio. He calls radio a paradox: the most involving and intimate medium which consumers tend to treat with indifference.

Until recently, Malaysian creatives could only cast from a pool of voice talent "pre-approved" by the broadcasting authorities. "Now fresh new talent can be used," Rueda reports. "The challenge to all of us is to discover raw, untested voices that can put more truth, flesh and blood into our radio characters." Rueda tried one of his writers, Alvin Ng, as the voice in a Nike radio commercial called *Anaconda*. "Written by Edward Ong, it went on to win Gold awards in the London International Advertising Awards and the New York Festivals." As Rueda observes, "Now that we don't have to sound like each other, the battle to stand out becomes even more complex."

Yasmin's advice to young creatives is applicable in markets beyond her own: "One, live and mix with society at large, so you've got your finger on its pulse. That way, your stories will always be relevant. Two, read or listen to radio ads that win awards all over the English-speaking world, so you have an idea of how to execute your work."

MEXICO

With 850 AM and 488 FM stations, Mexico's language is Spanish. English programmes are broadcast for the 250,000 Americans and Canadians living in Mexico City, as well as for expatriate retirees and tourists at the beaches of Cancun, Acapulco and Puerto Vallarta.

Vice president and creative director of BBDO Mexico Carl Jones observes that without dedicated radio creative companies, the agency copywriter is in control of directing the actors and the mix. "As a result, the level of quality isn't as good."

Horacio Mancilla, former senior writer at BBDO Mexico and now a deejay on Mexico City's ALFA 91.3, believes radio commercials should have "a sound, a word, or even a silence, that captures the listener's attention. Something that separates that single spot from the rest of the noise." In order to write dialogue-driven ads, Mancilla believes you need "to have an ear for the world you live in, to be able to repeat the words a taxi driver uses when he talks to you, or a politician in a speech. The secret is to listen carefully to how they speak the words they use, to sharpen your ear to that, and then just transfer it to paper."

Jorge Soldevilla at BBDO Mexico looks for funny situations that happened to him. "I see if I can relate them to the basic promise. If I can't, I start inventing stories that the target market can relate to." At the same agency, creative director Efren Murillo starts with the key benefit and seeks personal experiences, consumer insights, or sounds and words that provoke images which intersect with the benefit he wants to communicate.

Another senior writer Miguel Ullivari, formerly with Ogilvy, Leo Burnett and BBDO in Mexico, narrows his focus to aural references. "Radio draws on everything you have heard — music, jokes, conversations, dialogue, even bedtime stories. Explore them all. The more things you can remember, the more new ideas you can come up with."

Like their counterparts in other countries, Mexican creatives are preoccupied with their final mixes. A BBDO creative director Miguel Moreno mutes effects, one by one, to determine if they are important enough to be included in the final mix. "If you don't need it, take it out. If you really need it to help the idea, put it back again."

THE PHILIPPINES

Expect to hear parodies of politicians selling anything from instant noodles to bank loans — radio commercials happily celebrate the nation's unique political freedom, reports Philippine creative guru David Guerrero who once satirised Ferdinand and Imelda Marcos in a commercial. "It was based on the Marcos family escaping by chopper from the mob outside the Presidential Palace, and needing *Money Magazine* to plan their future investments."

According to Guerrero, co-founder of premier creative agency BBDO/Guerrero Ortega, radio commercials can be extremely inventive in the Philippines. "Lots of humour, dialogue, parody, and not as many jingles as you might think! However, the low cost of the medium leads to frequent excesses by advertisers and agencies alike. Full-length songs are not as unheard of as most people would like. And media plans are written with a view to overkill. On AM, the reverb button is rarely off, and noise and repetition are the order of the day. This can have a certain kitschy appeal to the outsider, but probably not so much to the audience."

Apart from political freedom, Guerrero observes that Filipinos are not afraid to make fun of themselves and their own accents. "There are many plays on Filipino quirks such as words beginning with 'p', which are often *misfronounced*!"

The Philippines was a pioneering radio nation. American businessmen issued with temporary permits set up the first stations in the early 1920s. Regular commercial broadcasting began officially on 30 December 1930 when KZRM went to air, owned and operated by the Radio Corporation of the Philippines, the distributor of RCA radios. By the mid-1980s, when FM radio sets became more affordable, listenership began shifting away from AM. Today, seven hundred AM and FM radio stations operate nationwide, AM broadcasting mainly news and talk shows in Tagalog, while FM concentrates on music and mostly broadcasts in English.

Guerrero says creatives are not afraid to experiment on radio, "sometimes embarrassingly so". Humour is always a staple, but tends to be formulaic. "There are some attempts to dig into real-life dialogue and situations, but too often the temptation to slip into easy stereotypes seems too strong for creatives to resist. Over the last few years radio has lacked a 'headline' commercial that has really got people talking and entered the culture, the way that TV spots have done." Crude over-branding is another concern. "People don't put six logos on ads, so why do they mention the name six times in a radio commercial?"

His creative director David Ferrer also calls for breakthrough radio. "Radio has been the favourite medium for writers around here for a long time. It has been the means to communicate with the masses. Through the years clients have gravitated towards jingles and spell-it-out approaches to reach their target markets. Recently however, fewer and fewer creatives have bothered to explore the strengths of the medium. Humour is still the popular way to sell. Some have injected humour into local customs and habits, some punch humour into current events. Still a lot of attempts are far too slapstick and contrived. In fact, in local award shows there are fewer radio entries compared to TV and print."

Guerrero believes radio offers lots of unexploited areas in terms of drama and characterisation if creatives invest the time and patience to develop them. "The biggest problem is allowing yourself to think big with radio and give it enough scope. There aren't that many great radio reels to listen to, so getting inspiration to get started isn't that easy." His advice to young creatives: "Write lots of speculative commercials. They cost next to nothing to produce, next to nothing to air, and consequently take next to no effort to sell. *It's probably the last medium left where no one has really taken ownership.*"

THAILAND

"The power of radio in Thailand is underestimated," asserts the doyen of Thai creatives Bhanu Inkawat, former chairman and executive creative director of Leo Burnett Thailand. "People in Thailand spend a lot of time in cars, frustrated by traffic problems. They have a lot of time to kill and listen to a lot of radio programmes. But most of the spots are boring. They don't play with emotions."

According to Inkawat, Thai radio commercials are one-way communications. Creatives, he says, should get to know the mood of the listeners and communicate with them in an interesting way. "But radio is the last thing creatives want to get involved in, it's not glamorous like TV and print."

Thailand's television creativity is recognised around the world for its engaging, often bizarre, humour. "Humour is the key," he believes. "People are sitting in their car, their minds are drifting, and they need something to lighten them up. We can tap into insights and touch them. We can put them somewhere else in their imagination. The most important thing is to make people feel they are taking part in the situation and in the commercial."

Inkawat says most cars are air conditioned so outside sounds do not intrude on the listener's attention. Creatives have the opportunity to experiment with sound effects, but should not lose sight of the message. He advocates natural-sounding commercials and will use any voice that is interesting and appropriate. "Once there were only two professional voices in Bangkok. We kept using them all the time. Now we find people off the street, even our own creative people, anybody — as long as their voices are natural, have real character and are interesting."

He references a radio campaign his agency developed for the Tourism Authority of Thailand to stimulate domestic travel. "It was about how people lived their lives every day, and how they promised themselves they would go away for a holiday, one day... It was entertaining, but touched a lot of people's feelings. They had forgotten what life means. They were missing out because of work and day-to-day pressures. The best thing they could do was pick up the phone, call the Tourism Authority of Thailand and find out about a good resort town..."

As Khanitta Khanittanan, director of creative resources at Leo Burnett Thailand, explains: "We wanted Thai people to take a break. They'd been working very hard day and night, and we wanted them to visit upcountry or a resort town for a long weekend, somewhere they hadn't been before. We got an idea from a famous speech given to Harvard graduates that started with the line, 'If I had anything to advise you...' and we added, 'it is to spread your sunscreen lotion...' We took a very honest, very sincere approach, like talking to a friend."

One commercial asked which is more important — money or your family? The listeners were given two choices: they could go to their bank, withdraw a lot of money, and take it home for the night. Or they could leave work early, go home, hug their wife and children, and stay a night with their family, and then compare the feelings.

In another commercial, the listeners were told they were locked in a lift with only enough oxygen to last fifteen minutes. In that moment, they were asked what they would be thinking, what hadn't they done? Had they been to see their parents, had they written a letter to an old friend, had they gone to visit their old teacher...?

A good ad will always stand out, Khanittanan says. Humour lets you ambush the audience. "We had ghost stories on radio, with the sound of a dog howling. We ambushed listeners by saying that if you're driving your car in the middle of the night, and you suddenly felt very cold, you'd better change your car's air conditioner."

She believes phone numbers have to be made memorable on radio. Another agency had turned the phone number of MK sukiyaki restaurant into a laugh to promote home delivery of Thai sukiyaki hotpot with transparent noodles. "In Thai, five is *ha*. So their number 248 5555 became *song si pad ha-ha-ha-ha...*"

Leo Burnett Thailand art director Andrew Bell is responsible for regional Asian radio campaigns for his clients. "They have to be based on strategy and advertising ideas," he stresses, "not 'funny voices'." He is involved in the briefing and approval process; each country then executes its own commercials. Bell favours involving deejays, "because they're the reason people tune to a particular station."

"Radio is always low budget, and never given great priority by anybody, because it's not a big income earner. It seldom engages creatives, and the creative director and art directors seldom get involved." Using "funny voices" is everybody's recourse in Thailand, he says, just as it is in the West. "The great failing of a lot of radio is that it's not based on ideas, it's based on 'funny voices'."

A MARKET WITHIN A MARKET: ASIAN AMERICAN RADIO

Asians are the fastest growing racial group in America, recording 49% growth in the decade since the 1990 census, reports Saul Gitlin, executive vice president of strategic marketing services at Kang & Lee. "While 11.2 million Asians represent only 4.2% of the American population, they boast the highest average household income (US$7,000 ahead of Caucasian Americans), the highest level of education and the highest rates of entrepreneurial activity. They possess the highest home computer penetration and the highest Internet usage." Well over 80% are clustered in a handful of centres — California, New York, Hawaii, Washington State, Texas, Illinois, Massachusetts, Washington DC and Georgia. Asian Americans are mostly Chinese, Filipino, Asian Indian, Vietnamese, Korean and Japanese, with a small percentage of Thais, Cambodians and Laotians.

Gitlin says over 600 media vehicles serve Asian Americans. Broadcast media is limited though, and radio is very cost effective: a prime 60-second spot in a major market may cost as little as US$50 to US$90. The value becomes even more compelling in southern California, where the single largest concentration of Asians lives. Along with their fellow motorists, they become a vast captive audience for drivetime radio.

Kang & Lee Advertising, now a division of Young & Rubicam, was founded in 1985 by two Korean American admen, Eliot Kang (now the president and CEO) and Kevin Lee. It is the largest full service agency focusing on the Asian American market, with specialist ethnic teams targeting different Asian audiences.

The agency's award-winning creative director Dennis Chang confirms that humour works in Asian American radio, but not dry humour or sarcasm. The Chinese language is rich with proverbs, idiomatic set phrases and, like Korean, has a high incidence of homophones or near-homophones. Word plays abound in radio ads. Chang recalls one of his own concepts: "The concept revolved around a play on words — 'cha' which means tea and 'chia' which means putting on medicine. The radio spot targeted Chinese taxi drivers and played on the notion of taking a break for tea. However, in this case, the commercial was for a local ointment for haemorrhoids and the driver was taking a break not for 'cha' but to 'chia'..."

While the agency uses media channels uniquely positioned to Asians, Chang argues that his target audience still resides in the greater US and is therefore constantly exposed to American culture. "Despite the fact that Asians in Asia may not be said to be as responsive to humour, our creatives need to consider the cultural context of the US."

Chang also recommends the use of sound effects to create more vivid pictures in listeners' minds. "For executions destined to be used across cultures and languages, sound effects have a more universal impact." His agency employs the same macro production techniques as mainstream American radio. "The best spots are those with great production values — high quality voices, music, sound effects. They stand out from the more common station-produced fare which is the norm."

GLOBAL RADIO: THE VIRGIN PERSPECTIVE

Radio keeps evolving. The day Sir Richard Branson's Virgin Radio launched in Britain in 1993, 3.2 million listeners tuned in — a remarkable achievement considering Virgin launched only in London and just as an AM station. Now Virgin is building an Asian radio network.

"There is a perception that Virgin is an innovator, slightly irreverent, and does things with a glint in its eye," explains Virgin regional chairman and chief executive Andrew Craissati. "The brand creates a certain degree of expectation and curiosity." Virgin leverages its musical legacy. "A lot of people still remember that we're the record label that brought them the Sex Pistols. There is this sense that we're not frightened of doing things, and I think people somehow like that." Virgin's passion for radio is driven by music. Today Virgin is probably the largest retailer of music in the world. "We probably sell close to 30% of all compact discs in the world, we have terrestrial radio, Internet radio, and we still have a record label."

Virgin's fundamental ambition is an Asian radio "network" — not a single programming format that runs across Asia, but more a portfolio of radio stations initially in China, India, Singapore and Thailand that have a consistency of branding and quality. Virgin's adult contemporary programming targets 16- to 35-year-olds, but the stations themselves would be very diverse in terms of format, language and culture. Craissati elaborates: "One of our points of difference is that many radio stations in Asia don't do much market research. Their programming is effectively a finger in the air to gauge the tastes of the market." Virgin, on the other hand, has developed strong analytical skills. Market research will shape the brand's connection with audiences across Asia. The implications for advertisers are clear. Craissati says the radio medium in Asia usually accounts for 4 to 4.5% of advertising expenditure, while in mature markets it is "north of 8%".

10

BE HEARD

Peter Souter once said that too often we are guilty of doing radio last, or with the most junior team. "If clients and agencies realised that, it would be so much easier to stand out on radio. If you did put a little more care into radio, if a specific tailored radio brief was written, you might be far and away the best people on the radio at that time."

Tony Hertz points to the overwhelmingly visual orientation of today's creative teams. And radio, he says, isn't seducing them. "TV's immense power and accessible production technology means that complex ideas can be expressed completely visually. The same applies to press. The Mac removed mental and geographic barriers and made advertising less language-based. While radio is capable of conveying exciting imagery, it is still mostly sold as a cheap tactical medium. So while TV and press have become mentally bigger, radio hasn't..."

RADIO encourages risk and forgives mistakes. It is the perfect medium for testing bold ideas for tentative clients. As lyricist Alan J. Lerner of *My Fair Lady* fame once observed, "I have always believed that only genuinely talented people can create something that is genuinely bad. Only the mediocre are always at their best."

"Radio is the one place an ad break can give a kid a big break," says Michael Newman. "Radio production is cheapish so you can do more ads for your bucks. You can experiment, stretch, evolve. You can practise becoming a perfectionist. That's a lot more difficult to do in TV, with a whole crew standing around waiting for lunch."

"With a TV commercial, there's so many people involved in the creation of it that nobody actually owns it," observes Alexsandra Lyall. "With radio, creatives can write it, select the talent, go into the studio, produce it and say 'this is mine'."

"Once you learn to write great radio, TV and film will come to you just that little bit easier," says Antony Redman. "Radio is the toughest medium because it lays you bare. You can't pass it over to a great director or disguise it with sexy images if you don't have a strong idea. But radio doesn't have the prestige of a big TV shoot. It doesn't get you a stamp in your passport. I've hardly ever seen a cassette of radio ads in someone's portfolio. Writing a great radio ad doesn't seem to get those extra zeroes in your pay cheque that everyone wants. And it's sad."

When it comes to radio advertising awards, the same names keep winning. Looking back to the early 1980s, Barbara Levy reflects: "Ninety percent of the radio people in America then are still in business now and still winning awards. Very few people are going in to radio production companies today. Radio has become almost like an afterthought, which I find quite funny for the simple reason that more and more people are spending more time in their cars." Observing a decline in radio creativity, Levy singles out music: "In all honesty, there is some excellent music being done now, but nothing remotely like the jingles of the 1970s and 1980s which to this day are recognisable." Citing today's music, she adds: "I don't think any of it will be recognisable 20 years from now."

Rowan Dean, chairman of the Australasian Writers and Art Directors Association, describes radio as "a medium ripe for creative rebirth".

"IF you haven't got passion, you haven't got anything," says Les Francis.

Great radio, like great anything, demands an obsessive hunger. George Bernard Shaw summed it up: "Artists must be selfish, it is in fact their duty."

"It is absolutely clear when someone has the discipline to say I'm not going to let anything out of the door that I've heard before, I'm not going to do a derivative ad," attests Street Remley. "If you listen to some of the great masters like Dick Orkin, guys who probably turn over a couple of hundred campaigns a year, never do they fall back on one of their earlier ideas. The truth is, you can hear when someone has gone to great pains to do something that is totally original. They say nothing is new, but that isn't true; there's a lot of stuff that's brand new and fresh to the advertising industry. The great commercials always break through, and that's why they make us say how did *he* think of that, or why didn't *I* think of that...?"

RADIO sparked Adrian Holmes' interest in advertising. Holmes, now chief creative officer of Lowe & Partners Worldwide, started off working in a photographic darkroom with a radio playing while he laboured. Tired of hearing one dreadful commercial after another, he tried his hand at writing better ones. That was when the station told him of the existence of advertising agencies and Holmes set his sights on a career in copywriting.

Scott Whybin, of Whybin TBWA & Partners Melbourne, got his first big break when his commercial for a provincial car dealer won a major Australian radio award. Within months he had jumped from the industrial city of Newcastle to the creative department of Abbott Mead Vickers in London.

"People who look down on any medium should not be in our business; they overlook opportunities." Michael Conrad recalls his early days writing radio copy: "When I started at Young & Rubicam in Frankfurt, I had to first work a lot on radio. All young creatives had to. At that time, we did not take radio as being second class, even though it was not a glamour medium like print."

Frank Todaro, one of the world's most awarded commercial directors, recalls his first job as an art director. "I quickly started taking all the radio assignments from my writing partner who hated doing radio. I loved directing the actors and putting it together the way I wanted."

Todaro later moved on to New York's Cliff Freeman & Partners, where founding partner Arthur Bijur gets beginners immersed in radio, learning writing crafts and gaining the confidence to direct talent. Bijur believes there is a correlation between doing great radio and crafting great television soundtracks. "That sensibility fine-tunes you to lots of little craft-related things that help you with television. It's all about tight performances, it's all about timing, it's all about working with a much more limited variety of sensory input than television. I've always been particularly pro-radio. I used to love going off to the studio and doing my own thing. It's one of the only opportunities in this business where you can just do something yourself, especially for a junior person. Radio teaches you to really think visually as a writer."

BRITISH advertising legend Mike Cozens shares a tip for young creatives. "Concentrate on doing things other people don't want to do. Become a great radio writer because no one else is," he advises, then move on from there.

Rob Martin Murphy agrees. "Don't hide under your desk when the radio brief comes around. Not many people can write great radio — that's probably why they're giving you the brief! There is a big opportunity to be one of the few who can, so grab it with both hands." And when that brief arrives, think ideas. "Don't sit there and sweat over blank paper trying to write the great radio script. Radio is just like print, TV and posters. The best stuff always has a great idea at the centre of it. So think ideas, ideas, ideas first. Once you have a great idea, the great script will come."

Mike Edmonds also suggests: "Seek out the radio briefs in your agency. They're usually the ones gathering dust under the TV and poster briefs. But they're fun and will get you noticed out there in agency-land quicker than big budget TV. TV takes forever and the strike rate of ideas-getting-made-into-actual-commercials is depressingly low, whereas radio is cheap and fast. You can actually sell a creative radio script more easily than a risky TV idea. And hey, a Gold Clio is a Gold Clio..."

Steve Elrick's advice: "When everyone zigs, zag. There is a dearth of good radio. 'No Awards Given' is a familiar refrain at award shows when it comes to the radio section, so a few good spots could mean that a young team could be taking a few walks up to the stage in a very unusual category. That will get you noticed and because it's radio, everyone will have to listen to it being played! Any creative director worth his salt will recognise people with the ability to create good ideas — it doesn't matter if they appear on paper, on television or over the radio."

Calvin Soh challenges young Asian creatives to create cutting edge radio. Soh worked at Fallon New York and returned to his hometown Singapore as president and creative director of the legendary agency's first Asian office. "Humour is more in evidence in the US, and there's a genuine attempt to entertain or engage. But I honestly can't think of one radio spot that has moved or touched me here in Asia…"

Cheap TV Versus Expensive Radio

Austin Howe's passion for radio has inspired many young American creatives. Howe is founding president and creative director of Radioland, now in its sixth year in Portland, Oregon. "I had been a copywriter and creative director at Saatchi & Saatchi and Cole & Weber, then owner and creative director of AKA, a small creative boutique like Australia's OMON. AKA was one of *Creativity* magazine's 'Hot Shops to Watch' in 1996. We had some juicy regional clients who always seemed to want to do TV, but never really had TV money. So we started talking clients out of 'cheap TV' and into 'expensive radio'."

Howe's rationale was straightforward enough. "We'd tell them, 'You're not just competing with other brands in your category. You're up against Nike and Bud and Coke, and these guys are spending upwards of a million bucks just to produce their TV spots. Good luck with your $20,000 commercial!' And then we'd promise them, 'For $20,000 you can have the very best radio spot on the air. Period'."

Howe's challenge generated a lot of success — and creative awards. "I had always had a weird love for radio," he confesses, "and now I was loving it even more. I partnered with all the top radio production companies at the time, and learned a lot from guys like Dick Orkin, Chuck Blore, Bert Berdis, Craig Weise, Stephen Kessler, Joy Golden, Paul Fey, and Terry O'Reilly at Pirate Radio in Toronto, Canada. I loved what Terry and his partner Rick Sherman were doing at Pirate, and we began discussing the possibility of me opening a Pirate Radio in the US. But in 1997 I had the opportunity to sell my agency and start Radioland, so I went for it."

But Howe did not start Radioland in the conventional way. He hired Emily Reed, an account planner from Goodby, Silverstein & Partners who had worked on *got milk?* and Porsche. "We sent her around to all the elite creative agencies in the US to talk with creative directors, writers and producers about their problems with radio. Those insights were hugely helpful in forming the basis for Radioland's business model, and they still drive us today."

"We got lucky early on," Howe recounts, "and landed some Nike work from Wieden & Kennedy who had never gone outside for help with radio creative before. We were also able to penetrate the walls of TBWA Chiat/Day, doing work for Levi's and AirTouch Cellular." Radioland was soon winning awards and getting assignments from Crispin Porter & Bogusky, Hal Riney, DDB, Saatchi & Saatchi, BBDO, Team One, FCB. For two years, Radioland produced all of Deutsch LA's radio. "Some agencies, like Wieden's and Chiat/Day, just briefed us and let us do the whole thing. Others, like Deutsch, would start with a script and we would tweak it, and try and 'plus' it at the session. We were also hired by advertisers directly and ostensibly became the 'radio agency' for Hardee's fast food chain, Gallo, Jiffy Lube, Cablevision and Adidas." By 1998, Radioland had opened a second office in Los Angeles and a recording studio to handle the volume of work coming in.

When Howe did his initial planning, one of the recurring themes was that radio did not have the same cachet as TV. "With the obvious exceptions of Cliff Freeman, DDB Chicago, Black Rocket, and to a lesser extent Goodby's, Crispin, and Deutsch, radio at nearly every agency simply isn't a priority. It isn't considered to be that important. One of my efforts to elevate the medium was something I called 'Directors For Radio', a concept that was met with great enthusiasm by agency people, the trade press, and even some heavyweight directors like Francis Ford Coppola and Rob Reiner. The notion was that you would never attempt to make a movie that was dialogue-dependent without a great director, so why would you ever try to make a radio commercial, which is entirely dependent upon dialogue, without one?"

Radioland signed deals with CAA and ICM to use their directors for radio commercials. The additional cost was significant, he says, but not astronomical. "We ran full-page ads in *Adweek* and *Advertising Age* and did one national Jiffy Lube campaign with Daniel Stern and I directing. But it didn't catch on as I had hoped. 'Too much money' was a common complaint. 'After all it's only radio.' I still believe in it. But it would require a significant investment of time and energy to make it part of the creative process..."

MAKE YOUR MARKET A RADIO MARKET

Perth is to Australian radio what Minneapolis is to American print and television advertising. With a population of 1.38 million, Perth is a state capital on the Western Australian seaboard. Yet despite its size and relative isolation, Perth has become a hub of radio creativity.

"Radio is the great equaliser," says Mike Edmonds, creative director of the Marketforce agency. "A writer in Perth knows he can make a radio commercial that sounds just as good as a New York writer's radio commercial. This is a very inspiring thought for an agency writer. It means he can achieve world-class commercials. The same can't be said for TV and print. With those media, you need tons of money to hire the right directors and photographers and talent, money that Perth clients don't have."

Edmonds identifies the ingredients that Perth has for doing great radio:

1. Enthusiastic creatives who love to actually write scripts, not just draw ideas on layout pads. The city's internationally awarded writers include Steve Browning, Adam Barker, Lindsay Medalia and Ric Cairns.
2. World-class sound production facilities with intelligent and creative sound engineers and producers like Marty Braine.
3. An incredibly supportive radio industry that challenges us to create better commercials for their listeners and rewards us when we do. MIX 94.5 FM awards an annual US$10,000 prize to the writer who pens the best spot on their station.

TITLE: GIARDINI'S RESTAURANT

The situation was continued across three consecutive commercials and dominated the break.

SFX: *RESTAURANT AMBIENCE THROUGHOUT.*

WAITER: Are you ready to order, sir?

MAN: Ahh … what kind of eggs do you have?

WAITER: We've got Eggs Florentine, Eggs Benedict, Scrambled Eggs, Fried Eggs Sunny Side Up, Sunny Side Under, Eggs Over Easy, Poached Eggs, Spanish Omelette, English Omelette, Eggs and Sausage, Eggs and Bacon, Eggs and Spam, Runny Eggs, Hard Eggs, Semi Hard Eggs, Eggs and Soldiers, Eggs à la Giardini…

FADE TO COMMERCIAL BREAK

WAITER: *(FADES UP)* Giardini Egg Combo, Scrambled African Egg, Fluffy Eggs, Curried Eggs, Macedonian Poached, American Omelette, French Omelette, Cheese Omelette, Kentucky Eggs, Bavarian Eggs, Turkish Eggs, Scrambled Turkish Eggs, Scottish Eggs, Giardini Egg Special…

FADE TO COMMERCIAL BREAK

WAITER: *(FADES UP)* Rocky Eggs, Eggs in a glass, Boiled Eggs, Pickled Eggs, Egg Divine, Egg Soufflé, Stuffed Eggs … that's pretty much all you can do with eggs.

MAN: Well, actually I've only got time for a coffee now.

WAITER: Latté, Flat White, Macchiato, Long Black, Short Black, Double Decaffeinated, Half Twist… *(FADES)*

MVO: Weekdays at Giardini's, you can have eggs any way you like. 135 Oxford Street, Leederville.

Perth is a radio market where 303 Advertising changed the usual paradigm to make the point that client Giardini's offers a huge choice of eggs. Written by Tiffany Wiltshire and Levi Slavin. Engineered by Martin Braine at Brainstorm.

4. A growing pool of voice talent who are keen to do free demo tracks and work on their craft, thanks in large part to guys like Marty Braine who go see all the local plays and shows to ferret out the good throats.

LIFTING YOUR GAME

Jack Vaughan has this advice to aspiring creatives. "Listen to as much comedy as possible. Comedians already capture all the precepts of timing, word plays, humour and surprise. Writer Steve Hayden, Apple *1984*, talks about devouring country and western music because of its verbal ideas, like, 'If I said you had a beautiful body, would you hold it against me?' Which is not a million miles from Pete and Dud, or was it Monty Python, who said: 'I must warn you, sir, that anything you say will be taken down and held against you.' 'Raquel Welch.' "

For Vaughan's money, nothing sharpens the wits like listening to them. "I was raised on *Mad Magazine*, Shelley Berman, Bob Newhart, Woody Allen, Tony Hancock and Henny Youngman. I'm certain it gives you an ear, or did for me. These days it's Billy Connolly and Stephen Wright whose verbal juxtapositions are inspirational — 'Did Roman paramedics call IV's fours?' — to say nothing of Seinfeld and the galaxy of comedy store tryouts who teach observation. There are more of them accessible now than there's ever been. Not a hard assignment for radio copy students..."

Andrew Craissati shares similar advice: "Understand comedy. Years ago I was involved with a production house in the UK that was owned by Mel Smith and Griff Rhys Jones, and they turned out radio commercials that I thought were works of art. They were literally award-winning pieces of conversation. Radio is a wonderful medium for humour. I would encourage any creative to upgrade their grasp of comedy, try and avoid too much basic slapstick, and make it more sophisticated and intelligent."

"As with any medium, experiment," says Steve Henry. "Look at what radical artists are doing, whether they're musicians or deejays or comedians or playwrights. Then do what all the original artists are doing anyway, and nick the idea. Put your own spin on it, as the radical artists do, but don't be afraid to nick ideas from anywhere."

"Experiment with monologues, dialogues, funny group scenarios, sound design, music," Ken Bennett suggests. "Never be afraid to try new things. Realise that radio is an incredible creative canvas with almost infinite potential. Have fun with radio and never view it as the poor stepchild of TV."

"Don't be afraid to fail," Andy Lerner says, "because at some point it's inevitable." Lerner started in the business as a recording engineer, doing music at night and commercials by day. He soon found himself gravitating towards commercials. Clients were relying more and more on his opinions and ideas, inspiring him to eventually operate a casting, writing and production service. If you are doing humour, cautions Lerner, make sure it's funny. "Show it to people. Perform it for people. See if they laugh. If it isn't funny, throw it away and start over. I usually end up throwing away 90% of the stuff I come up with. Take the time to see if you're doing your idea the best way it can be, see where it leads you. Your good idea can lead to a *great* idea. Read your ideas aloud or perform it with others in the agency to really get a *sense* of it. You'll be surprised how differently it works from when you read it to yourself while you wrote it." Agencies, he says, tend to throw radio assignments at young creatives. *"Don't turn down any opportunity."*

Remley issues an invitation to creatives. "I would encourage them to come into the studio, let me book the actors, come in with nothing but the brief, and let's invent the script in the studio. That would open their eyes to the nakedness of doing such a thing, but more importantly to the potential of what you *can* do when people aren't encumbered with mundane thinking, a sloppily written script, or scripts that are done without enthusiasm. I think I could jar them into a new frame of mind if they came in with nothing more than just the basic brief and let me show them what can be done on the spur of the moment with good minds and good talent who are keen, fresh and original."

JIM BERINSON advises young creatives not to listen to other radio commercials. "Don't think they're the benchmark. There really isn't a formula for doing good radio. You should write what you'd *like* to write. You can paint all kinds of pictures and each listener will change them in their mind's eye. I find that fascinating…"

ADVICE FOR YOUNG CREATIVES

From Ian Reichenthal,
Creative Director, Cliff Freeman & Partners New York

Edit your script.

Edit it some more.

Be honest. Is there something — even one line — that could be better?

Yes there is.

Edit some more.

Is the script to time?

Seriously, is it to time?

No, I'm really being serious. Stop timing it in that fast voice. You're not fooling anyone.

Edit some more.

Go to the casting sessions.

Did you learn something from the casting sessions? Did the actor stumble over a line you've written? Was something less funny, or less clear, or less "anything" than you imagined?

Maybe it's your cast. Cast some more.

Maybe it's your script. Edit some more.

Show it to someone whose opinion you respect.

Show it to someone else whose opinion you respect.

Did they manage to find any flaws in your script that you hadn't noticed?

Curse them.

Then thank them.

Then go back to your office and edit some more.

Great. You've finally got a tight script and a good cast.

Now just show up to the recording session.

"Open your mind," urges Brad Power. "Don't just fit into what everyone else thinks a radio ad is."

"The last place you should be looking to learn is other radio ads," concurs Chris Kyme. "You'll just get cornered into the same old approaches." Kyme suggests studying radio as a medium. "In countries rich with great radio, where you have first-class dramas, great talk-radio and interview programmes, you can learn a lot from the masters."

Carl Jones suggests listening to the old radio soap operas and the successful radio comedies like *The Goon Show*. "Read theatre scripts, reading like actors do at an audition; you don't have to act, just reading aloud helps. Listen to *War of the Worlds* — even now it is a very strong piece of drama."

"IMAGINE for a moment that the written word was banned," says Steve Owen. "Now convey the message using sounds, voices and music. Now explore that world..."

"Take advantage of radio's visual possibilities," urges Keith Reinhard. "As my friend Charles Osgood says, 'See you on the radio...' "

Listening to TV spots is a good discipline for young creatives, advocates Kenn Delbridge. "Close your eyes and see how much of it makes sense without visuals. Learning to get a message across without pictures is your biggest hurdle. Radio commercials have to rely on the spoken word and sound effects only." Delbridge suggests listening to old radio dramas that are now commercially available on audio cassettes and CDs. "Listen to brilliant work from Orson Welles and others who used the format of radio to tell stories and painted brilliant pictures in the minds of their listeners."

"Don't let the radio spot just hit a listener's ears, but the space in between them," says Ravi Deshpande. "Therefore, have an idea in the commercial and, as far as possible, entertain while selling." Be versatile, he says, don't just follow one particular style, and have the courage to improvise on the spot. "Brief the talent and producer thoroughly, but don't be bullied. Stick to the mood, tone and message you want to get across. Go to a studio with the best technology and make sure you book enough time."

DAVID ALBERTS cautions against following the same, stereotyped structures: "Twenty seconds of funny, and then ten seconds of straight voice-over that explains the relevance of the funny. It's like you've entertained them for twenty seconds and then you just dump them. You have to break that format. These days we're internally saying to creatives that they are not allowed to have anyone explaining their idea at the end of the commercial. They have to make the product central to their idea."

Newman also suggests trying to subvert the shape and structure of the usual radio ad. "Please don't start your commercial with the phone ringing. I'm sure the *Guinness Book of Records* will prove it is history's most common opening for commercials. Everyone is used to formula, especially the long-suffering listeners." Even conventional commercial lengths can be challenged and subverted. "I once asked for the shortest possible commercial lengths for a retail campaign when I realised all I needed was an announcement that 'Everything advertised on this radio station can be bought considerably cheaper at Preston Market'." Newman urges young copywriters to grab every available opportunity. "Senior creative people are too mesmerised by the glamour of TV to bother with the radio extensions to their campaigns. Offer to do everyone's radio. Use your art director. Write a radio script to accompany every print brief you're asked to do. And every direct mail brief. Write a topical radio ad from something happening in the news — today."

"Be willing to self-disclose," advises Christine Coyle. "Abandon the use of clichés and tired ad jargon. Put aside your desire to write sketches for *Saturday Night Live*. Radio is the most intimate of mediums. It can get the consumer emotionally closer to the product or service than any other medium. Focus on what story you can tell that demonstrates the unique selling proposition dramatically and effectively."

Today, young Australian Emma Hill is a senior writer at Clemenger BBDO Melbourne. Born in Tasmania, she started writing at Clemenger Hobart in 1993. Long before she started winning awards, she worked for five years on reception and in media, accounts, and account service. Her advice resonates for other young writers: "Clients just seem to give you more freedom with a radio script. They don't place as much importance on radio, and on the briefing and process and production of it, as they do on television. The briefs will be really simple, like 'just say that', whereas for television they'll give you so much more information. For the production of it they won't come to the session, they'll just let you go." Hill treasures this freedom to develop better work for the clients, as well as develop herself as a writer. "You've got to grab it with both hands as an opportunity every time. Think really simply. Relate to real people. Have a moment from real life that makes people laugh at themselves and put a tag on it. If you've got a complex brief that needs a whole lot of information in it, try and get help to simplify the brief. And try to develop a relationship with a production company you can really trust."

Creative freedom underscores Nigel Dawson's love of radio. "One of the things I like best about radio, and why I still try to snaffle radio briefs that are floating around the agency, is that you have no interference. I do the creation and the crafting. I do the production with the only other people involved — a producer and engineer. It really is entirely one's own baby. And it's good to be entirely to blame, be it for the commercial's success or failure."

HERTZ articulates his passion for radio: "Very early on in my advertising career I found that I had more control over radio than everything else I did. My measurement of successful work, on a personal level, is did it end up the way I thought it was going to end up? And whenever I've done print or television, it rarely does. The selfish side of me likes radio because *I* get to do it. I get left alone. It's just me and the actors, and the engineer who is an extension of me. So if I heard something in my head, like Brooke Bond Tea, it came out the way I intended."

Hertz regrets that the same kind of strategic thinking and minimalism that goes into print and TV is not applied to radio. "Radio is treated somehow differently, as though it doesn't count in the same way. You should apply the same thinking, the same intellectual disciplines to radio that you apply to everything else you do. And take your time. Good radio needs as much creative time as good TV and print, more if you're not used to it. It's worth fighting for. Yes, radio commercials can be written one day and on-air the next, but that doesn't mean they ought to be. Great radio needs careful pre-production — casting, timing and blocking — and enough studio hours to allow for crafting, reflection and inspiration. You will hear the difference."

His advice to aspiring radio creatives: "Learn to listen to the way people speak and the relationship of the sounds that go on in your own life…"

RALPH VAN DIJK is another advertising agency copywriter who became a radio creative guru. Starting out in New Zealand, he switched from agency life to become creative director at a number of radio stations. He moved to London in 1989 and co-founded Eardrum a year later. Eardrum is recognised as the UK's most successful radio specialist, having produced countless award-winning campaigns as well as comedy-based programming for both the BBC and commercial radio. He is also a director of the character voice agency Earache.

Why the switch to radio? "I've always loved writing and had a good ear — something you develop quickly when you have Dutch-speaking parents! When I worked on radio jobs at agencies I loved the speed of turnaround from concept to completion. I also found that radio combined many of my passions like music, drama and comedy."

Van Dijk tells young creatives to think visually. "If you can picture the scene, chances are the listener will, too. Push the boundaries and avoid the obvious radio clichés. An experienced radio director will hopefully point them out for you, but they include:

1. two blokes chatting in a pub,
2. ads that start, 'This is the sound of…,'
3. radio programming parodies."

His final word of advice: "Use a director."

"LISTEN to what people talk or mumble about in real life," counsels Yukio Nakayama. "Spoken words are 'live', and the language is what we cannot expect. We are dying to listen to human words, not information." Nakayama advocates mining real-life dialogue and conversations for unpredictable gems that few writers could ever write. "There are always small ideas around you. Who knows, they could become big ideas…" Whatever you do, he says, do not think of a big budget first. "Do not try to show off… Listen to the deepest voice of your own."

"Radio is a great medium for young creatives to learn the craft of writing and improve their skills," says John Immesoete. "If a writer can write a good radio spot, they can write good TV or print. To learn the skills I'd first look towards other writers whose work you admire. Talk to them, get to know them, don't be afraid to ask for help or criticism. Too many young writers are young turks afraid to ask for help or criticism either because they think they don't need it or can't take it. Wrong on both counts. Thoughtful old pros can help make your shiny new ideas shine that much brighter." Immesoete urges writers to resist the temptation to put themselves above the medium of radio. "Some older writers don't do radio because 'there isn't any money in it' or 'no one cares'. They don't do it because they can't, because they never learned how and now they're embarrassed about it. Don't be a victim or follower of this precious elitism because it isn't true. Writing for the radio can be the most rewarding thing a copywriter can do. You can be creative, original, recognised, independent in spirit, and truly effective as a writer. It's a skill worth learning to do well."

VIOLINIST Itzhak Perlman, stricken with polio as a child, has braces on both legs and walks with the aid of crutches. Gaining the stage, he must reach his chair, set down his crutches, and undo the clasps on his legs before he can play. On 18 November 1995, during a concert at the Avery Fisher Hall in New York, one of the strings on his violin broke. Undaunted, he closed his eyes and signalled the conductor to continue. Recomposing the piece as he played, changing and compensating note after note, bar after bar, he coaxed sounds from the remaining strings that they had never made before. Finishing the performance to screams of applause, he waited a moment before saying quietly, "Sometimes it is the artist's task to find out how much music you can still make with what we have left."

In radio, without visuals, with simply voices and sounds, it was ever thus.

BIBLIOGRAPHY

Blanc, Mel and Philip Bashe. *That's not all Folks!: My Life in the Golden Age of Cartoons and Radio.* Warner Books, Inc., New York, 1988.

British Broadcasting Corporation, The. *Broadcasting House.* BBC, London, 1932.

Crook, Tim. *Radio Drama.* Routledge, New York, 1999.

Jones, Colin. *Something in the Air: A History of Radio in Australia.* Kangaroo Press Australia, 1995.

Kent, Jacqueline. *Out of the Bakelite Box: The Heyday of Australian Radio.* Angus & Robertson, Sydney, 1983.

Lane, Richard. *The Golden Age of Australian Radio Drama 1923–1960: A History Through Biography.* Melbourne University Press, 1994.

Lwin, May and Wee Chow-Hou. "The Effect of an Audio Stimulus: Accents in English Language on Cross-Cultural Consumer Response to Advertising". *Journal of International Consumer Marketing*, Vol. 11(2), 1999.

Mackay, Ian K. *Broadcasting in Australia.* Melbourne University Press, 1957.

Schulberg, Pete. Revised edition of Schulberg, Bob. *Radio Advertising: The Authoritative Handbook.* NTC Business Books, Chicago, 1996.

Walker, R. R. *The Magic Spark: The Story of the First Fifty Years of Radio in Australia.* The Hawthorn Press, Melbourne, 1973.

INDEX

ABOUT THE AUTHOR

Jim Aitchison, an Australian, was former creative director of Singapore's Ball Partnership and Batey Ads. He has won hundreds of awards and judged many of the world's top shows. He has also written radio serials and co-hosted morning drivetime. His first two books, *Cutting Edge Advertising* and *Cutting Edge Commercials*, have become international bestsellers. After twenty years in advertising, he is now a full-time author.